You CAN Retire Young!

How to Retire in Your 40s or 50s Without Being Rich

Copyright © Larry A. Ferstenou, 2002. All rights reserved. No part of this book may be reproduced or transmitted in any form or by any means, electronic or mechanical, including photocopying, recording, or by any information storage and retrieval system, without permission in writing from the publisher.

Published by
American Book Business Press™
325 East 2400 South, Salt Lake City, Utah 84115
http://www.american-book.com
Printed in the United States of America on acid-free paper.

You **CAN** Retire Young!

Designed by Joe Nendza, joesdesign@earthlink.net

Publisher's Note: *This publication is designed to provide accurate and authoritative information in regard to the subject matter covered. It is sold or distributed with the understanding that the publisher and author are not engaged in rendering legal, accounting, or other professional service. If legal advice or other expert assistance is required, the services of a competent professional person in a consultation capacity should be sought.*

Library of Congress Cataloging-in-Publication Data is available upon request.

ISBN 1-58982-008-8

Ferstenou, Larry A, You **CAN** Retire Young!

Special Sales

These books are available at special discounts for bulk purchases. Special editions, including personalized covers, excerpts of existing books, and corporate imprints, can be created in large quantities for special needs. For more information e-mail orders@american-book.com or call 1-801-463-3942.

You CAN Retire Young!

How to Retire in Your 40s or 50s Without Being Rich

Larry A. Ferstenou

In memory of my dad, Edward R. Ferstenou:

From whom I acquired financial self-discipline;
and whose untimely death at age 52
inspired us to work hard and save even harder,
to achieve the goal of retiring young.

Contents

Introduction

Surveys reveal that most people would like to retire young—55 or younger—and many would choose their 30s or 40s if they could. But can they? Absolutely. And so can you. It's going to take more than wishful thinking, however; it's also going to take some effective strategies and a sufficient net worth. This book will cover why you should, and how you can, turn that dream into reality; the rest will be up to you.

The more money you earn, the easier it will be to retire early. Regardless of income, however, the 3 Keys to retiring young delineated in the following pages will be your guide to spending less, saving more, and investing wisely. You *can* take control of your future, retire as young as possible, and start enjoying what should be the best years of your life. But in order for that to become a reality, you must start focusing on the future *now*.

THE THREE-LEGGED STOOL

Perhaps you've heard of the "three-legged stool." Traditionally, retirement has been possible because of this stool. The first leg was employer-funded pension income, the second leg Social Security income, and the third leg personal savings. In the past, those three income sources provided most retirees with ample financial security. But the stool is getting wobbly and you cannot depend on it for your future retirement. What happened?

Leg 1: Employer-funded (defined-benefit) pensions have declined markedly. In fact, according to the latest annual report from the Pension Benefit Guaranty Corporation (www.pbgc.gov), employer-funded pension plans peaked at approximately 114,000 in 1985 and have since declined to a low of about 38,000. Because these plans became too expensive to fund and administer, and the financial burden would increase rapidly as the baby boomers—those born between 1946 and 1964—began retiring, many employers took a preemptive step and switched from employer-funded pensions to employer-sponsored plans like the 401(k) where employees primarily fund their own pensions.

Employers may match their workers' contributions up to a certain limit in these plans, or they may not. That means the pensions of most future retirees will depend on how much they contribute themselves—and few are contributing enough. In fact, only about 42 million U.S. workers participate in a 401(k) and nearly twice that many (75 million) have no employer-sponsored plan at all.

Leg 2: The old standby, Social Security, is in financial jeopardy. Chapters 12 and 13 focus on the problems surrounding this federal program and, once you read them, you will understand why there is mounting concern about the viability of this potential income source in the future.

Leg 3: That leaves personal savings. If more money were being invested in IRAs and other retirement accounts, and/or in other mutual fund accounts (taxable or not), this leg wouldn't be as much of a concern. But the personal savings rate in America in 2000 fell to its lowest level since the Depression—and it was only a little better in 2001. Surveys further confirm that few people are saving anywhere near enough to support themselves in retirement.

If the future of the three-legged stool appears grim, rest assured that it's going to impact some more than others. The reality for all of us is that we will not be able to count on the federal government and our employers to take care of us in retirement like they are taking care of today's senior citizens. So what can we do?

START TAKING CONTROL

Almost everyone will retire one day. For some it will be when they turn 65 or 66, for others perhaps 70, and for those who do not prepare, it may be 80 or later. And what about you? That's going to depend on how much effort you start putting into it now. While some kind of retirement will eventually be a reality for most of us, let me ask you a few questions about your feelings today.

- Would you like to have more time to spend with family and friends?
- Do you have hobbies you would enjoy pursuing if you had the time?
- How about getting up every morning knowing that you can do whatever you want?
- In fact, have you given serious thought to how great it would be having 52 weeks of vacation each year instead of two or three?

If these sound good to you, then you should focus on retiring not when you are 65 or 70, but while you are young, healthy, and motivated to take full advantage of what early retirement has to offer. Enjoy the *freedom* to do what *you* want to do, when *you* want to do it. You can't imagine how good that feels. Or maybe you can and that's why you're reading this book! It's a holiday everyday...a perpetual vacation...your ticket to a better life.

One reality, however, is that while most people would like to retire young, the majority will not be able to financially afford it. Most lack the motivation and self-discipline necessary to take control, plan ahead, and accumulate the net worth needed. That's okay. We need people like that, too; people who spend all the money they make. They help boost the economy that, in turn, helps generate continued growth in the investment portfolios of us early retirees. But is that where you want to find yourself—financially unable to retire young or maybe *never* able to retire? We certainly didn't, so we took control and did something about it. You can too.

NOT RICH, BUT NOT POOR

I wrote this book to convince you that retiring young is an attainable goal and one you should strive toward. And what about money? Don't you have to be rich to retire young? Absolutely not! We retired in our early 40s without being rich; but neither were we poor. The net worth you are going to need will depend on the lifestyle you want to live (which will be thoroughly discussed in chapters 6 and 9). Over our 18-year careers we averaged $47,300 per year in after-tax income—which included interest, dividends, and capital gains. Millions of couples earn well above that today.

If you earn and/or save more than we did, or if you are fortunate enough to get a windfall or have a forthcoming military, civil service, or corporate pension to look forward to, then you can possibly retire in fewer years than it took us. Earn less or save less than we did and you can expect it to take longer. But there is yet another option for those who earn less or haven't managed to save the net worth necessary to fully retire: part-time work during early retirement can give you far more freedom than you have now while providing sufficient income to make retiring young possible.

Don't think you can realistically save enough money on your current income? In chapter 6 you will learn about a couple that had a dream of owning a big farmhouse in the country. But with virtually no net worth, an income that averaged less than $30,000 per year and four children, it seemed impossible. Did they meet their goal? You will find out later. But if they did save enough under those circumstances to achieve their dream (and a good guess would be that they did), then perhaps others can learn from their experiences and strategies too.

GIVE YOURSELF THE CHOICE

If you can believe a guy who retired at 42, who has been retired nearly nine years, and who has no plans of ever returning to full-time employment, there is simply no other goal to pursue than to retire as young as possible. The choice will be yours—to retire young or to keep working—but only if you plan ahead and follow the 3 Keys to retiring young that will allow you to build the net worth necessary to give yourself that choice in the future.

You may love your occupation now, but what about in 10, 15, or even 20 years? Enthusiasm for your job or career can change dramatically. And with the number of layoffs we have seen in past years, whether you have a job or not in the future may not be your choice. So take control of your life now and prepare yourself for whatever may come. If you choose to, you *can* retire young; this book will show you how.

Chapter One

Do What You Want, When You Want

Have you ever read a book that changed your life? My wife and I did, in 1992. The title of the book was *Cashing In on the American Dream: How to Retire at 35* by Paul Terhorst (please refer to the appendix for more information on all book titles referenced in these chapters). A year later, at ages 42 and 40, we retired from full-time employment. My goal in writing this book is to also change your life.

- If you are in your 20s or 30s, it will provide the guidance you need to retire in your 40s or 50s.
- If you are already in your 40s or 50s, you may be closer to retirement than you think. That is what we discovered. We had a sufficient net worth, but we didn't realize that it could (or should) become a reality so early in our lives. Perhaps you will find the same is true for you.

- If you don't earn enough to retire in your 40s or 50s, but you want to retire as early as possible so that you can take advantage of what should be the best years of your life, then this book will also provide the strategies needed to meet your retirement goal.

We have been early retirees for almost nine years. Regrets? Not for a minute! Early retirement has been too much fun. I wrote this book to convince you that there's more to life than work, and retiring in your 40s or 50s is the goal to pursue. But even if you cannot afford to retire until later, considering ongoing medical advances and increased life expectancy, you may still be young relative to your ultimate life span. And you'll want to be sure you have the financial resources for a comfortable retirement at that time. So how do you know if you are a good candidate for early retirement? That's easy; just answer the following questions:

- Do you derive immense satisfaction from your job or profession?
- Do you have sufficient time to pursue all the activities you *most enjoy*?
- Do you have all the time you would like to spend with family and friends?
- Do you look forward to workdays more than days off?
- Would you be bored if every day was vacation and you could do whatever YOU wanted to do?

If your answer is "yes" to those questions, early retirement is not a priority for you at this time—but it could be in a few years when circumstances change. On the other hand, if most of your answers are "no," then maybe it's time you started doing something about that. For starters, you might try taking the interactive quizzes offered at the Web site of the American Savings Education

Council at www.asec.org. (Note: Since Web sites are periodically updated, the directions given throughout these chapters for finding different Web pages may not be applicable by the time you read this book. If that turns out to be the case, look for the key words I've highlighted and you should find the pages if they are still available on the updated site.)

- Click on **Savings Tools.**
- Click on **Retirement Personality Profile (RPP)** and take the quiz.
- Then click on **Retirement Readiness Rating (RRR)** and take that quiz.
- You might also enjoy doing the **Ballpark Estimate.**

Fidelity Investments also offers a six-question interactive quiz on its Web site at www.fidelity.com that tests your attitude about retirement. To take this quiz:

- Click on **Planning and Retirement** at the top.
- Then click on **Retirement Investing Center.**
- Scroll down to "I'm nearing/considering retirement" and click on **Plan for Life After Work.**
- Under #1 Envision, click on **Test Your Attitude.**

These tools are meant to be fun and motivating. They provide insight into your current situation and help you to see where changes in your thinking or actions might be beneficial to meeting your early retirement goal. If you don't have a computer and access to the Internet, try your local library.

GETTING AWAY FROM WORK

What do you like to do on vacation? The beach seems to be popular. You lie around, relax, basically do nothing, and try not to think about work for a week. Maybe you like to travel and see the country or the world. Or perhaps you prefer to stay home and catch up on things you don't otherwise have time to do. Whatever your vacation getaway, time always seems to pass too quickly. Why? Because you are having fun doing things you enjoy. And that's the advantage of retiring young—so you can go to the beach, travel, or do whatever makes you happy, every day for the rest of your life.

Here's a crucial point though: you should not retire just to get away from your work. If you don't like your job, then maybe you should change jobs, or switch careers. But if you can afford it, and you have sufficient personal activities you want to do that genuinely give you pleasure and make it fun to get up each morning, then you are a definite candidate for saying good-bye to some full-time job or career you would rather not be doing. However, the age at which you can retire, and what you can afford to do in retirement, will depend on your financial resources.

The fact that we hung it up in our early 40s (given the investments we had at that time and without any kind of corporate or government pensions) meant there would be some limitations to what we could do. For us, scaling down our assets and simplifying our lives was an easy trade-off for the reward of early retirement—freedom from *having* to work. If your goal is to one day be a guest on "Lifestyles of the Rich and Famous" or to make the Forbes 400 list of the world's richest people, then you will have to work longer to accumulate the money you need to support those aspirations. As long as you are happy with that choice and enjoy doing whatever you are doing, then by all means, keep working. But if you are not happy, then maybe it's time to restructure your future plans.

WHAT TO DO

So what would you do every day as an early retiree? Some experts suggest that if you cannot compile a list of at least 30 things you would like to do, you might not be a good candidate for early retirement. Based on my experience, I'm not sure you need that many because one or two items alone could encompass significantly more time than others. Take an early-retiree friend of ours as an example. Golf is his favorite recreational activity. He plays 18 holes several days per week for most of the year and that takes nearly five hours per round. In addition to being a rather time-consuming activity, it is also good exercise since he walks the course carrying his golf bag. He retired in his 40s while still young and healthy; continuing to walk the golf course, rather than riding in a cart every time, will help to keep him that way.

An endless list of activities is available for you to do during early retirement—more than you could do for as long as you live. What might some of your choices be if you had the time and money? How about these examples?

Exercise/Recreation/Sports: Participation in different sports and recreational activities can be beneficial in maintaining a level of fitness (mental and/or physical) that can help you stay healthy and improve your life. Which activities you choose will depend on personal interest, but some possibilities include: aerobics (floor or water), badminton, basketball, biking, bowling, canoeing, fishing, golf, hiking, horseshoes, in-line skating, kayaking, martial arts, racquetball, running, skiing, snowboarding, softball, swimming, table tennis, tennis, volleyball, weight lifting, and yoga.

Reading: Wouldn't it be great being able to read all the current best-selling books and the latest magazines for fun, rather than only having time to read the professional journals and books related to your work?

Music: I have met few people who wouldn't enjoy being able to play a musical instrument. Early retirement can be the perfect opportunity to pursue that dream.

Dancing: Western line and square dancing, as well as ballroom dancing and modern dance, may all be available where you reside. If you don't know how to dance but would like to learn, college adult continuing-education programs often offer such classes.

Cultural: You can enjoy ballets, concerts, operas, dance troupes, and stage plays—from professional productions to those offered at a local college.

Writing: Many people enjoy writing, or at least they would if they had the time. Now you do. This can be your opportunity to write as much as you want for fun, or you may decide to try turning it into profit!

Socializing: For the first time in many years you have time to visit with friends and family you haven't seen for a long time. Some people also enjoy playing bridge, poker, or other card and table games with others.

Education: Most colleges offer extended learning or continuing education classes for adults. Study history, archeology, genealogy, psychology, or anything else you have wanted to learn more about but never had time to pursue.

Crafting: Crafts such as woodworking, metalworking, glass staining, tole painting, ceramics, canvas painting, and sculpting can be personally satisfying and sometimes profitable. You can apply the talents you already have or take classes to learn new crafting skills.

Traveling: The opportunities for travel are limited only by your interest and net worth. If you would like to see more of the country or the world than you can afford, take on temporary part-time jobs and designate that extra money specifically for your "travel budget."

Investing: Though your retirement funds should be in long-term investments, some early retirees enjoy taking a small percentage of their portfolios to trade stocks for fun and additional income (hopefully).

Volunteering: Join one of the many local charitable organizations that need your help. There is usually flexibility to work as few or as many hours as you like.

Movies: If you enjoy movies, this is your opportunity to see all the recently-released shows; watching the Academy Awards will actually have meaning. Be sure to take advantage of the cheaper matinees and/or discount movie theaters.

One other activity requiring special attention is the Internet. If you don't think the World Wide Web can keep your attention, then either you have never been on the Internet or you are extremely difficult to please. The Internet allows you to be in contact with the world. The amount of information available to you with a few mouse clicks or keystrokes is nothing short of phenomenal. Here are a few ideas of what you might do on the Internet:

- Read newspapers from countries throughout the world.
- Read hundreds of online magazines.
- Tap into the Web sites of companies to get information about their products.
- Research any topic of interest.
- E-mail your friends and relatives on a regular basis.
- Chat with people from all over the world.
- Tap into one of the auction Web sites to buy and sell items (that might even provide a means of earning extra spending money while in your early retirement).
- Develop your own Web site for fun or whatever reason.

Most people who have tapped into the Internet now wonder how they ever got along without it. But few people have the time to fully utilize it like early retirees do, whether that involves some research activity, catching up on the news and sports, reading the joke of the day, registering for free money or prizes, or playing checkers with some unidentified person from across the globe.

Only your interests and financial means limit the activities you can pursue during retirement. Many of the activities suggested in the list above are either free or low-cost—the kinds of things you can do to enjoy your early retirement if you are not one of the fortunate who retires rich. We have discovered activities that are relatively expensive and others that are not. We gravitated toward the latter and found many simple, low-cost activities that can be as much fun as those which cost a lot. Make a list of the activities you would like to do if you had more time and money. If you cannot readily compile a list that will constructively fill each of your days and motivate you to look forward to tomorrow, then retiring from full-time employment may not be right for you at this time—or maybe you should start developing new interests.

You might also consider working part-time, which can have several advantages for early retirees. In addition to partially filling newfound time off, part-time employment can help retirees: get out of the daily grind when they don't otherwise have enough money to do so; bring in extra income that will allow them to do activities they can't otherwise afford on their retirement budgets; and keep their skills sharp in the event they later elect to return to full-time employment (not everyone is necessarily a good candidate for early retirement and some may choose to return to work). The advantages of part-time work for early retirees will be thoroughly discussed in chapter 15.

HOW YOUNG?

Retire as young as possible. Traditionally, retirement at age 62 has been considered early. After all, that is when we supposedly can begin collecting reduced Social Security benefits. But too many things can happen to your health between birth and 62 to wait that long. For the 18 years prior to retiring, our goal had been to retire when I turned 50. Under that scenario, and assuming an average life expectancy of about 76, my full-time working years would have totaled 27 (from age 23 to 50) while retirement would have totaled roughly 26 years (from age 50 to 76). That's about 50-50 and seemed fair to me. Currently, most people work 40 years or more (to age 62 or 65) and then enjoy retirement for only 10 or 15 years. Does that seem right to you?

If you retire in your 40s or even early 50s, you can tip the scales the other way—you can enjoy the advantages of retirement for as long or longer than you work. We never know when we might be one of those statistics that dies before the average age, or when we might be involved in an auto accident or contract some dreadful disease that will not allow us to pursue the things we most want to do in our retirement. So consider early retirement as giving up full-time work at the earliest opportunity it is financially feasible. Realistically for many people, that could be their 40s or 50s. For those earning less money or who are unable to save enough, it will be later. But that's okay too—it can still be earlier than would otherwise be the case if the strategies in this book are not followed.

And if you do retire early, does that mean you will never work again? Absolutely not. You may decide to continue working part-time, or you may decide to return to work full-time. We know people who have done both. In the latter situation, it is merely a matter of taking a respite sometime in your life; and that may be exactly what you need to carry you through another five or ten years of full-time employment.

Remember, as is true for most early retirees, the lifestyle you want to live largely determines how early you can retire. Should you retire in your 40s and you are not pleased with the lifestyle your net worth affords you, working a few more years should allow you to retire in better style the second time around. Of course, part-time work may fulfill the same objective while also allowing you to enjoy many of the benefits of early retirement.

Chapter Two

The 2-Minute Survey on Work

Why do you work? Think about it for a minute. What is your *real* motivation for getting up and going to your job each day? Do you enjoy it so much that you can hardly wait to get there, or would you rather be doing something else? Would you work if you didn't have to—if you could afford not to?

Upon retiring at age 42, my answers to those questions were well defined, and I had suspicions as to how most people would respond. But they were merely assumptions, perhaps incorrect, prompting the question: What is the point of writing a book on how to retire young if everyone loves their job and no one wants to retire early? A short, focused survey on work and retirement seemed the answer and shortly thereafter the 2-Minute Survey on Work was born.

Let me clarify that this was not a "scientifically conducted" survey and it has limitations. It was not stratified by age, sex, or ethnic origin to reflect the proportional population characteristics of the entire United States. The survey never asked ethnic origin and, though I requested age and sex demographics, not everyone filled that part out. But while that information might have been interesting, it was not deemed critical. Rather, the purpose of the survey was to gather opinions from a diverse group of people in different cities and states concerning their outlook on work and retirement. In all, responses were gathered from over 500 people with roots in 28 different states—from Alaska and Hawaii to all parts of the continental United States.

JUST DO IT

You will find this chapter more interesting if you first complete the survey before going on to the discussion. Take a couple of minutes now and write down your answers to the seven questions in the reprinted survey below, then we will discuss the results.

THE 2-MINUTE SURVEY ON WORK
This is a research project on work and retirement.
Your honest answers are appreciated.

1. **WHY DO YOU WORK?** Check all that apply. (If retired, why did you work?)

_____Support myself and/or family
_____Enjoy the challenge
_____Want or need the "benefits"
_____Prestige or ego
_____Self-esteem
_____Greed (want more money)
_____Socialization with coworkers
_____Help other people
_____Something to do
_____So my kids get an inheritance
_____Can't afford to retire yet
_____Other

2. Now rank the **3 PRIMARY REASONS** you work (or did work). Note: 1 = most important, then 2 and 3.

    _____Support myself and/or family
    _____Enjoy the challenge
    _____Want or need the "benefits"
    _____Prestige or ego
    _____Self-esteem
    _____Greed (want <u>more</u> money)
    _____Socialization with coworkers
    _____Help other people
    _____Something to do
    _____So my kids get an inheritance
    _____Can't afford to retire yet
    _____Other_________________

3. How much money would you need in the bank/invested to **CONSIDER YOURSELF "RICH"**? _________________

4. At what age do you **PLAN TO RETIRE**? _______
   At what age would you **LIKE TO RETIRE**? _____

5. Are you counting on receiving a **SOCIAL SECURITY PENSION** when you retire? _______

6. If you **COULD AFFORD NOT TO WORK**, would you still do so? _____ If yes, would you work:
   Full-time paid? ___ Part-time paid? ___ Volunteer? ___

7. What percent of your household income **DO YOU INVEST YEARLY** for retirement? ________

FOR STATISTICAL PURPOSES, THE FOLLOWING WOULD BE HELPFUL:

Age_____ Sex_____ Occupation: ____________________

In which of the 50 states have you lived the longest? ________

Education Completed: __H.S. __2-year College

__4-year College __17+ years education

Annual Household Income: __$0-25,000 __$25-50,000

__$50-75,000 ___$75,000+

THANK YOU VERY MUCH

Copyright © 2000 by Larry Ferstenou

AND THE SURVEY SAYS

The survey results supported my assumptions above, but with a couple of surprises. To summarize the main points of the findings:

- People work for many different reasons, but the predominate reason they work full-time is money.
- Nearly two-thirds of all respondents defined "rich" as having at least one million dollars.
- Half of all respondents are counting on Social Security in their retirement.
- If they could afford not to work, 77 percent would continue working anyway. Most would choose to work part-time paid and some would volunteer.
- Most people would like to retire at 55 or younger, but few believe they will be able to meet that goal.
- Most respondents will need to save and invest more than they currently are if they want to retire young.

Now let's look at the rationale behind each question and the results derived from over 500 survey participants.

Question 1: WHY DO YOU WORK? Check all that apply.

This may seem like an obvious question, but there are many reasons why people work. Not unexpectedly, 91 percent responded that they work to support themselves and/or their families. The second highest scoring reason was for the "benefits" that many employers provide—like medical insurance, vacation, 401(k), and paid holidays. I anticipated that "can't afford to retire yet" would be number three, but it was edged out by "enjoy the challenge." While many people may be challenged by their jobs, it appears that they would retire nonetheless if they could afford it. Here are all the reasons people work and the percent that chose each one:

91% Support myself and/or family
59% Want or need the "benefits"
49% Enjoy the challenge
47% Can't afford to retire yet
37% Self-esteem
34% Socialization with coworkers
22% Help other people
19% Something to do
17% Greed (want more money)
10% Prestige or ego
6% So my kids get an inheritance
5% Other

Question 2: Now rank the 3 PRIMARY REASONS you work (or did work).

Question 2 was written to confirm my suspicions as to the real reasons people work. Given an opportunity in question 1 to indicate all the reasons why they work, it was not uncommon to see six or more items checked. But limiting the choices to three, and then ranking them in order of importance, provided insight into why people *really* work.

It was no surprise that support of self and family again far outscored everything else. Money and the related employee benefits are the only gains paid employment can give you that you cannot get from non-paid activities. Among other things, volunteer work can do wonders for self-esteem, allow you to socialize, give you something to do, challenge you, massage your ego, and allow you to help other people. So while volunteer work can fulfill all the other reasons listed here as to why people work, what it cannot do is provide the monetary support for you and your family. The three primary reasons people work, listed in order of importance, were:

78% Support myself and/or family
41% Want or need the "benefits"
22% Can't afford to retire yet

The fact that *all* of the participants did not choose "support myself and/or family" demonstrates that, as seen in question 1, some people have other reasons for working. The relatively low percentages for the second and third primary reasons are due to: (1) the responses being widely spread out among the twelve choices, and (2) many people marking only one primary reason for working—support myself and/or family—rather than three as requested.

Question 3: How much would you need in the bank/invested to CONSIDER YOURSELF "RICH"?

The subtitle of this book, *How to Retire in Your 40s or 50s Without Being Rich,* needed confirmation and credibility. While the range of responses was wide, I was not surprised to see the majority of respondents (64 percent) define rich as having a million dollars or more. Since a million dollars is not necessary to retire young, you can stop worrying about having to be rich if you would rather retire early than work the rest of your life.

Question 4: At what age do you PLAN TO RETIRE? At what age would you LIKE TO RETIRE?

This question was written to confirm the main premise of the book: that people work for the money and would retire young if they could afford it. If everyone loved working, then the ages at which they "plan to retire" and would "like to retire" would be relatively late in their lives—probably in their 70s or maybe "never" as some indicated.

Conversely, if people work predominately because they have to, not because they want to, then the age they would "like to retire" would be relatively young and probably significantly lower than when they "plan to retire" (because most cannot financially afford to retire as young as they would like to).

A significantly high 76 percent of the survey participants expressed a desire to retire at age 55 or younger; a slight majority of the participants (51 percent) indicated age 50 or younger. Numerous participants answered that they would like to retire "now," which was anywhere from their current age of under 30 to over 60.

There was no doubt, as a result of this survey question, that most people would like to retire young—younger than they believe they will be able to. Whereas only 21 percent of respondents *wanted* to work past age 60, over three times that many *planned* to retire at age 60 or later (presumably for financial reasons).

Plan To Retire:	60 or older	= 66%
	55 or younger	= 30%
	50 or younger	= 15%
Like To Retire:	60 or older	= 21%
	55 or younger	= 76%
	50 or younger	= 51%

Question 5: Are you counting on receiving a SOCIAL SECURITY PENSION when you retire?

Because chapters 12 and 13 are devoted to Social Security and its impending insolvency, the purpose of question 5 was to determine how many people are counting on that pension for their retirement. Considering that the traditional three-legged stool (employer-funded pension, Social Security, and personal savings) is slowly collapsing, how many baby boomers and younger adults are expecting to receive Social Security?

This question was scored for those participants who identified themselves as age 50 or younger. In my opinion, those older than 50 have less concern about receiving higher Social Security payments upon turning 62 or older than those under 50, especially those who are in their 20s or 30s. Age 50 was arbitrarily chosen as the cut-off for tabulating these responses.

This was the biggest surprise of the survey as only a few responses separated the two groups. It was so close that the scores were calculated to tenths of a percentage point. In retrospect, it would have been interesting to pursue how much of a pension those who answered "yes" think they are actually going to receive.

Yes = 49.3%
No = 50.7%

Question 6: If you COULD AFFORD NOT TO WORK, would you still do so? If yes, would you work: full-time paid, part-time paid, or volunteer?

The results from this question were also unexpected. While initially I anticipated that most people would either choose not to work at all or they would do volunteer work, a surprising 71 percent expressed a preference for working and indicated that, rather than volunteer their time, they would choose to work part-time paid. (That finding is reasonably consistent with the "2001 Retirement Confidence Survey" found on the Employee Benefit Research Institute's Web site (www.ebri.org), wherein 61 percent indicated that they plan to work for pay after they retire.)

A surprisingly low 39 percent expressed an interest in volunteer work, although some respondents marked both part-time paid and volunteer (which is why the numbers do not add up to 100 percent). As you will read in chapter 15, there is nothing wrong with pursuing part-time paid employment when you retire young; in fact, it can provide several significant benefits.

Would you work?	Yes = 77% No = 23%
If yes, would you work:	Full-time paid? = 16%
	Part-time paid? = 71%
	Volunteer? = 39%

Sixteen percent of the respondents would continue full-time employment, even if they could afford to not work at all. This group was comprised of those who work for reasons other than money (as revealed in question 1), as well as those who added a comment that they would switch from working for someone else to a self-employment venture.

Question 7: What percent of your household income DO YOU INVEST YEARLY for retirement?

The last question was included to compare the retirement savings rate of the people surveyed to the national average. The biggest concern about the findings from this question is whether most people know the percentage of annual household income they are saving; the number of people who left it blank or entered a question mark on the line supported that. And were they considering solely what they set aside, or what their employer is also contributing to their retirement account? The question wasn't detailed enough to provide those answers. But if not totally accurate, at least the question provides a breakdown of how much people *think* they are saving.

Savings Rate	Percent Who Believe They Are Saving That Amount
0%	16%
1 to 5	23
6 to 9	9
10 to 14	27
15 to 20	18
21 to 30	5
31 to 40	0
41 to 50	1
51%+	1

According to these survey results, 61 percent of our participants believe their household savings are more than 5 percent of their annual income. That is well above the 1.6 percent personal savings rate in 2001 and the 1.0 percent in 2000 as reported by the U.S. Department of Commerce, Bureau of Economic Analysis (www.bea.doc.gov). The higher the savings rate, and the higher the annual household income, the better the odds for retiring young. One-quarter of the survey respondents think they are saving a relatively high 15 percent or more of their income, while 2 percent believe they are saving more than 30 percent (the minimum per year we saved on average).

STATISTICS

A statistical section was included in order to define the survey population. The figures below reveal that a wide range of individuals in terms of age, sex, education, household income, and occupation participated in the 2-Minute Survey on Work. For those interested in statistical information, the demographics of the survey participants were as follows:

AGE:

Under 20	= 4%
20-24	= 9%
25-29	= 7%
30-34	= 11%
35-39	= 15%
40-44	= 19%
45-49	= 15%
50-54	= 9%
55-59	= 5%
60-64	= 3%
65+	= 3%

SEX:

Female	= 59%
Male	= 41%

EDUCATION COMPLETED:

High School	= 39%
2-Year College	= 31%
4-Year College	= 20%
17+ Years	= 10%

ANNUAL HOUSEHOLD INCOME:

$ 0 to 25,000	= 19%
$25,000 to 50,000	= 38%
$50,000 to 75,000	= 26%
$75,000+	= 17%

EXAMPLE OCCUPATIONS REPRESENTED:

Although not inclusive of all the occupations identified on the response sheets, the following provides a fairly extensive representation of the range of employment backgrounds of those completing the survey.

Accountant
Account Executive
Accounting Clerk
Administrative Assistant
Aircraft Mechanic
Aircraft Technician
Airline Executive
Appraiser
Artist
Banker
Bank Teller
Benefits Administrator
Business Analyst
Buyer
Case Manager
Cashier
Certified Nursing
Assistant Chiropractor
Circulation Director
Clerk
Closing Officer
College Instructor
Computer Programmer
Computer Technician
Consultant
Cook
Cosmetologist
Counselor
Crew Planner (Scheduler)
Customer Relations
Data Entry
Dental Technician
Dentist
Department Manager
Director of Advertising
Director of Operations
Dog Groomer
Employment Specialist
Engineer
Farmer
Financial Analyst
Flight Attendant
Flight Dispatcher
Florist
Foreman
General Manager
Graphic Artist
Grocery Checker
Grocery Manager
Highway Patrol Officer
Human Resources
Manager Insurance Sales
Representative
Investment Broker
Journalist
Mail Carrier

Laborer
Librarian
Loan Assistant
Loan Officer
Machinist
Mortgage Loan Underwriter
Musician
Music Therapist
Nurse's Aide
Nurse Practitioner
Office Manager
Operating Engineer
Optometrist
Paralegal
Payroll Clerk
Physician
Physician's Assistant
Pilot
Pipe Fitter
Plans Examiner
Police Officer
Produce Worker
Professor
Psychotherapist
Purchaser
Quality Assurance Auditor
Quality Control Inspector
Receptionist
Records Manager
Registered Nurse
Rehabilitation Counselor
Rental Agent
Sales
Secretary
Security Guard
Social Services Worker
Stock Clerk
Teacher
Technical Writer
Title Officer
Training Coordinator
Truck Driver
Vice-President Marketing
Waitress
Writer

WHERE DO YOU STAND?

How did your responses compare to the survey group? Are you working primarily for money or for other reasons? Like most of the survey respondents, would you like to retire younger than 55? If so, then how do you transition from working full-time to ultimately enjoying the freedom that early retirement brings?

And what about the work ethic—that you should work because you are young and physically able? If you have a strong work ethic but would also like to retire young, you may perceive a conflict.

We did. If that is an issue for you, then the next chapter should be beneficial in planning your early exit from full-time employment.

Chapter Three

What About the "Work Ethic"?

One of the most difficult aspects of retiring in your 40s or 50s may be overcoming the "work ethic." Having come from the Midwest where the work ethic is reputed to be strong, retiring in one's 40s was not a concept with which we were familiar. We grew up with the expectation that people grind away until age 65 (or later, for many) and then retire on Social Security. When we first discussed the idea of retiring in our 40s, the issue of not working until at least 62 repeatedly came up between us—as did questions of how friends and relatives might react.

EFFECTIVE RATIONALIZATIONS

Frankly, both of us struggled with the repercussions that our decision to retire so young might have. We both had been called workaholics in our businesses and somehow not working just didn't seem right. Since we could afford not to work, why should retiring early be an issue? It came down to one thing: the work ethic. It was so ingrained in us that you work until at least age 62 (and more likely 65) that we had difficulty accepting the alternative. It took awhile, but obviously we overcame that perceived incongruity. How? Effective rationalizations:

- Considering the excessive hours during our years of self-employment, it seemed like we had already worked a lifetime in our 18-year careers.
- Early retirement may not be forever; perhaps it will only be a respite for a couple of years. (However, we also realized that if it turned out to be everything we expected and we could continue to afford it, early retirement would become permanent.)
- We may work part-time to earn IRA money and a little extra "mad money." The fact that we might do some work made the idea more defensible. We also decided that if we were to do volunteer work, we would still be contributing to our community and society as a whole.
- Working hard and saving/investing an exceptionally high percentage of our income compared to most people allowed us to accumulate a net worth sufficient to no longer have to work. That is reason enough.

By the time we actually retired, we had resolved that it was okay not to work. But admittedly, we discussed this issue again and again. It is unfortunate that we had not come across the book *Your Money or Your Life* by the late Joe Dominguez and Vicki Robin prior to retiring, because it may have led to less need for rationalizing. The authors attempt to put work, money, and life in perspective and assist the reader in understanding his or her relationship between life and money. Joe Dominguez had been a technical analyst and institutional investment advisor on Wall Street. He retired at age 31 after deciding there had to be more to life than work. Mr. Dominguez and Ms. Robin developed their book and early retirement program to help readers focus on:

- How much money they have earned in their lifetimes
- How much they have to show for it
- What it really cost to get it
- How to track what they earn and spend
- How satisfying or fulfilling spending money really is
- How they can minimize spending and maximize income
- When they have "enough"
- How to manage what they have

Of the numerous retirement-related books I have read, *Your Money or Your Life* was one of the most unique. The authors feel strongly about life and the planet, and the relationship they establish step-by-step between life and money is worth reading for anyone contemplating early retirement. Their ideas and procedures fit well with the guidelines in this book.

If you still perceive a conflict between the work ethic and early retirement, try to spend some time around people who have taken an early exit from the workforce. When you get young retirees together, their enthusiasm seems almost infectious and that should boost your eagerness to follow suit. Of course, the difficult part is finding early retirees to talk to; few people retire in their 40s or 50s because most do not have the motivation or discipline needed to save and invest so they can meet the net worth required for early retirement. I hope *you* do.

LIVING GUILT-FREE

After moving to Utah, we met a 46-year-old man who had also recently left California and retired in St. George. Upon meeting for the first time, I asked if he was retired (not an unusual question in a gathering of mostly retired people). He seemed uncomfortable as he responded, "I'm currently working part-time." Not until I admitted to being a bona fide early retiree did he confess to the same, though it was also true that he had a temporary job working a few hours per week. The point is that Kris and I weren't the only ones who experienced some guilt at first for being able to do whatever we wanted to while virtually everyone else our age was going to work day after day. Doesn't the work ethic require that people in their 40s be gainfully employed?

Our friend's story was similar to ours in many ways. For years he had worked far more hours than the average person and had saved a lot of what he had earned. When the opportunity presented itself for him to retire and spend his days engaging in activities he enjoyed, there seemed to be no other alternative. In the six years we have been friends now, there is no question that we all truly appreciate the situation we are in; it's hard to imagine others not actively working toward the same goal.

If you plan to retire young but begin to experience the guilt trip, reread the fourth rationalization above. If you have made the trade-offs that most find necessary to retire early and, as a result, you have managed to accumulate a sufficient net worth, there is no reason to feel guilty. Enjoy doing whatever you want to do each day while everyone else your age goes to work. You earned it.

THE WORST THAT COULD HAPPEN

For over eight years we have had one response for those questioning our retirement at such a young age: The worst that can happen is some day we may *have to* go back to work. If that day should come, then at least we will have genuinely enjoyed ourselves for however long we managed to stay retired.

Think about this for your early retirement. The downside is that if the stock market totally collapsed, you may have to return to work—possibly part-time, maybe even full-time. That still beats having had to work all along. But assuming the market continues in its historical pattern and your investments remain relatively stable, you can be free from *having* to work for as long as you live. Doesn't that seem like a risk worth taking? And consider this: If the stock market totally collapsed, having to return to work until it turns back around will seem rather trivial compared to the problems millions of others (those who are not financially prepared and do not follow the 3 Keys to retiring young) will experience.

AND WHAT WILL YOUR FRIENDS SAY?

One of our concerns as we discussed the idea of retiring in our 40s was what our friends would think. Would they be supportive and wish us well? Would they think we had lost our minds? Did it matter what they thought or said? All of our friends were actively engaged in their jobs or careers. For us to suddenly quit working to "do nothing" (as many people think retirees do) seemed something they would not understand. And what about relatives still living in Wisconsin where we learned our work ethic? Although what our relatives thought would not impact us much since we lived 2,000 miles away, we questioned what impact it might have on our parents who still live in small Wisconsin towns and see the relatives all the time. How many parents want to see their children perceived as too lazy to work?

Once we completed the rationalization process discussed at the beginning of this chapter, we began sharing our decision with friends. Most questioned whether we could afford it; if so, then they thought it was a great idea. Two friends predicted we wouldn't make it longer than six months, since they perceived us both as workaholics. Obviously they were wrong. While visiting friends and family in Wisconsin shortly after retiring, we talked with several retired senior citizens. Their comments were similarly reassuring: "Don't wait to retire until you're too old and crippled up to have fun," and "If you can afford it, go for it."

After approximately one year in St. George, we rented a home (and then later bought one) in a townhouse complex comprised largely of retirees who followed the traditional path of working until 62 or older. In that regard, we were quite an anomaly. Following the usual comment, "You're too young to be retired" was the question of what we had done for careers that we could afford to retire in our early 40s—a legitimate question. Explaining about our workaholic days, not having any children, and living on a budget usually sufficed. And after we got involved in activities related to our townhouse complex, people were vocally appreciative of the fact that we were young and ambitious enough (and had the time, of course) to volunteer lots of hours in helping to set up and run our homeowners' association.

AFTER THE FACT

One interesting situation occurred nearly four years after we retired. While attending a Christmas party, an attendee unknown to me asked what it was we had done prior to retirement. A second participant whom I knew commented, "I hear you sold your business and made a huge amount of money." Without asking where she heard that, I set the record straight. We did not sell our businesses; rather, we locked the doors and walked away. We were able to retire early because we are financially self-disciplined individuals who live within our budget.

That incident was amusing because certainly most people (and definitely the person who made the comment) have a hard time understanding how people in their early 40s can retire without being rich. In fact, the person who made the comment about us selling our businesses and making a huge amount of money generally spends as much in a month as we do in six months. But then most people, and especially the group engaged in that conversation, could probably never see themselves living on our budget. It is all relative and early retirement without being rich is possible, for us and for you too.

Since announcing our decision to retire early, we have only heard one or two negative comments and, of course, it is sometimes difficult to know when someone is kidding or serious. Those comments came from past business associates and referred to our not paying our share of taxes any longer; of course, that was relative to what they pay and to what they knew we paid when running our businesses. Certainly we would not be paying the same level of federal, state, and FICA taxes we had become accustomed to; after all, that was one of the motivators for retiring early.

Over the past eight years, comments from people who find out we retired in our early 40s have been overwhelmingly positive, and numerous times we've hear the comment, "It must be nice." Of course, that shouldn't be surprising. After all, most people would rather have freedom and control over their lives than continue working in the day-to-day grind. Most remark that they wish they could do (or could have done) the same. With sufficient focus, determination, and effort, many could.

That goal will be easier to achieve if you have an upcoming defined-benefit pension (corporate, military, or civil service), you plan to marry into money, or you intend to be the recipient of a big inheritance. But assuming most people will not encounter these circumstances, virtually everyone wanting to retire early will need to apply the 3 Keys to retiring young, detailed in the next chapter, to make their dream come true.

Chapter Four

The 3 Keys to Retiring Young

For as long as I can remember, being rich seemed like the goal to achieve—there simply didn't appear to be any advantages to being poor. While there is more to life than money, you can do so much with it (good or bad) and so little without it. To one day be independently wealthy was a motivator throughout much of my life; to not have to work until the day I died was another.

Relatively early in our careers, we set a goal of retiring "rich" when I turned 50. We intended to work hard, become rich (which we defined as having a net worth of at least a million dollars), and then never work again. Did we reach that goal? Not exactly. We never got close to that magic figure of one million and we didn't retire at age 50 either. We actually retired at 42 and 40, but without being rich. So what happened to that goal of having a million dollars and how did we manage to retire so early without being rich?

In our case, accumulating wealth meant working far more than the standard 40-hour workweek. For several years, we worked six and often seven days a week, including holidays. It was not unusual for either of us to work 16-hour days, and when there didn't seem to be any other solution, I even managed 100-hour workweeks. Working as hard as we did to reach that goal of accumulating a million dollars took its toll after several years and the reality surfaced that one or both of us would probably be dead long before that lofty ambition came to fruition. Was the pursuit of a million dollars in order to retire at 50 necessary? We thought so at first, but later realized it was not.

SETTING A GOAL

In 1977, one year into our marriage and while in our mid-twenties, we seriously started talking about retiring at age 50. What precipitated that ambitious goal at our young ages? The primary reason for choosing age 50 was the death of my father of a heart attack at age 52; I was 26 at the time. My dad was a long-haul truck driver who delivered bulk milk from Wisconsin to other states. It was a sedentary, stressful job accompanied by a greasy-spoon truck stop diet.

Seeing my dad die at a relatively young age without ever having had the opportunity to retire and do the things he would have been happier doing, had a significant impact on us. It provided the motivation to accomplish our goal of early retirement, a goal that was later reinforced by accumulating evidence of a link between heredity and heart disease. Since my dad died at 52 of a heart attack, the wise move seemed to be to retire at 50 and, assuming heredity had me following in his footsteps, at least have a couple of years to fully enjoy doing the things we wanted to do.

But that incident also prompted an increased awareness of the number of people who die or experience severe disabilities at relatively young ages as a result of injuries and illnesses. Watching television, reading the newspaper, and talking to friends further confirmed that retiring as early as possible should be a goal to pursue because the future is too uncertain to assume one will retire healthy at the current target ages of 62, 65, or older.

The logic of retiring as young as possible was again reinforced approximately three years after we retired, when my brother-in-law died of cancer at the young age of 33. We never know if there will be a tomorrow. If you need a daily reminder of that, check the ages of people in the obituaries when you open the morning newspaper. Since none of us are immune from early death or disability through illness or accident, it makes me feel better knowing that, whatever should happen tomorrow, we haven't worked up to the day we die and we have thoroughly enjoyed each and every day of our lives since retiring young. Return to full-time employment? Not a chance for this couple.

Although my career in vocational rehabilitation provided a degree of satisfaction for many years after completing graduate school, burnout was a significant factor in quitting. To have a job or career that one truly loves would be ideal, and had that been the case, this early retiree might still be working. It is those rare individuals having real passion for their careers who often continue to work beyond what they have to from a financial standpoint.

But for the rest of us, our passions tend to be avocational. For me, *retirement* has long represented what life should be about—the freedom and opportunity to do what *we* want to do every day while we are young and healthy enough to take advantage of it. Early retirement became my goal and motivation for working. Although there were many interesting and fun coworkers and clients over the years, and there was satisfaction in helping others plan career changes, it was not something I wanted to do for the rest of my life. I did not need or want a rigid schedule, daily commitments, stress, and lack of time to do the things in life that were more enjoyable to me than working.

Retiring early will require establishing a financial goal and then conscientiously accumulating a sufficient net worth to reach it.

Over the years we have seen and utilized numerous tables, charts, graphs, and formulas printed in magazines and books that allowed us to compare our net worth to target figures considered necessary for retirement. Those exercises can be fun and beneficial to your planning, so take advantage of them when you can. They can be good reinforcement for your efforts and can help you to get or stay on track. In chapter 9 you will learn about retirement planners/calculators, which are excellent resources for establishing a financial goal and tracking your progress in meeting it.

We always outpaced the chart/graph recommendations for our age group; we accomplished that by initiating an uncommon degree of financial self-discipline—the goal being to save enough money to retire at age 50. But we aren't the only ones who *can* do it! Later in this book I describe in detail how we accumulated a sufficient net worth to retire in our early 40s (without being rich) and how you can too. For now, though, it's time to introduce what I believe are the 3 Keys to retiring young which most people will need to follow to fulfill their early retirement dream:

Simplify Your Life
Embrace Financial Self-Discipline
Invest Wisely

While we had little difficulty with the first two keys, we made several expensive mistakes on the third. Having never had anything but savings accounts and certificates of deposit (CDs) throughout our lives, moving into actual investing was a learning experience. And whereas we started investing when California was booming and you could make money in virtually any kind of real estate, we also got caught in the economic downturn that hit California in the late 1980s, early 1990s. We made a number of investing mistakes that you will not need to make if you learn from ours. You will find our investing nightmares described in chapter 10.

SIMPLIFY YOUR LIFE

This first key to retiring young sounds much easier to do than it is, judging from the pace of retail sales the past few years and everything we see, read, and hear. But it is one of the essential strategies for most people to retire early. Numerous articles and books are dedicated to simplifying one's life. Some may go to extremes, but most explain the rationale and provide ideas for putting the concept into practice. If you need help figuring out how to simplify your life, or why you should, read the following books:

- *Cashing In on the American Dream* by Paul Terhorst (this has been out of print for years but may still be available at your library).
- *The Simple Living Guide* by Janet Luhrs.
- *Your Money or Your Life* by Joe Dominguez and Vicki Robin.
- The *Tightwad Gazette* books by Amy Dacyczyn.

You can find hundreds of books and articles on frugality and simple living listed on Internet Web sites, or you can spend hours reading online by typing "tightwad books," "frugal living," or "simple living" into one of the Internet search engines. One Web site dedicated to simple living is www.thefrugallife.com.

About a year ago I joined an Internet forum dedicated to early retirement. One couple on the forum likes to travel and live in different cities (or countries) for six months to a year at a time. Their strategy is to move to a city, buy all their furnishings at thrift stores or garage sales and then donate them to charitable organizations when they decide to relocate again. The money they save in moving costs alone more than pays for refurnishing their household each time they move. It's a good strategy that allows them to remain flexible to do what they enjoy doing—traveling and living in different areas and cultures. And, yes, they do subscribe to the simple living theory so that they do not accumulate anywhere near what the average household does.

Simplifying your life breaks down to this concept: **The less you own and have to take care of, the less complicated your life and the less it costs to live.** Decreasing assets not only saves money, but it also saves time and, in many cases, aggravation. Put your money to work earning more money to live on and forego the depreciating assets and frivolous trinkets. Vicki Terhorst, of *Cashing In on the American Dream*, commented in a 1993 *Money* magazine interview, "We cherish a favorite coffee cup instead of a coffee table." That seems to convey the essential concept in simplifying your life—not that you shouldn't own furniture, but that you keep in perspective the number of assets you own and must maintain.

We have owned homes, furniture, cars, TVs, stereos, VCRs, and many other common household assets that provide enjoyment in our lives. For most people, life (and retirement) would not be complete without owning the things they enjoy. Just remember to keep the accumulation of assets in check. We avoid purchasing the latest fads, fashions, and technology; we don't need one of everything manufactured; and we don't feel a need to keep up with the Joneses. If you have those needs, then you are probably not a good candidate for retiring young—unless you adjust that thinking or you have the income to support all of that and still retire.

Neither of us has ever seen any benefit to smoking, drinking, gambling, or taking illegal drugs. On the contrary, what those activities can do is waste your money, defer your retirement, and ruin your life. Generally, we found that the more hours we worked the less money we spent and the faster our net worth grew. If you are content not living in the "fast lane" or keeping up with your friends and neighbors, and if you can make the trade-offs necessary to spend as little as possible and save as much as possible, you can find yourself in a good position to retire young.

During our first year of retirement I saw an interview on CNBC with a young couple in their 30s who had a combined income of

$70,000 per year and a goal of accumulating $500,000 so they could retire early (age 55 they said). At the same time, they owned a new 3-bedroom home in southern California with a mortgage payment that exceeded $1,300 per month, had two fairly new BMWs, and admittedly lived the lifestyle they enjoyed. It was obvious to me as a program viewer, and to the financial planner with whom they were talking, that although they may reach their financial goal by age 55, it would be much easier if they cut expenses and invested more of their income dollars. However, they were choosing a higher standard of living and better lifestyle now with hopes of also reaching their preferred early retirement by age 55.

Living the lifestyle one wants to live today and maybe having to retire later in life is certainly an alternative to the other approach, which we took, of foregoing some material possessions and other "wants" now and retiring earlier. Of course, the ideal situation would allow for living the lifestyle one wants today while also retiring early. Then again, if you can afford that, you probably don't need to read this book.

The authors of *The Millionaire Next Door,* Thomas J. Stanley, Ph.D. and William D. Danko, Ph.D., found through their years of research that accumulating wealth requires discipline, sacrifice (perhaps better described as trade-offs), and hard work. We found the same. The question therefore becomes: Are you willing to make those trade-offs in order to have the option of quitting full-time work in the future if you want to?

Paring Down

Once you retire, many expenses associated with work can easily be pared down, such as clothing allowance, number of vehicles owned, commuting expenses, and meals eaten out. But making such lifestyle adjustments as much as possible years prior to exiting the workforce, can go a long way toward increasing your net worth to meet your early retirement goal.

For starters, you can simplify your life by getting rid of those once-valuable items that are now gathering dust and taking up space. If you have been living in the same place more than a few years, it is not unusual to have accumulated a lot of unused and no-longer-needed items. Don't continue parking your valuable autos in the driveway while piling up less valuable unused stuff (in some cases, junk) in your garage. The same reasoning applies to filling drawers and closets with items you no longer use and taking up otherwise usable space merely because you don't know what to do with all of it. Sell unneeded items or give them to charity.

Prior to leaving California for Utah, we had three moving/garage sales to simplify our lives. We sold the majority of our remaining business assets and numerous personal items that we did not think we would *need* in the future, with the exception of some gifts that had been handcrafted by family or friends. What we did not sell we gave away. Our thinking was, rather than hold onto items that we may seldom or never use, why not make some money, not have to worry about storing them, and then if we *really* need an item in the future, we will buy another.

Over the years we have found that only a few of those items (and none of great value) could have been used later. However, balancing that with the hundreds of items we did sell that we have not had to store over this period of time, either in a storage unit or in a bigger house than we need, having the garage sales was the smart move. The more you simplify your life the less expensive it will be to live and, ultimately, if you choose to retire young without being rich, the less complications in your life the better.

You can have as much as you want as long as you can afford it and still meet your retirement goal. Some people will retire with a much larger net worth than others and that will allow them to own more assets if they choose. But for those who would like to retire early without a huge net worth, what is important is having only what they need and needing less than most people.

If you think simplifying your life is going to be difficult, keep your focus on the future. Balance how much you don't want to have to work the rest of your life with what you want to buy today. To give you some help in saving money, specific strategies will be delineated in later chapters.

You might also want to do a net worth statement every quarter like we do (total all your assets, subtract your debt, and that will leave you with your net worth). Watching your net worth grow can be fun and it reinforces your efforts—like losing weight after starting a diet. You change your eating to try and lose weight. If you fail to lose any, you quit the program. But if you start dropping a pound at a time, that provides sufficient reinforcement and encouragement to try harder. Saving, investing, and watching your money grow is no different.

Simplifying your life means buying less of the things you don't *need*. And closely integrated with that is the second key to retiring young: financial self-discipline.

FINANCIAL SELF-DISCIPLINE

Simplifying your life means not having to have two houses, three cars, four stereos, five televisions, and six telephones. Financial self-discipline, on the other hand, involves conscientious and savvy buying when you do make purchases, as well as not spending frivolously. It is a crucial element in planning for early retirement because it also means saving a higher percentage of what you earn, especially as income increases; ultimately, that will be a major factor in determining when you will be able to retire. Think of financial self-discipline as:

Spending your money in a prudent manner and saving (investing) as much as possible to reach the goal of retiring young.

I have always had a penchant for saving; fortunately, Kris also shares that characteristic and perhaps that had a lot to do with our relationship running fairly smoothly all these years (since money is one of the most divisive factors in marriages). Our tendency has always been to establish priorities and save for bigger goals rather than frittering away money on trinkets and items we considered a bad value or wasteful. But most people do not retire young because they establish different priorities for spending their money, and saving for the future is not foremost on their minds.

Some good examples of the value of financial self-discipline come from my career as a vocational evaluator. For 17 years, I assisted individuals in career planning and/or returning to work. Most of my clients had suffered some kind of job-related injury and were involved in the state workers' compensation rehabilitation program. For several years I also worked with "economically disadvantaged" clients—another term for those receiving welfare. Having already begun a fervent effort to accumulate wealth, it was an eye-opener to see the amount of money many of my workers' compensation rehabilitation clients earned while concurrently failing to save for their futures.

One representative example involves a client who earned his living as a welder. While I was earning $25,000 or so (in 1986) with my master's degree in rehabilitation, this client without any college had been earning in the range of $70,000 per year. However, upon suffering a back injury that precluded his returning to his occupation, he had no reserve funds to help him in his time of need. Upon inquiring as to why he did not have any money saved that could be assisting him now, he responded, "We ate well—steak and lobster every night. We bought everything we wanted."

While this welder was making far more money than my wife and I combined, he admitted to having none when it was really needed. In the meantime, while earning roughly half as much money between us, Kris and I had already accumulated our first

$100,000 in net worth. But then, we were not eating steak and lobster every night and buying everything we wanted.

Many of my other industrially-injured clients told similar stories, and given that many of them had been working in construction-related jobs during the California housing boom years, their annual incomes also exceeded our combined income. However, few of the hundreds of clients I worked with in California had saved enough to help them meet their financial obligations when their injuries forced them out of the competitive job market (much less having begun saving for retirement). Their incomes were reduced to less than $1,000 per month in workers' compensation payments and, for some, their next stop was food stamps.

Working with welfare clients provided other examples. They weren't all inter-generational welfare recipients. In fact, some earned good wages at one time but lacked the financial self-discipline to save. Discussions with my clients revealed that illegal drugs and alcohol were common within their families and some admitted that potential financial savings had been blown on vices that could have been avoided in the first place.

Don't underestimate the role of discipline in retiring young. But there's no magic pill. If you are not born financially self-disciplined, you will have to learn it. And you can. When people want something, they usually figure out a way to get it, which requires some degree of discipline. You need to develop, strengthen, and channel that discipline to achieve your goal of retiring young. Whether applied to your finances, career, or personal life, self-discipline is comprised primarily of focus and determination.

To apply financial self-discipline in your life, start by writing out a specific goal you want to achieve, such as cutting spending a defined amount or accumulating a specific dollar figure in your retirement accounts—make sure it's realistic. Then write out the steps you need to take, and the trade-offs you need to make, to reach that goal. Focus and determination will then be the essential elements in attaining it.

Concentrate on achieving your goal and adhere to the steps you have devised to accomplish it. Convince yourself that the results emanating from fulfilling your written goal are more important than other things you want. If you stay focused and reward yourself by charting your progress along the way to confirm that you are making positive movement forward, you will accomplish your goal, step by step. If you keep your goals realistic and if you want them enough, focus and determination will get you what you want. That is the application of self-discipline and one of the essential factors in changing your life.

For more on learning self-discipline, read *Take Control: Master the Art of Self-Discipline and Change Your Life Forever* by Michael A. Janke. The author is a former Navy SEAL who reveals, among other strategies, techniques utilized by elite commando units to develop self-discipline (and they are unquestionably some of the most disciplined people in the world). His book centers on learning discipline in several areas of your life: personal, physical, mental, nutritional, and professional. His "100 Secrets of Power Living" offer many valuable ideas for self-improvement that, in turn, can increase self-discipline and change your life.

How early you want to retire, the lifestyle you want to live in that retirement, and the amount of money you earn, will determine how financially self-disciplined you will need to be. Specific strategies and techniques for applying financial self-discipline will be covered in chapter 7, which is dedicated to this important topic.

INVEST WISELY

While simplifying your life and becoming financially self-disciplined are important, it is wise investing that will make or break your early retirement possibilities. Depositing money into a savings account or certificate of deposit (CD) is not "investing" in the same manner that purchasing stocks, bonds, or real estate is, where assuming more risk (the possibility of losing money) earns a higher return on that investment. In later chapters we will discuss different types of investments, how we saved enough money to retire early, and how you can, too. While all types of investments have inherent advantages and disadvantages, it is important to balance risk with potential reward in planning for early retirement.

Most people are comfortable with CDs and savings accounts, but these choices will not allow you to accumulate a sufficient net worth over time to retire young. What can help you grow that net worth is the stock market. According to figures obtained from the Vanguard Group, from 1926 through year-end 2001, the stock market (in this case the S&P 500 Index) averaged 10.7 percent return per year, while U.S. corporate bonds averaged 5.7 percent, and U.S. Treasury Bills (which earn returns similar to CDs, higher than that of savings accounts) averaged a mere 4.0 percent. Although the stock market has its ups and downs—and some of those downs have been for fairly long periods of time—given a long-term horizon of 20-plus years, the stock market has been the logical choice for investing your money and accumulating the net worth needed to retire early.

At the same time, you have probably heard stories about how so-and-so lost money in the stock market and that is likely true. But they lost money because they panicked and sold when the stock market went through one of those short-term downturns, or they were invested in a specific stock (company) that went bankrupt or had some other problems. Those who maintain a diversified portfolio—which can be easily done with mutual funds—and who continue to hold those funds over the long term (20-plus years), have the opportunity to accumulate a net worth well above that which can be achieved with most other investment vehicles.

People who invest in the stock market become owners of the companies in which they invest. They invest because they believe those companies will make money and that, in turn, will pay dividends and/or increase the stock prices. You can choose to invest only in the United States or in countries across the globe. Mutual funds invest throughout the world and can be used for a variety of investments appropriate for growing net worth to retire early.

The argument against CDs or bonds for accumulating wealth is inflation. Their rate of return does not exceed inflation sufficiently to allow you to accumulate wealth (or if you are about to retire early, to draw enough income above inflation to not have to worry about outliving your money). But over the long haul, stocks have out-distanced inflation by a wide margin and the stock market has proven to be a viable place to build net worth. This essential third key to retiring young—investing wisely—will be discussed at length in chapter 10.

APPLYING THE 3 KEYS

Let me refer you once more to *The Millionaire Next Door* since many of the authors' findings fit well with the concepts and strategies discussed in this chapter, and much of this book. By studying wealthy Americans for 20 years, the authors found several commonalities among them. Most millionaires and multi-millionaires rarely give the impression they are rich because they tend to live below their means (live simply), are frugal (embrace financial self-discipline), and invest nearly 20 percent of their income each year, with nearly 95 percent owning stocks (invest wisely).

In other words, most millionaires got where they are by following the 3 Keys to retiring young discussed herein. In terms of being frugal and saving for the future, the authors found that wealthy people derive more pleasure from watching their net worth grow than from spending their money on possessions that may impress others, but which depreciate in value. I couldn't agree more.

The higher your annual income, the easier it should be to retire young. However, regardless of how much your income is, for the majority of early retiree hopefuls it will be difficult to accumulate sufficient net worth to retire early without applying all 3 Keys described in this chapter. **Simplifying your life** will reduce your need to buy and accumulate possessions and **financial self-**

discipline will save you money on what you do buy, while also increasing your percentage of annual income saved (especially as your income rises). Those savings can then be **invested wisely** so that you can accumulate the net worth necessary to retire young. Using the 3 Keys as your guide, you will have the primary strategies necessary to retire early without being rich.

Chapter Five

Today or Tomorrow?

Six months after we retired some friends came to visit and, of course, early retirement became a conversation topic. My friend was still in the field of vocational rehabilitation and was eager to quit. Like most of the friends we talked with regarding early retirement, this couple saw only advantages. In fact, they had recently embarked upon a new part-time business venture that they were optimistically projecting would grow and allow them to retire in three years (at which time they would be close to 50 years of age). In addition to discussing the benefits of earning more money, we initiated a discussion on "living for tomorrow" versus "living for today," an important concept in allowing most people to meet their early retirement goal.

Living for today refers to wanting things now—without giving much thought to the future. In the context of this book, living for today means not worrying about retirement tomorrow and hoping that Social Security is still around so there is some meager income when one turns 62 or older. In contrast, living for tomorrow means working hard today and giving up some of life's immediate pleasures to save more for the future. Done correctly, that can mean having the option while you are young to choose whether you want to work or not work (a choice you'll relish when the time comes).

Of course, there are those who believe living for today is the only way to go—that if they die tomorrow, they will have had a good life. But statistically, most people live into their 70s and in the future more will be living into their 80s and 90s. So the bigger concern should be, what will our lives be like when we are in our 60s, 70s, 80s, or older? Since most people live into their 70s now, don't we need to prepare for that?

We have seen and heard too many stories of elderly people trying to make it on a meager Social Security payment. Based on a September 2001 fact sheet from the Social Security Administration, less than 10 percent of today's elderly live in poverty; were it not for Social Security, it would be 48 percent. With the Social Security program headed toward insolvency in 14 years, is living at or below the poverty level where you want to be in your 60s, 70s, or 80s? It's certainly not in our retirement plan!

A COMPROMISE

A compromise is needed between the "live for today" and "live for tomorrow" philosophies. If you live only for today, you may find yourself living below the poverty level when you are older, or at least not being able to live the lifestyle you want. In contrast, if you live only for tomorrow—being a workaholic until age 62 or 65 or until you are rich—you may never get the chance to enjoy the money you have worked so hard to save. The compromise involves having fun while you are younger, but it also emphasizes simple living, financial self-discipline, and wise investing so that you can experience the freedom of retiring young. You *can* do both.

Retiring young doesn't require depriving yourself of the things you enjoy. But most spending will involve trade-offs. For example, continue to take vacations, but choose less expensive ones. Buy a new vehicle, but pass on the Mercedes or buy a used one. Purchase a new TV, but give up the home theater or HDTV and get a 27-inch for much less. In the meantime, the money saved from those trade-offs is invested for the long term. By charting the growth of your net worth, you will see how those trade-offs on current depreciable assets are leading to your ultimate early retirement. You trade the big house, luxury vehicles, and newest high-tech gadgets for being able to choose later whether or not you want to continue working. Once you decide you want that choice and control over your life, then the trade-offs become easier.

If you decide you want to retire young, place an emphasis on living more for tomorrow than today. Follow the advice and strategies provided throughout this book and you can enjoy life today while giving yourself a choice for tomorrow. Enjoy the option of retiring in your 40s or 50s (or as young as possible) while others will work the rest of their lives because they only lived for today.

ONE POWERFUL INVESTMENT STRATEGY

What is one of the most important steps you can take toward living for tomorrow and achieving the goal of retiring young? Whatever effort is required to accomplish the following, do this:

Accumulate $100,000 (minimum) in tax-deferred retirement accounts as fast as possible.

That may sound like a lot of money, but it is critical to your early retirement for one simple reason: **the power of tax-deferred, compounded growth of your money.** Can you believe that $100,000 invested in a tax-deferred account at a 10 percent average annual return (which is less than the average 10.7 percent the stock market has been returning for the past 76 years), will grow to $672,000 in only 20 years? Better yet, that initial $100,000 will grow to one million within 25 years. And that is if you never add another penny to the account. Now imagine what will happen if you continue to add to your 401(k), 403(b), Keogh, Simplified Employee Pension (SEP), or other retirement plan each year. It is not difficult to accumulate a large retirement nest egg over a period of 15 to 20 years. But it requires a focused effort and financial self-discipline to accumulate that much money in your tax-deferred retirement accounts as fast as possible.

> Note: What if your employer does not offer a tax-deferred retirement plan? Then max out your IRAs and continue to save as much as possible in minimally-taxed mutual fund accounts (which will be discussed in chapter 10). Your money will not grow as fast, but at least it will grow.
>
> Another option might be to invest after-tax dollars into tax-deferred annuities. But do your research and pay attention to expenses, because these types of accounts can cost you a lot over time. Another primary disadvantage is that the earnings are taxed as ordinary income rather than capital gains when you start withdrawing your money. Check out annuities offered by some of the large no-load mutual fund companies because they generally have the lowest expenses. For a good discussion on the pros and cons of annuities, read *The Courage to Be Rich* by Suze Orman.

To estimate how much your money will grow in a tax-deferred account, you can use the "rule of 72." It works like this: **Divide the rate of return on your investment into 72 and the result tells you how long it will take for your money to double.** For example, if you have $100,000 invested at 3 percent, such as in a savings account, it will take roughly 24 years to double your money (72 ÷ 3 = 24). However, if you invest that same amount in mutual funds that return 10 percent per year, your $100,000 will double in about seven years, grow to $380,000 in 14 years, surpass $800,000 in 22 years, and exceed $1.7 million in 30 years. The table illustrates the power of tax-deferred compounding.

Initial Investment of $100,000 with an Average Annual Return of 10 Percent Growing Tax-deferred:

After	You Have	After	You Have
Year 1	$110,000	Year 14	$379,750
Year 2	121,000	Year 15	417,725
Year 3	133,100	Year 16	459,497
Year 4	146,410	Year 17	505,447
Year 5	161,051	Year 18	555,992
Year 6	177,156	Year 19	611,591
Year 7	194,871	Year 20	672,750
Year 8	214,359	Year 21	740,025
Year 9	235,795	Year 22	814,028
Year 10	259,374	Year 23	895,430
Year 11	285,312	Year 24	984,973
Year 12	313,843	Year 25	1,083,471
Year 13	$345,227	Year 30	$1,744,940

The totals above assume that you never add another dollar to that initial $100,000 account. Realistically, you will continue to add money every year and increase the amount you are adding as your income rises. Another factor to consider is that you will not withdraw all of the money at one time. If you accumulate $500,000 after 17 years, you could retire early and withdraw a percentage of that each year while allowing the remainder to continue growing for another 20, 30, or however many years you choose. The less you withdraw each year, the more that is left to continue growing.

Note: Although it is possible to tap your retirement accounts penalty-free prior to age 59½ by taking substantially equal periodic payments, most early retirees will probably find it preferable to wait. That will require other income as might be derived from non-retirement accounts, an employer-funded pension, and/or part-time work.

The faster you accumulate $100,000 in a tax-deferred account, the quicker it begins doubling. For a two-earner couple, you need to save $5,000 per person each year for 10 years to accumulate $100,000; that's what we did on a combined average annual after-tax income of $27,700. Assuming you earn $50,000 to $75,000 per year, that will mean saving in the range of 15 to 20 percent of your earned income—surely an achievable goal if you are motivated and follow the 3 Keys to retiring young. If you invest more than that, you can build your tax-deferred account beyond the $100,000 and watch your retirement funds grow even faster.

One thing should be obvious from the preceding table: The earlier you start investing, the better off you'll be later. Your money grows much faster toward the end of any given period than at the beginning. For example, it takes roughly 17 years for $100,000 to grow to $500,000, but just eight more years to see it double again to over one million dollars. The earlier you start, the more tax-deferred compounding of interest works in your favor.

TAXABLE VERSUS TAX-DEFERRED

And what if you don't use a tax-deferred account? Let's take that same $100,000 we used above invested at 10 percent and look at the difference. Assuming you are in the 27 percent federal (the new tax rate as of 2002) and 7 percent state tax brackets, what are your accounts worth after 20 and 25 years?

Investment	Taxable Account	Tax-Deferred Account
$100,000 after 20 years	$359,000	$ 672,800
$100,000 after 25 years	$494,200	$1,083,500

By using tax-deferred accounts, you will have nearly twice as much retirement money after 20 years and *over twice* as much after 25 years. That should be sufficiently convincing evidence that, to retire in your 40s or 50s (or any age), you must invest as much as possible in tax-deferred accounts. But this wide gap can also be deceiving. You will have to pay taxes on those tax-deferred accounts when you withdraw the funds, whereas you have paid all along on your taxable account money. The gap will narrow when you pay taxes on those deferred funds, but you'll still come out thousands of dollars ahead by investing as much money in tax-deferred accounts as you can.

Realistically, you will probably build your net worth the same way we did—by continuing to add to your accounts year after year until you retire (and you may even continue to add thereafter). By the end of our first 10 years of marriage, we had that $100,000 nest egg. According to the table above, had we just let that money grow, we would have had $214,359 in the next eight years, not enough for us to retire in our early 40s. But what we did during those eight years was continue to save and invest at even a faster pace than the first 10 years as our annual income grew.

While our initial nest egg may have grown to a little over $200,000 leaving it alone, the additional investments we made each year into both tax-deferred and taxable accounts, and the growth of those funds over the next eight years, allowed us to retire with over twice that amount. Watching your money compound and grow is great, but continuing to add to it and watching it grow twice as fast is even better.

It requires self-discipline to save and invest while so many others spend all their money (and sometimes more) to have everything they want *now*. But there can also be great satisfaction in watching your retirement accounts grow and knowing that, in the future, you will have the choice of working or retiring young (or semi-retiring—working part-time at whatever you feel like doing) while all the reckless spenders are still plugging away and burning out on their full-time jobs because they have no other choice. You will get the last laugh. To have that opportunity in the future, however, you must start focusing on the long term *now*.

IRAs

At a minimum, everyone should have an Individual Retirement Account (IRA). Up until now, an IRA by itself would likely not provide enough income to retire young—unless it is supplemented by an upcoming pension and/or future Social Security payments that are sufficiently high. But your opportunity to retire early with only an IRA has improved with the passage of a new tax law in 2001 (assuming the law is not rescinded along the way and that you maximize your IRA contributions each year as allowed). The Economic and Tax Relief Reconciliation Act of 2001 increases traditional IRA and Roth IRA contributions as follows:

Year	Maximum IRA Contribution
2001	$2,000
2002 – 2004	3,000
2005 – 2007	4,000
2008	5,000
2009	$5,000 plus indexed to inflation

Beginning in 2009, the IRA limit will be indexed to inflation and increased in $500 increments. And for those 50 and over, from 2002 to 2005 the new law will allow an additional $500 per year to be invested in IRAs as “catch up” contributions; that will increase to $1,000 per year in 2006 through 2010. Without question, for the next nine years an IRA will be an improved retirement plan. But one caveat: unless Congress and the president extend these higher IRA limits, they are scheduled to expire at year-end 2010. So be sure to take advantage of this new law while the opportunity exists.

For simplicity's sake, and because the new tax law expires in nine years with no guarantee that it will be continued, let's look at an example of IRA growth potential based on the current $2,000 per person that can be invested into an account. Let's assume you and your spouse recently graduated from college and landed your first career positions. You contribute $4,000 per year ($2,000 each) into tax-deferred IRA accounts starting at age 22. Considering a 10 percent average annual return once again, how fast will your retirement money grow?

Starting at Age 22 Invest $4,000 per year	**IRA Account**
After 10 years	$ 64,000
After 20 years	229,000
After 30 years	658,000
After 35 years	$1.1 million

At age 52, after 30 years of saving your IRAs, you probably will not have enough to retire because a 3.5 percent inflation rate will have reduced that $658,000 to an equivalent of $332,000 in today's dollars. If you wait 35 years to retire, you will have an account worth almost $1.1 million ($473,000 inflation-adjusted). You will be 57 years old and will have contributed a relatively small percentage of your income per year. Whether that will be enough to retire on will depend on the lifestyle you want to live. But one thing for sure, it will keep you from starving. And take note: Maximizing your IRA contributions over the next nine years should be the extra boost needed for many to be able to retire at 57 with an adequate net worth.

If you earn $50,000 annually, an investment of $4,000 per year into your IRAs is a mere eight percent of your income. It should be clear by now that if your goal is to retire young, you need to invest as much as possible each year. Following the 3 Keys to retiring young can help you do that. But if you don't have enough money to retire when you are otherwise ready, you can always consider supplementing your retirement income with part-time employment.

PICKING UP THE SAVINGS PACE

What would happen if you saved an average 30 percent per year like we did—that would be $15,000 per year on a household income of $50,000? Again, invested in tax-deferred retirement accounts at 10 percent starting at age 22, you would amass the following (rounded to the nearest thousand dollars):

$15,000 Per Year Invested at a 10 Percent Average Annual Return Starting At Age 22

After 10 years	$ 239,000
20 years	859,000
30 years	2,467,000
35 years	$4,065,000

After 20 years, and at the "old" age of 42, you would be a little short of a million dollars—which you would have after 21 years. Continue working another ten years and you would have nearly $2.5 million by age 52. And what about inflation? Factoring in a 3.5 percent inflation rate, the purchasing power of your tax-deferred retirement accounts would be as follows:

Before Inflation	Inflation-Adjusted
$ 239,000	$ 200,000
859,000	569,000
2,467,000	1,246,000
$4,065,000	$1,775,000

The actual inflation rate in the future, and its impact on your specific situation and budget, will determine if you have more or less money than you think you need to retire young. In this example, many people could happily retire as young as 42 with over a half-million inflation-adjusted dollars in their retirement accounts. Or they could retire a little older, and even more comfortably, with an inflation-adjusted $1.25 million at age 52.

As you will learn later, we were saving and investing upward of 60 percent of annual income in our peak earning years. We focused on early retirement and living for tomorrow rather than today. Even though most of that money was not going into tax-deferred retirement accounts, which were already fully funded, it was still growing relatively quickly in no-load mutual funds.

The more you increase the percentage of annual household income that you are socking away for retirement, the quicker your nest egg grows and the earlier you can retire. Earning an average of $47,300 per year after taxes, we were able to accumulate a net worth sufficient to retiring young in only 18 years. It may take you longer if you earn less and/or if you save less. But do you need to retire in your early 40s? Would 50 be acceptable? Even 55? That's still years ahead of when most people will retire. In fact, those without high incomes who live only for today rather than tomorrow may *never* be able to retire.

If you are in your 20s and just getting started in your career, you have tremendous potential and opportunity in front of you to establish and achieve your future goals. Thousands of young people are graduating from college today with degrees in computer/information technology and other fields where many will earn more money than we could imagine when we graduated and started our careers earning $25,000 to $30,000 per year between us. According to the U.S. Census Bureau, millions of couples today earn $50,000 to $75,000 or more per year. A couple with no dependents earning $75,000 or more after taxes should be able to choose what age they want to retire and plan their lives accordingly.

Of course, not everyone is so fortunate to make that much money and many will have to retire later in life. Similarly, those with children and/or other dependents may find their savings potential slowed. But in either case, any individual or couple who wants to expedite retirement should immediately begin implementing the 3 Keys to retiring young to have the best opportunity of achieving that goal.

AND START EARLY

Here's one last example of the power of tax-deferred investing. Let's assume once more that two 22-year-olds are getting started in careers they absolutely love and believe they will continue pursuing until they retire at age 67. Spouse A starts an IRA and invests $2,000 per year for 10 consecutive years ($20,000 total) and then never adds another dollar but lets the account ride at a 10 percent annual return. Spouse B procrastinates and doesn't start investing in an IRA until age 32, but then puts away $2,000 every year for the next 35 consecutive years ($70,000 total) at the same 10 percent return. Who will have the most money when they retire at age 67? Would you believe Spouse A, and it isn't even close?

Invested			Total at Age 67
Spouse A	$20,000	Age 22 to 32	$900,000
Spouse B	$70,000	Age 32 to 67	$545,000

It simply cannot be any clearer. While it is never too late to start investing for retirement, the sooner you start the faster your money grows and the younger you will be able to choose whether or not you want to retire.

UNSHACKLING THE BALL AND CHAIN

We can no longer imagine working full-time the majority (or all) of our lives—having a ball and chain on our legs keeping us from doing the things we want to do. But that's what many experts are predicting for a majority of the baby boomers—and those younger—in the future. The three-legged stool (employer-funded pension, Social Security, and personal savings) upon which so many in the past and present have relied, will not be able to support all the baby boomers, much less future generations.

As the situation stands today, most people will not have a sufficiently large pension (if any at all), they will not be able to depend on Social Security, and they will not have adequate savings. A four-legged stool will become far more common in the future and that fourth leg will be continued employment—part-time for many, full-time for some. The question is: Will that fourth leg be your choice because working part-time allows you to retire early or spend a little more in retirement? Or will that fourth leg be perpetual full-time employment because you do not have the financial resources to retire at all? A robust economy is fueled by the desire of people to live for today, not tomorrow. While living for today is necessary to derive sufficient reinforcement for your long hours of work, living for tomorrow is essential for not having to work the rest of your life.

Your tax-deferred accounts represent the true nest egg for retirement because they grow faster than the investments you pay taxes on each year. Whereas you will eventually have to pay taxes on those accounts when you draw the money out, by then you will be retired and probably be in a lower tax bracket. Of course, if you are fortunate enough to have accumulated a huge retirement nest egg, you could be in a higher tax bracket. But that is not the worst problem you could have. What could be worse is having little or nothing in your retirement accounts!

In 1998 the Roth IRA was introduced. Currently you can invest up to $2,000 in after-tax dollars (refer to the section on IRAs earlier in this chapter for the new limits through 2010) but then all of the interest that accumulates can be withdrawn tax-free when you retire. Of course, that assumes Congress doesn't change the rules between now and the time you start withdrawing it. And that's always a possibility.

Your annual income and success at following the 3 Keys will determine how much money you will be able to save and invest each year. The more you contribute to your retirement accounts, and the earlier you sock it away, the faster you accelerate the date when you can choose to work or not work. You *can* unshackle your ball and chain and you *can* turn the fourth leg of the retirement stool—continued employment—into optional rather than mandatory work. But in order for those to become realities in your future, you must start planning today.

Chapter Six

How Much Is Enough?

Why do people work who can afford not to? For one reason, because they don't have to. Most of us enjoy doing things we *don't have to do* more so than the opposite. Several other reasons why people choose to work when they don't need to financially are:

- They have a drive to accomplish a particular goal or fulfill a specific need.
- They genuinely enjoy what they do and/or are exceptionally challenged by it.
- Some want to garner more prestige, elevate themselves to a higher social status, and own more status symbols.
- Some want a more luxurious lifestyle—now and later.
- And sometimes people continue working when they can afford not to, or go back to work after they retire, because they have never developed sufficient interests outside work to replace the number of hours they work.

That is the point of a book titled *Get A Life: You Don't Need A Million to Retire Well* by Ralph Warner. His book emphasizes the need to develop interests and relationships with others well before you retire so that when you leave that 40-plus hour workweek, you are prepared to fill your time productively with activities you genuinely enjoy doing. *Get A Life* presents valuable planning information for those serious about pursuing early retirement.

YOU DON'T NEED TO BE RICH!

How much money do you need to retire young and never work again? It depends on the lifestyle you want to live. But one thing for sure, *you don't need to be rich!* According to the 2-Minute Survey on Work, 64 percent of the respondents defined rich as having saved/invested a million dollars or more. While being rich would have its advantages, it isn't necessary. What is necessary for most people, however, is that they simplify their lives, embrace financial self-discipline, and invest wisely. And, of course, how fast you can grow net worth to the level needed for early retirement is going to have a lot to do with how much you earn.

According to the latest available statistics from the U.S. Census Bureau ("Money Income in the United States: 2000"), of 106.4 million American households, 15.5 percent had total annual incomes in the $35,000 to $49,999 range, *nearly three times* that many (42.7 percent) earned $50,000 or more, and almost 24 percent had a household income of at least $75,000. Interestingly, the income sector with by far the largest percentage increase since 1981 has been the $100,000 and over group. Translating those figures into raw numbers, it should be obvious that there are a lot of potential early retirees in America today:

- Income of $ 50,000+ = 45.4 million households
- Income of $ 75,000+ = 25.3 million households
- Income of $100,000+ = 14.3 million households

Clearly, millions of Americans could wave good-bye to full-time employment in their 40s or 50s if they were motivated to achieve that goal and followed the 3 Keys. Realistically, unless you have a good employer-funded pension to look forward to, retiring young is probably going to require an annual household income of $50,000 or more (of course, the number of dependents being supported is going to make a difference). But that is not to discourage you from planning an early retirement if you earn less.

Let's take the example of Amy and Jim Dacyczyn who were briefly mentioned in the introduction. Upon marrying in 1982, they dreamed of raising a large family in a big farmhouse in the country. The problem was they had a net worth of practically zero and an income of less than $30,000 per year. Contrary to popular belief, the Dacyczyns set out to prove their dream could be achieved. (You can read more about their story in her book *The Tightwad Gazette*, or in a magazine article titled "They're living the good life on $17,580 a year" which you'll find in *Money*, January 1997).

Through a program of frugality that would amaze the average person, Amy Dacyczyn wrote in her first book that they saved $49,000 in less than seven years (while raising four children) and purchased $38,000 worth of big-ticket items like vehicles, appliances, and furniture. At the end of those seven years they were also debt-free. How? Ms. Dacyczyn attributes it to *saving 43 percent* of their gross income per year. Their savings were sufficient for the down payment on their country home and they subsequently added twins to their other four children. Their dream had been fulfilled.

As you will read throughout this book, the percentage of gross (or net) income you save and invest each year will be a primary determinant in your early retirement. The Dacyczyns found that they could reach their goals by saving more rather than earning more. What they did, and how they did it, is certainly impressive. Their story should be an inspiration to all those hoping to retire young but who are not sure they can afford it; in fact, *their story should be an inspiration to all who think they do not earn enough to save money.* While most people would probably not go to the frugality extremes that the Dacyczyns did, the point is they proved that if you want something enough, there is usually a way to get it. They were unusually thrifty, but the end can justify the means.

After proving that it could be done, Amy Dacyczyn became a crusader of thrift and frugality, started a newsletter, wrote three books, and found herself doing interviews and talk shows throughout the country. As a result of all those activities, their lives underwent yet another change. In *The Tightwad Gazette III*, Ms. Dacyczyn wrote that the unexpected financial success that accompanied her books and newsletter, together with their continued life of frugality, allowed them to retire early. Although her business was doing well, she commented after giving it up that the freedom of not having to work was preferable to owning more material goods. We couldn't agree more.

The Dacyczyns represent the early-retiree mentality that you will read about throughout this book. The freedom of not having to work can be more satisfying than purchasing additional assets that necessitate working longer to acquire and maintain them. The Dacyczyns accomplished their goals largely through frugality—an essential strategy in building sufficient net worth to retire young. You may find many of the suggestions in her books a bit extreme, but those books are also packed with ideas and suggestions that can help you save money and build net worth.

If you don't earn $50,000 or more per year, it may take longer to reach your early retirement goal, but you can still reach it. Or you might consider working part-time to supplement your investment income (see chapter 15) so that you can retire earlier. It is not unrealistic that a couple without children earning *less than* $50,000 may be able to retire earlier than a couple with children who earn well above $50,000, depending on their lifestyles. The higher your household income and the lower your number of dependents, the easier it should be to accumulate the net worth necessary for living your early retirement dream.

Another factor that could make the difference in retiring young is an employer-funded pension from a previous career, as might be the case for someone who had done a 20-year stint in the military, or who worked 15 or 20 years for some employer before moving to a second career. Don't underestimate the value of your defined-benefit pension—more on that later in this chapter.

HOW DO YOU KNOW HOW MUCH YOU NEED?

Previously I alluded to the issue of how much is enough to retire young. Although you would like a simple answer to that question, there isn't one. How much is enough for you will depend on your preferred lifestyle and retirement goals. In other words, if one of your goals is to live in Beverly Hills and fly your own Lear jet for a hobby, you will need a lot more money than if your goal is to live in rural Mississippi and spend the majority of your day sitting in the house reading and watching television.

A personal example of lifestyle differences comes from meeting up with an old friend I hadn't seen in 25 years. Knowing that Kris and I were early retirees, he asked how much money he needed to retire early. My answer, of course, was that it depended on the lifestyle he wanted to live and that we have been able to retire on approximately $1,500 per month. After a good laugh, he explained that he and his wife live in a $2 million house and she spends $60,000 per year just to have fun. Since I didn't get the impression they planned to alter their lifestyle and simplify their lives anytime soon, needless to say, we would need large differences in net worth to support our chosen retirement lifestyles.

To look at differences in lifestyle (which is basically defined by your budget) so that you can get an idea of what retirement might cost and how much is enough, let's examine two different budgets **(theoretical and over-simplified to make a point).**

Example 1

Let's assume that reading and watching television make you exceedingly happy; you and your spouse want to do that 16 hours per day and sleep the remaining eight. If that were the case, then the bulk of your expenses would be for housing, groceries, health insurance (which would seem a necessity in most every budget), and electricity for your reading light and television. Your budget would be pretty slim and you could probably retire fairly young. Of course, where you choose to reside will make a difference, since the cost of living can vary significantly from one part of the country to another (more on this in chapter 14). Example 1 will be referred to as the Reading/TV Budget:

Reading/TV Budget

Example 1	Monthly Expense Budget
Housing/Rent	$ 400
Groceries/Dining Out	200
Health/Auto/Home Insurance	250
Utilities	100
Miscellaneous	50
Total Monthly Expenses	**$1,000**

Assuming a 10 percent return on your money (which we will discuss in chapter 10), you could theoretically retire on this budget with approximately $120,000 invested.

Income: $120,000 x 10% = $12,000 per year
Expenses: $1,000 x 12 months = $12,000

While this first example provides an initial look at determining how much you need to retire young, and it is a budget that is probably within the reach of everyone reading this book, would it fulfill anyone's retirement dream?

Example 2

On the other hand, let's assume you want to entertain frequently, travel to exotic destinations, and live in an upscale neighborhood most of the year while also having a winter or summer condo. For purposes of comparison, we'll call Example 2 the Luxury Budget; it illustrates how much more money you would need to retire with these expenses:

Luxury Budget

Example 2	Monthly Expense Budget
Housing/Rents	$ 2,400
Groceries/Dining Out	1,000
Health/Auto/Home Insurance	1,000
Utilities	300
Entertainment/Travel	2,000
Miscellaneous	300
Total Monthly Expenses	**$7,000**

Assuming a 10 percent return on your money once again, you would need approximately $840,000 to retire on this budget.

Income: $840,000 x 10% = $84,000 per year
Expenses: $7,000 x 12 months = $84,000

Neither of these budgets takes into account the adjustments and additional income needed to offset inflation or pay federal and state income taxes. Of course, in the Reading/TV Budget example there would be no federal taxes due (at least not for a married couple based on 2001 tax tables) and probably minimal, if any, state taxes—and you could consider moving to one of the states that does not have an income tax. But the Luxury Budget example would find that couple in the 27 percent federal tax bracket (the rate as of 2002), which would increase expenses several thousand dollars at tax time.

While these are over-simplified examples, they are presented to demonstrate the basic thinking involved in planning for early retirement and the impact that one's lifestyle has on that decision. They provide a first look at "how you know how much you need." Deciding the lifestyle you want to live will be the primary determinant in how much will be enough for you to retire young.

It's not impossible that you could have a monthly budget in the range of Example 1 above. Granted, most people would not consider sitting in front of the television all day an enjoyable retirement; maybe when they're in their 80s, but not in their 40s or 50s. But if rent was lower or the house was mortgage-free so that most of the housing/rent expense category could be allocated to other items like recreation and entertainment, then $1,000 per month might be enough for those who have simplified their lives appreciably. The long-term impact of inflation on that net worth, however, would be the primary concern.

Could you live within budget Example 2 above? Most likely. However, spending $24,000 per year on travel and entertainment and another $28,800 on housing would require either: (1) a very high annual household income now and an exceptionally high savings rate, or (2) an early retirement that may not be so early. Only you can decide what will make your retirement enjoyable. There may be a compromise between those two budgets, though, that will allow you to do what you want without having to wait until you turn 62, 66, or 70-plus to do it—because, by then, you may not be physically or mentally able.

The best reason to retire early is newfound freedom—so that you can look forward to getting up and facing each new day, rather than dreading it. What you do and when you do it will depend on your net worth and retirement income. If your net worth does not support the things you would like to do in retirement, remember that part-time work can provide you with extra money to meet your budget, or additional income to meet those "off-budget" expenses discussed in the next chapter.

ENOUGH FOR MANY

Everyone who retires early will have a different definition of how much is enough and a different budget to go along with it. When we retired in 1993, the book that helped us make that decision (*Cashing In on the American Dream*) had recommended $400,000 to $500,000 as a general rule, though a bare-bones retirement plan was presented for those having as little as $100,000.

On the Internet forum for early retirees mentioned in chapter 4, the question arose last year as to how much is realistically needed to retire early. Of those retirees who responded, a net worth of $500,000 (or $2,000 to $3,000 per month income from all sources) was still considered reasonable for early retirees who are willing to simplify their lives and cut spending. That was further supported by a book I recently read titled *How to Retire Early and Live Well With Less Than a Million Dollars* by Gillette Edmunds in which he comments, "Most middle-class Americans, including me, could live comfortably on the investment returns from $500,000."

At a conservative 8 percent return, which should be attainable with a combination of stock and bond mutual funds, $500,000 in net worth would provide an early retiree with a $40,000 annual income. A 10 percent return calculates to an annual income of $50,000, less any set-aside for taxes and inflation. Of course, one problem with having your money invested in mutual funds is that the return is not consistent from year to year. Although you may average 8 or 10 percent per year over time, some years you should do better and some years your portfolio may decrease in value.

For eight years we have comfortably lived within our average budget of $1,375 per month (in reality, our expenses have averaged only $1,200). However, we also spent $300 per month on average in off-budget expenses funded by our part-time jobs—expenses we could do without if we needed to (although they have contributed to a more enjoyable retirement), or we could easily increase our budget $300 per month and give up the part-time jobs. But combined, we have lived on about $18,000 per year for eight years (not including taxes). Many people could do the same and be happy with their newfound freedom from work. Of course, the bottom line in how much it is going to cost you per month to retire young will depend on your chosen lifestyle.

An 8 to 10 percent average annual return over time on a $400,000 net worth invested in mutual funds would generate an annual income of $32,000 to $40,000 per year. After a 3.5 percent inflation set-aside, that would leave $18,000 to $26,000 minus taxes. Certainly the latter would be sufficient for many; however, even the $18,000 would work for some, especially if supplemented by part-time employment. Personally, we have done just fine on about $18,000 per year and no one has yet brought a "CARE Package" to our house assuming we were destitute.

For those averse to investing their retirement money in the stock market (regardless of what the facts and figures illustrate), but who would still like to retire young, a more conservative strategy could be implemented. Let's assume you are happy with your current lifestyle, you pay off the mortgage on your house, and you plan to never work again. You lock up your remaining $400,000 in CDs at 7 percent (a rate that has been rather scarce the past few years), and generate an income of $28,000 per year. After the standard deduction and personal exemptions, a married couple would pay approximately $2,200 in federal income taxes based on the 2001 tax tables, and significantly less in state taxes (or none) depending on the state. After taxes, you end up with an annual retirement income in the $25,000 range.

That would be sufficient for many young retirees to live on. However, the downside is that, without an inflation set-aside, your principal erodes some each year and, over time, you have less and less principal generating monthly retirement income. Set aside 3.5

percent to cover inflation and your retirement budget shrinks to about $11,000 per year. Could you comfortably retire on that?

In my opinion, a net worth of $400,000 to $500,000 (or $2,000 to $3,000 per month income) diversely invested remains viable for early retirement as long as you simplify your life and embrace financial self-discipline. However, $400,000 will probably be a little on the short side for many and additional trade-offs in lifestyle or the pursuit of part-time employment will be necessary. But each young retiree will be different. Many people will laugh at the thought of living on $18,000 per year and want nothing to do with it; yet, there will be others who can live on less—especially if it means not having to work for the rest of their lives.

DON'T UNDERESTIMATE YOUR PENSION

Because most employed workers will not have an employer-funded pension to look forward to, I wrote this book primarily for those without such pensions to delineate how they can build a net worth on their own sufficient for retiring young. If you will receive a monthly pension (and/or believe Social Security will comprise a fair share of that $2,000 to $3,000 per month that many people could happily retire on), then retiring early can be easier for you.

Once you figure out the amount of money you will need each month to do the things you want to do—your retirement budget—calculate your projected monthly income from all sources: employer-funded pension; employer-sponsored pension like your 401(k), 403(b), 457, SEP, or SIMPLE; Social Security (but read chapters 12 and 13 first); and savings to confirm that they match. If your income is less than your budget, you may have to work longer, save more, get a higher return on the investments you have, work part-time, or adjust your retirement budget.

A defined-benefit corporate, civil service, or military pension, which could be available to you after 20 years of service (maybe less) and while you are in your 40s, could comprise a significant portion of your retirement income. If that's the case, you will need less net worth than would otherwise be necessary to generate the same monthly income. You may easily meet $2,000 to $3,000 per month with income from investments or a part-time job.

Not all employees realize how valuable their future employer-funded pensions are and what a significant part they will play in retirement. For example, a $1,000 guaranteed monthly pension is equivalent to having $150,000 in an investment account earning 8 percent annually, or $120,000 earning 10 percent. A $2,000 monthly pension is equivalent to $300,000 in an investment earning 8 percent per year. And some pensions are even adjusted annually for inflation. Anyone with a defined-benefit pension will not need nearly as much in net worth to retire young with the same monthly income as those of us without pensions.

We have friends who will not only have employer-funded pensions, but who will also have lifetime medical coverage paid by their employers. Since health insurance is a significant line item in the budget of most early retirees, such coverage paid by an employer is another benefit that could allow someone to retire young with a lower net worth than those without such an advantage.

If you do not feel you are earning enough to retire young, but you will receive an employer-funded pension, do not underestimate the value of that pension. It can easily compensate for a lower net worth at the time you retire young and you should find yourself in a better position than many of us without any guarantees.

In the next three chapters we will look at financial self-discipline, tracking income and expenses, and taking control of spending—all of which are important for planning early retirement. Once you have estimated your retirement budget, the kind of lifestyle you want to have will be defined. That, in turn, will determine how much net worth you will need (in other words, how much is enough for you) and how much you will need to save to achieve your early retirement goal.

Chapter Seven

Financial Self-Discipline

As briefly discussed in chapter 4, financial self-discipline is an essential key to early retirement for most people. Think of it as spending your money in a prudent manner and saving/investing as much as possible to reach your goal of retiring young. Spend and save judiciously and you will come out well ahead of most people. This chapter will reinforce the need to apply financial self-discipline in order to save as much money as you can, as fast as you can, so your investments start compounding tax-deferred.

ACCUMULATING OUR NET WORTH

Before starting a discussion on financial self-discipline, however, it is time to reveal how Kris and I accumulated enough money to retire in our early 40s. Did we start our marriage with a big nest egg? Did we come up with some big windfall along the way? Were we born into money or earned so much that anyone in similar circumstances could retire young? While most early retirement books are authored by employed accountants, attorneys, or financial planners who pull down incomes much higher than the customers reading their books, most of you reading this will probably better identify with our story.

The condensed version is this: We grew up in working class families, started our married life in debt, never inherited a penny, never won the lottery or were lucky enough to get any other windfall, have no employer-funded pensions (military, corporate or civil service) now or in the future, and we didn't make a big bundle from our businesses when we retired because we locked the doors and walked away rather than selling them. If you can relate to that, then read on. Here's our story—how we started, how we managed to accumulate the net worth to retire in our early 40s, and how we did that through financial self-discipline and focusing on the future. It wasn't all uphill; in fact, there were times when we took one step forward and two steps back. You will see that, if we could do it under our circumstances, so can you.

We started tracking income and expenses in 1976. Net worth (total assets less debts) was calculated at the end of each calendar year so we could measure our progress and determine whether or not we were meeting our long-term goal of increasing net worth by $10,000 annually. One note before discussing actual figures: Net worth normally includes estimating the market value of your house less your mortgage. We did not do that in our net worth calculations each year because it involves too much guesswork (and usually results in thinking one's house is worth more than it is). Rather than play that game, we calculated our net worth each year based on our actual cash assets plus the down payment we had in our house. We figured we could at least get that back since our houses were always worth far more than our down payment.

Our net worth calculations changed some, however, once we started investing in the stock market. We calculated net worth based on the price or net asset value (NAV) of each stock or mutual fund on the last trading day of the year. In effect, those are "paper profits" because, unless you actually sell them and get that price, they are only on paper and may not exist the next day (kind of like estimating the value of your house). But it is customary to value stocks and bonds in this manner and we followed suit.

From Wisconsin to California

Our road to early retirement began in Wisconsin when we married in May 1976. I was two weeks from finishing graduate school and Kris had completed her first year of full-time teaching. Prior to that, we were both college students working part-time to help pay our way through school. We did not have much money.

In fact, upon getting married and pooling our financial resources, we started with approximately $5,000 between us—some of which was residual school loan money and the rest was income saved from Kris's first job as a physical education/health instructor at a small high school in Wisconsin. But we also brought a combined $11,000 in student loan debt to our marriage (loans which helped fund our way through college along with each of us working part-time). The bottom line is that we started our married life with a level of debt more than double our savings.

Two weeks following our nuptials, we moved from Wisconsin to Wichita, Kansas where I began working as a counselor/evaluator for the Wichita Unified School District at a starting salary of $13,400 per year. The competition for the few teaching positions available in Wichita was keen and the school district found itself in the enviable position of being able to hire fully-qualified teachers as aides. Although Kris had credentials and experience as a physical education/health instructor, she began working under the title of teacher's aide in the fall of 1976 for roughly $2.65 per hour while actually being responsible for the same class load as a full-time teacher. Of course, the purpose of starting as a teacher's aide was to get her foot in the door and eventually move up to a full-time teaching position.

It should be obvious that, not only did we start our marriage $6,000 in debt, but we also began our careers with salaries that weren't anything to write home about. In fact, in our first year of married life we had a combined income from wages of $15,600. Our debt was half of our annual take-home pay.

Kris secured a full-time teaching position the following year at a salary of approximately $10,000 and we both received raises up until we left Wichita in June of 1979 and moved to California. Had we stayed in Wichita the entire year, our combined salaries would have been in the $30,000 range; but we didn't. And while you might suspect that we moved to California for considerably more money, that was not the case. We left Wichita because it was too large for us small-town folk and we wanted to get away from the crime and traffic, as well as the snow, cold, and ice storms that we had tolerated in the Midwest all of our lives. Unfortunately, moving to California set us back financially for some time.

We moved to Santa Maria after I secured employment at a rehabilitation center. The starting salary of $15,000 per year was less than the nearly $19,000 I had climbed to in Wichita. However, a more important factor was that the move once again left Kris unemployed (but no one needs to feel sorry for her because she was the initiator and willing participant in that move out west). Upon setting foot in Santa Maria, we had an income about 50 percent of that which we had left in Kansas—from roughly $30,000 in Wichita to $15,000 in Santa Maria, assuming Kris did not find a job.

In addition, whereas our monthly mortgage payment in Kansas was $425, our new mortgage in Santa Maria was $700 per month. Even now as this story unfolds, it makes me wonder what would prompt a couple to voluntarily cut their income in half while increasing their expenses, and then pay for the move on top of that!

After moving to California we learned that, although Kris had already taught both elementary and secondary school for four and a half years, she needed to return to college for another year to earn a California teaching credential (which included a semester of practice teaching). Since requiring practice teaching for an experienced teacher appeared a waste of time and Kris objected on principle if nothing else, she elected instead to begin a full-time bookkeeping trainee job in the fall at $5 per hour.

Because our move to California occurred in the summer of 1979, we earned a little more money the first half of the calendar year while still in Kansas, and a lot less the second half; our combined wages for the year were a little below $25,000. In our new location and with new jobs, you would think we had bottomed out from an income standpoint. But that was not the case.

In 1980 Kris returned to school to study accounting and our combined wages dropped to $21,000. We earned that much only because Kris worked part-time while attending school full-time and I took on another part-time job in addition to my full-time position. A year later Kris completed school and started teaching accounting at a private business college. For the first time in our six years of marriage, and with four college degrees between us, we finally reached a major hurdle and surpassed $30,000 per year in combined income. While I stayed at the rehabilitation center for six years, Kris switched jobs two more times in an effort to acquire additional accounting experience.

In 1984, eight years after we got married, Kris went to work for a CPA firm and our combined income finally reached $47,000 per year. A rational person would think the sky had to be the limit from there. But they would be wrong. The following year we purchased all the vocational evaluation equipment from the rehabilitation center where I had worked the previous six years and I started my own business in September. It took the remainder of the year to get things going, which involved a lot of hours but not a lot of income. In fact, our start-up expenses resulted in a loss for the business over those four months and our annual income dropped $10,000 from the previous year. But things did take off after that.

Working for Ourselves

Self-employment for me started in September of 1985 and lasted through May of 1993 when we retired. Initially, I worked the business myself, answering the phone, scheduling and evaluating clients, writing reports, sending out billings, purchasing supplies, and cleaning the toilet; Kris maintained the books and also helped where she could when we were exceptionally busy. We started hiring employees the second year when the business grew and it was too much for me to handle alone.

The main difference between operating my own business versus working for someone else was the control factor—the full decision-making authority to run the business as I felt it needed to be done. I had all of the responsibility, and all of the income. It meant working far more hours than I ever had before, but it also brought the opportunity to earn considerably more money.

Kris started her consulting business in 1990. She assisted small companies in converting from manual to computer accounting and then trained their bookkeepers (a combination of her teaching and accounting backgrounds). She had no employees. Having her own business and being good at what she did also meant more control, far more hours, and the potential for a higher income.

For the first 10 years of our careers (1976–1985), our average annual income was $30,900 pretax ($27,700 after taxes). We earned $15,600 our first year out and it took until 1983 before our combined incomes reached $40,000 per year gross, including interest on our savings accounts and CDs. However, the following eight years (1986–1993), were quite another story. With the opportunity to work lots of hours but also earn all the money, we averaged $96,000 pretax annually ($71,900 after taxes) when interest, dividends, and capital gains income were included. Averaging out those 18 years leading to our early retirement, our annual income was $59,900 pretax ($47,300 after taxes).

Now relate that to your current situation and it should give you some perspective for planning your early retirement. We never had children and undoubtedly that was a significant factor in being able to grow net worth over 18 years sufficient to retire. But then a lot of you reading this book are earning considerably more money than the $47,300 after-tax income we averaged (which you may recall was more than just salaries, wages, or business income, as it included interest, dividends, and capital gains income, too).

A MOTTO FOR RETIRING YOUNG

So how did we manage to grow our net worth sufficiently in 18 years to retire in our early 40s? The answer is financial self-discipline. It is fortunate that both of us have been financially self-disciplined all of our lives so we never had a conflict concerning such an essential component to meeting our long-term goal of early retirement. As our income grew over the years, the annual percentage we saved increased and, subsequently, so did our net worth.

We set a goal early in our marriage to increase net worth an average of $10,000 per year. Though we struggled some those first years, we were close to meeting that goal by the end of our first ten years. The key was to set a goal, remain focused, and structure our life to meet that goal. You will need to do the same. If you want to retire young, copy this and hang it on your bathroom mirror:

Live simply and be prudent in your spending,
especially as your income rises
Or
To phrase it another way,
LIVE BELOW YOUR MEANS

Unfortunately, most Americans don't do that. As income increases, spending increases and they never get ahead. Most people seem to have a need to acquire more and more assets until they can't afford them any longer. Those people will never retire early.

We embraced the concept of simple living and prudent spending, both when our income was low and as it increased. By the end of our first 10 years together (1976–1985), our net worth had grown to $97,000. Most of this money was sitting in savings accounts and CDs. Based on a pretax income averaging $30,900 per year ($27,700 after taxes) those first ten years, we had come close to meeting our initial goal of increasing net worth $10,000 per year. That reflects an average increase in net worth of approximately *35 percent per year* on an after-tax income that many would agree wasn't that high!

As our income grew over the next eight years, we began investing the maximum into our tax-deductible, tax-deferred retirement plans and an additional amount into taxable mutual fund accounts. If you want to retire young, you must not make the common mistake of spending all of your increases in household income.

To illustrate how we managed our income growth, we calculated savings and expenses during our leaner years (1976–1985) as compared to our three peak earning years (1990–1992). As the chart below reveals, income during our peak earning years averaged $48,100 more annually than during our leaner years. Yet, expenses increased only $11,000. The $37,100 difference was invested for retirement. Our standard of living improved because we spent part of our increased income (23 percent); but we invested more than three times that amount for retirement (77 percent). Try doing the same as your household income increases.

	Leaner Years (1976 – 1985)	**Peak Years (1990 – 1992)**	**Diff.**
Avg. Annual Income	$27,700	$75,800	$48,100
Avg. Annual Expenses	18,000	29,000	11,000
Avg. Savings Per Year	9,700	46,800	37,100
Percent Saved	35%	62%	27%

Whereas we could have spent a lot more per year based on our $75,800 after-tax income those peak years, we chose to spend less and invest the difference so that we could meet our goal of retiring young. We felt that spending $29,000 per year was sufficient for two people looking at the long term and saving for the goal of retiring at age 50. We had what we wanted and we didn't need more. That's how we managed to acquire a sufficient net worth to retire in 18 years. Calculate how much you would save if you invested 60 percent, or even 30 percent, of your after-tax income for retirement and you will see how fast your net worth could grow, too.

With good growth in our retirement and non-retirement mutual fund accounts, net worth continued to increase so that we could choose to retire in our early 40s. The point that needs to be emphasized is this: As our income increased over the years, we did not spend all of it; in fact, on a percentage basis, we spent significantly less and saved the difference—and that's how you grow net worth so that you can retire young.

LIVING BELOW OUR MEANS

What we did not do was waste money just because our income far exceeded our basic expenses. Though our average after-tax income of over $70,000 those last eight pre-retirement years would have allowed us to live a more luxurious lifestyle and to have a house full of depreciating assets, we lived below our means. Although we bought a different house in 1986, it was smaller and less expensive than our income would have allowed us to buy. Our vehicles were not luxurious European imports; in fact, we drove our 1980 Plymouth Champ until we retired in 1993 and our 1984 Toyota Camry until 1999. We patronized discount stores for our clothes and most other items, buying as much as possible on sale. We became regulars at Costco once they came to town, used coupons at the grocery store, had rabbit ears standing upside down on the floor for television reception rather than cable television, and still frequented the early-bird specials at local restaurants.

We did not need more or better than that and our long-term goal of saving enough to retire at 50 was the motivating factor. Financial self-discipline worked for us and it can work for you—if you set a goal and remain focused, determined, and motivated to achieve it. We also found another strategy for retiring early: the more hours we worked, the less time we had to shop and spend.

But we enjoyed spending money too. Occasional business lulls provided the opportunity to get out to see what we could and spend some of the money we were working so hard to earn. We took in attractions primarily on the West Coast (some several times)—Disneyland, Knott's Berry Farm, Universal Studios, Sea World, the San Diego Zoo and Wild Animal Park, Yosemite and Sequoia National Parks, and the giant redwoods. We also visited Zion and Bryce National Parks and other attractions in Utah and made other shorter trips within the surrounding states. In addition, we continued to fly back to the Midwest to visit our families when we could. We worked hard but enjoyed the occasional times we could get away. Our goal was not only to live for tomorrow so that we could retire at age 50, but also to enjoy today as circumstances allowed.

When we decided to retire in May of 1993, we had enough money to live our chosen lifestyle. Again, the concept was that we had enough and early retirement became far more of an attraction than *more money.* So if there is any chance you have not grasped the concept by now, it deserves repeating. As your income grows, increase the amount saved appreciably more than the amount spent. Continue to live on a reasonable percentage and save/invest the rest. *Live below your means. It's that simple.*

SPENDING LESS/SAVING MORE

It should be evident from our personal history that financial self-discipline is an essential component in being able to attain the financial security required to retire in your 40s or 50s (or as early as possible). Yet you do not have to live like paupers. We did not deprive ourselves of the things most people would consider entertaining; however, we didn't throw much money around at things we considered frivolous, either. What we did instead was set priorities and make trade-offs—choosing one thing over another because it allowed us to save more or because it was a better choice in another way for meeting our long-term goals. The key to our success was the ability to spend prudently and save money at a significantly higher rate than the average American family does. This philosophy can work for you too!

Do you know what the average after-tax personal savings rate of Americans is today? The U.S. Department of Commerce reports that it was 1.6 percent in 2001 and 1.0 percent in 2000. According to a chart on their Web site (www.doc.gov), from 1959 to 1982 the annual personal savings rate fluctuated between 7.2 and 10.9 percent, with the peak savings rate being in 1982. It has been creeping downward ever since and 2000 saw the lowest rate since the Depression. Although the rate turned up in 2001 rather than continuing its decline, it's far below the level needed to retire early.

If you want to retire young (or for many people in the future, to retire at all), you need to follow our lead and start saving far more than the average American. In our first 10 working years (1976–1985), while the average American was saving 9.7 percent, Kris and I were saving close to 35 percent. And during our peak earning years (1990–1992), while the average personal savings rate was 8.3 percent, we were saving about 60 percent.

Our savings/investment rate was well above the average for most American households and that, in essence, was the major factor allowing us to accumulate sufficient net worth to retire in our early 40s. The need to spend less and save much more than is common to most Americans cannot be over-emphasized if your goal is to retire as young as possible with a sufficient net worth.

SHOP UNTIL YOU DROP

Most Americans like to buy things and cannot seem to spend enough. They like to have as much as they can and they like the biggest, newest, best, and fastest of everything available. But do they *need* all of that? Do *you* need all of that?

Financial self-discipline means prudent spending based on future goals—living for tomorrow rather than today. It means looking at the newest expensive technology and saying, “We don’t really need that. Maybe when prices come down. Maybe not at all.” If you don’t mind working, spend all you want. But if you *do not* want to work the rest of your life, then you need to trade off some of the things you want, but don’t need, to save more money.

Most people work to support their assets. They work to have a bigger and better house, two or more vehicles (and not necessarily cheap ones), large screen TV/home theater and/or HDTV, stereo and compact disc player, the fastest computer available, DVD, MP3 player, PDA or pocket PC, cell phones, boat, jet ski, snowmobile, ATV, ad infinitum. They like lots of clothes and shoes, exercise equipment they don’t use, meals eaten out at nice restaurants, and all the newest toys for the kids. There is not enough money to buy all the things people would like to have. And that sums up the problem and explains the steadily declining savings rate. Now if people decided they didn’t need all of that, they might actually have some savings at the end of each month.

Kris and I grew up with the same innate ability to save, so we were compatible in that regard and it has worked well for us. We were also both fortunate in that we grew up in families without a lot of money, but with a sense of frugality (prudent spending) and financial self-discipline. Everyone is not so lucky. Had we grown up with role models that had to have the newest and best of everything and who spent all that they earned, perhaps we would not be where we are today. Or maybe as adults we still would have seen the benefits of not working all of our lives and adopted a savings/investing mentality anyway.

We once had a discussion that included the observation, “Just think how far ahead we would be financially if our parents had been stock investors and had taught us about the market and mutual funds when we were young." That may be true. But then there is the other side. We learned something equally valuable: how to save and spend our money wisely. In the long run, that may have gotten us as far or maybe further. Investing knowledge may not be particularly valuable if you don't know how to save; first learn to save and then how to invest. This book will help you do both.

Financial self-discipline means spending wisely and getting the best deals on the items or services you do buy. It means convincing yourself that you do not need the newest and best of everything produced. And it requires looking beyond the immediate and toward the future—trading off some short-term wants for long-term goals. Focus on what you really want and then actively pursue it.

By the time you finish reading this book you should have made a decision about retiring young. If that becomes your goal, then apply the principles and strategies herein to reach it. On the other hand, if you decide you would rather have the nice big house, luxury vehicles, and all the latest technology, then that is okay, too. But if your income does not support all of those assets, in addition to an appropriate savings/investment program, then early retirement will turn into late retirement—or maybe no retirement at all. The choice is yours.

FINANCIAL SELF-DISCIPLINE STRATEGIES

Assuming you choose retirement in your 40s or 50s, it is essential that you immediately initiate a program of financial self-discipline. You must decide how much you want or need things and then go from there. Not buying items you want but don't need, results in money saved and invested. You might try applying one of our techniques. Every time you want something (and we all want things), ask yourself, "Do I want that item enough that I'm willing to work longer (and retire later) so that I can have it?" If you are already retired, then ask yourself, "Do I want that item enough that I'm willing to go back to work to pay for it?"

The more times you answer no to that question, the more money you save. We have been applying that technique for years and have found it effective for us. If you decide you need or want something, then the next question to ask yourself is whether you need to buy that item new, or if one could be purchased used. You can save lots of money buying used items in like-new condition.

Many magazine articles and entire books are devoted to frugal living, so my intention is not to make this a guide on 1,000 ways to save money. But I would like to share my simple philosophy on purchasing any item: Why pay more if you can pay less? It fits well with the concept of financial self-discipline and can be a critical factor in your effort to accumulate net worth. There's no challenge in paying full price—anyone can do that. The challenge, fun, and satisfaction come from buying things for less and saving the difference to expedite or maintain early retirement.

Some of our efforts to pay less include maintaining a wholesale club membership (Costco has been in our last two cities but Sam's Club may be an option for others), and what we don't buy there, we pick up at discount stores like Kmart, Target, and Wal-Mart. We specifically look for sale or clearance items so that we get the best *value* for our money. In addition to that general philosophy on paying less, strategies we have used over the years to spend wisely and save money include the following:

Buy Reliable Vehicles Infrequently: Since our marriage 25 years ago we have purchased four new autos. We drove our first vehicle eight years, our second 13, our third 15, and we have had our current vehicle five years with a new one not included in the retirement plan for another three to five years. Purchasing a new vehicle every two or three years costs a lot and can drain your savings, especially if you finance and pay even more for it via interest.

You can save thousands of dollars by purchasing a two- or three-year-old vehicle because depreciation is greatest the first three years. Had we come across the right used vehicle in the past 20 years, that is what we would have done. Since we didn't, we opted instead to buy new and hold onto them for a long time. It is far less expensive to keep up a reliable older vehicle than to buy a new one every two or three years.

Research Prior To Buying: We read *Consumer Reports* magazine and frequently buy items based on their test results—not necessarily the specific items they recommend because they are not always available, but items based on their comments and especially the reliability charts. This strategy has worked well for us when buying vehicles, electronics, appliances, and most other things. We have had few repairs on items purchased over the years.

Electronics: We bought our like-new 26-inch living room television set used when friends upgraded to a large-screen, and our cordless phone was given to us when friends upgraded to a newer model (both are name-brand, high-quality models that are still working fine five years later). In 1986 we paid $99 for our stereo receiver—since it still works as well as it ever did, there's no reason to replace it. Our 266 MHz computer was purchased after the 350 MHz models came out—we saved a lot by doing that.

For many electronics products, buy older models being closed out to make room for the new, as there is often little difference between them except price. Consider buying used if someone you trust is upgrading. You won't have the latest and greatest technology, but you can own high-quality products at a fraction of the cost. Save the difference for retirement and it will compound over time to help you fulfill your early retirement goal.

Movies: We limit our movie-going to the discount theaters. So what if the movie is six months old? It's still the same movie. Think about how much you could save over time by frequenting discount theaters, or at least going to the $4 matinees rather than paying $7 to $10 in the evenings.

Clothing: Buy winter clothes during the spring clearance sales, which can begin as early as January, and summer clothes during the fall clearance sales, which can start as early as July. Here are a few examples of items we purchased this past year: I bought $15 summer shorts for less than $4 each, a $25 jacket for $5, a $9 sweatshirt for $2, a $16 pair of jeans for $2, a $40 heavyweight robe for $10, and the warmest shirt I've ever owned for $6 rather than the $25 regular price. Kris bought $12 shorts and $10 blouses for $2 to $3 each, a $66 blazer for $8, several pairs of $40 dress slacks for $10 or less each, $13 jeans for $3, and a couple of $6 scarves for $0.50 each. I think one would have a difficult time finding better deals than those.

We enjoy buying most of our clothes—the same clothes we could have purchased a month or two earlier at full price—for 75 percent off their original price (sometimes we'll pay a little more or less, depending on the item). Although we can't always find every bargain in our size, it's easier when we catch the clearance sales early. Any time of the year you walk into a store, head for the clearance racks and check out your options. You may be surprised at what you find and how little you have to pay for it.

Thrift stores and garage sales can also be a source of good used clothes—like the rarely-used sport coat in excellent condition that I picked up at a thrift store and had dry-cleaned for a total cost of $8. People buy high-quality, name-brand clothes and later end up donating them to thrift stores or having a garage sale. That gives you the opportunity to buy those same quality clothes for a fraction of their original cost.

Clearance Merchandise: If you want to save money to retire young, try to buy as much non-clothing clearance merchandise as possible. Not unlike the 75 percent discounts you read about above on spring and fall clearance clothing, you can find all sorts of other items at fantastic prices in the clearance sections of stores.

Here are several examples to illustrate the variety of items we purchased for ourselves or for gifts in the last year: a $45 business/computer case for $12.50, a $30 carry-on travel bag for $12, a set of $25 sheets for $4, a $20 telephone headset for $8.50, a small $10 travel hair dryer for $2, several 3-ring zipper binders regularly priced at $9 for $1.50 each, a box of $9 stationary for $1, an $8 set of three flashlights plus batteries for $1.50, a $7 wallet/purse for $1, and the list goes on.

We have found excellent clearance buys at several different stores in our city, but Staples, Target, and Wal-Mart are our regular stops. If St. George were larger, we would have even more retailers to check out. Shopping for clearance items is not only a great way to save money, but it's fun, too. You never know what you are going to find that's too good of a deal to pass up.

Dining Out: An article in the July 2000 issue of *Consumer Reports* magazine reported that Americans eat out 18 times per month on average, and our generation is spending 300 percent more on meals outside the home than the generation before us. Four suggestions are given for getting better *value* when dining out:

- Dine at off-hours
- Share an entrée
- Consider *either* the food *or* the salad bar
- Join a frequent-diner program

While living in California we frequented restaurants that had early-bird specials. Since moving to southern Utah, we have found discount coupons (a lot of buy-one-get-one free) and bargain meals aplenty and we take advantage of them regularly. This should give some a laugh but, as a result, we rarely spend more than $6 each when eating out. Of course, it's a different story when we travel and can't take advantage of all of our local coupons and discounts.

For those who wonder how we can eat so cheaply, I might add that food and ambience are not a big deal to us. You can't eat ambience, but it can cost you a lot. As long as a restaurant is clean and relatively quiet, that suffices for us. We eat to survive more so than because we derive immense pleasure from it. We like the food (or value) at some places better than others, but eating out is more about convenience and variety than a delectable dining experience.

Needless to say, steak and lobster or other fine dining is not one of our priorities. Actually, I prefer buffets because of the variety of food and the fact that they offer the best value when eating out (you will notice the emphasis placed throughout this book on seeking the *best value* for your dollars so that you can save more money to achieve or maintain early retirement). Eating out four or five times and not having to cook or wash dishes afterward makes more sense for us than eating out once for the same money. We eat out weekdays rather than weekends, lunch rather than dinner, and usually get plenty to eat at less cost.

We also take advantage of a local $25 two-for-one dining program, which includes other entertainment and household discounts as well. Similar programs exist in other cities so ask around or check the Yellow Pages under "Restaurants." After finishing our meal, we present our card to the cashier and the cost of one entree is subtracted. Merchants have accepted our discount card with as much enthusiasm as we see them treating others who pay full price. If you enjoy fine dining, you may find some of the more expensive restaurants participating.

One can only imagine how much money we have saved over our married lives through the use of early-bird specials, two-for-one dining cards, frequent-diner cards (where you buy so many meals and then get one free), and coupons. We have also been lucky to win several restaurant gift certificates in local drawings and to periodically receive certificates from friends and family. They make great gifts and reduce the amount we spend out-of-pocket. It helps to keep this budget item low.

On the other hand, if dining out is one of life's few pleasures for you, then increase the amount in this category and cut back on something else. It's merely another of the trade-offs most of us will make in our budget (and in our lives) to retire young.

Groceries: Groceries can be a hefty budget item, but it is also one category where smart shopping can again save you lots of money. Try these six suggestions:

- Watch for sales and then stock up on nonperishable items that you use most often.
- Buy store brands over name brands.
- Use bothersome coupons.
- Shop discount warehouses like Costco and Sam's Club.
- Don't grocery shop when you are hungry.
- Make a list of items you need and stick to it.

But you may be wondering where you would put 48 rolls of toilet paper, 20 boxes of cereal, a case or two of vegetables, and all of those other bulk items purchased. There are always places to put things if you simplify your life and get rid of the stuff you do not use or need. Here are six suggestions:

- Closets, drawers, and cabinets: Just clean out the clutter.
- Dishwasher: If you don't use it or decide you can get by without it—which also saves water and energy—a good supply of canned goods can be stored there. We've been utilizing that space for 25 years.
- Storage shelves: Again, assuming you simplified your life and cleaned out the garage, you may be able to build shelves along the walls. If you cleaned out the basement, there should be plenty of room for shelves, or you could possibly build some along the stairway.
- Attic: Great storage area for infrequently-needed items.
- Storage benches: Good for sitting, too.
- Under the beds: Works well for larger flat items.

Library: Libraries normally have a good selection of the most recent books and, if they do not have what you are looking for, you should be able to obtain what you want through the interlibrary loan program. Our library allows patrons to request books for purchase and then the library staff decides whether the request is appropriate for other patrons served. Several times that has allowed us to read new releases we were interested in. Our county library also allows us to check out back issues of magazines after they are a month old. So we have the option of reading the current magazine on-site or waiting a month and then taking it home.

The library is a great resource for all kinds of entertainment. In addition to books, they usually have videos, cassette tapes, compact discs, and now DVDs that can be checked out, as well as computers with Internet access for patrons. They often host lectures, seminars, and other educational-related events. As an early retiree, you have the time to take advantage of these offerings. If you aren't retired but take the time to utilize the resources your library has to offer instead of buying those same items, you will save money for retirement. Many libraries are now going online so that their card catalogs can be accessed from home computers.

Thrift Stores: While we have purchased numerous books since retiring, all but three have been from thrift stores. Although you cannot expect to find the current top 20 best-sellers, we occasionally find non-fiction books that are one or two years old and still plenty current in their content—and we often pay a dollar or less per book, whether trade paperback or hardbound. For fiction books, thrift stores and garage sales have an endless supply. (Note: For newer books, "remainder" bookstores are a good source for steep discounts. Major publishers sell off books after 6-12 months to these discount stores who, in turn, sell them for as little as 25 percent of original cover price. Also check the clearance sections of regular bookstores for similar deep-discount deals. And don't forget used bookstores, which usually buy as well as sell.)

Thrift stores can be a great source for all kinds of items. Prior to retirement we only occasionally shopped in thrift stores, but now you can find us there at least every couple of weeks. We used to donate perfectly good stuff to thrifts and other people do the same—items they have gotten tired of storing. Sure there's junk, but we make some great buys, too. Because you never know what you might find, shopping thrift stores is fun and it doesn't cost much. We then turn around and donate other stuff so that we don't accumulate too much and the stores can make a few more dollars. It's a good deal for everyone involved.

PRIORITIZING

Throughout our married life we have not deprived ourselves of assets we want and activities we enjoy doing. At the same time, we have tried to balance our wants with our long-term goal of increasing net worth so that, by age 50, we could retire and maintain a comfortable lifestyle. That was our goal from the time we were in our mid-20s and we ultimately were able to retire in our early 40s. It would not have happened without exercising control over our spending. You need to decide if spending less now to have the choice of retiring in your 40s or 50s is worth it to you. Clearly, there were not enough assets we could have bought during our working years to compensate for the freedom and joy we have experienced in nearly nine years of early retirement.

How can you apply financial self-discipline to your life? Start by asking yourself how much you need all of those major assets that are costing you money for purchase, maintenance, and depreciation. Is it possible you could get by on less? Here are some questions to focus your thinking and get you started.

- How large of a house do you need? Considering that your mortgage will be one of the most costly items you pay off in your lifetime, can you live in a smaller, less expensive house? Not only will you pay less up front, but maintenance and utilities will also be lower.
- Do you need expensive autos or would cheaper models suffice? Is a big vehicle necessary or could you get by with a smaller, more fuel-efficient one? Do you need two or more vehicles or could you share one and tolerate a little inconvenience? Do you need a new vehicle every three

or even five years? Choosing the less-expensive option in each of these situations could ultimately save thousands toward your early retirement.

- Is that large screen TV/home theater system or HDTV so important that you are willing to work longer and retire later to own it? Or would a 27-inch set be adequate?
- Do you need 500 compact discs and a new $2,000 stereo system on which to play them? Or could you get by with a $500 stereo, an FM antenna, and 100 compact discs?
- Is eating lunch out every day necessary or could you take lunch and save money? It should come as no surprise that we brown-bagged it throughout our careers.
- How about that big shiny new boat? Could you be happy with a smaller, less shiny boat knowing that saving more money once again will allow you to retire earlier so you have more time to spend at the lake?

You need to go through all of your expenses, determine your priorities, and ask yourself this question: Do I need that, or is there a less expensive alternative that would still give me pleasure but allow me to invest more money for early retirement? Focus on the long term (tomorrow) and then set your priorities today.

In order to embrace financial self-discipline, you need to know exactly how much money you spend and where you spend it. The next chapter will focus on tracking income and expenses. This is essential to getting control of your spending so that you can increase your savings and investing to reach your goal of retiring as young as possible.

Chapter Eight

Tracking Income and Expenses

If you are not already doing so, and most people aren't, you need to start tracking your income and expenses. With a computer and software such as Quicken or Microsoft Money you can track, categorize, total, and analyze expenses, as well as create a household budget. But I wouldn't necessarily go out and buy a computer and/or special software solely for that reason.

We have always recorded our income and expenses in a small notebook, account book, or planner and then at the end of each month we categorize them by entering all numbers into a spreadsheet. Our method is actually twice the work since all expenses could be directly entered into the computer rather than into a notebook first. But if we had to turn on the computer each time we wanted to record a couple entries, we wouldn't get all of our expenses recorded and it would defeat the purpose. So buy a cheap notebook or planner that can be easily carried with you to record expenses (or left at home for writing them down without having to turn on the computer). Whether you later categorize those expenses with your computer or do it by hand (which is how we started), at least they will be accurately recorded.

THE OLD-FASHIONED METHOD

If you don't have a computer, or if you would prefer to do it the old-fashioned way, a simple form like the example below is convenient, easy to use, and quite adequate. Draw columns on a sheet of paper for the categories you need to track that will ultimately comprise your budget. Enter rent or mortgage, food, gas, utilities, insurance, and so on across the top of the sheet in those columns. Then write each day of the week or month down the left-hand side, leaving a line to total everything at the bottom.

Record income on the days you receive it and enter your daily expenses under each appropriate category so that you only have to total the columns at the end of the week or month, whichever you prefer. Use our budget in chapter 9 as your guide for categories.

Sample Tracking Income/Expense Form

Days of Month	Income	Rent or Mortgage	Groc.	Dining Out	Utilities	Insur.
1						
2						
3						
4						
Totals						

Every time you buy something, get a receipt. If the clerk does not give you one, ask for it; otherwise, you will likely not remember multiple purchases by the end of the day. Record your expenses in your account book or directly onto your Income/Expense Tracking Form. At first, make an effort to record every penny you spend so that you can accurately analyze where your money is going. And remember, the less you spend, the easier this project is!

At the end of each week or month, total the expenses in each column. I assure you that if you have never tracked your expenses, and if you do it right, you will be amazed at how much money you spend and in what different categories you spend it. This can be fun as well as enlightening.

In *Your Money or Your Life*, Joe Dominguez and Vicki Robin take a novel and interesting approach to tracking expenses. It is more work than what I suggest above, but for many people it might be a better way to approach it. They show you how to set up forms, relate each expense to how it impacts your life and whether it was worth it or not, and then evaluate whether each of your expenses would be the same if you did not work. They also show you how to graph income and expenses to help reinforce saving. By the time you finish the book and complete the various projects, you will be perplexed by what you have done with all of your money. At the same time, by following their procedures you can turn that around, take control of your expenses, and establish savings goals to get you where you want to be in the future.

Even though we had been retired several years before reading *Your Money or Your Life*, the concepts presented were well worth reading; it certainly will give you something to ponder in terms of prioritizing your life. If your local library does not have the book, try their interlibrary loan program (some libraries charge a fee for that service so be sure to inquire first). You might also request that the library purchase it; if they decline, try a used bookstore. If one of your passions is buying new books, an updated edition was published September 1999 (which I have not read). Since it's over two years old, you might try looking for it at a discount bookstore.

Tracking your expenses may only take a couple of months for you to get a rough idea of where your money is going—and where it should be going. Actually, you can get a jump on tracking expenses by going through your checkbook and credit card receipts and recording your main expenses for the past 6 to 12 months. Obviously that won't include all of your expenses because you've probably used cash for many purchases, but it will be a start.

Finding out where your money is being spent is the first step toward making rational spending decisions in line with your early retirement goal. We have kept an income/expense journal since 1976 and we will continue to do so. Not only does it keep us focused, but it has also come in handy while writing this book!

Tracking expenses, together with a new philosophy on financial self-discipline, will guide you toward meeting your long-term goals, like retiring in your 40s or 50s (or as early as possible). Once you know how much you spend and where you spend it, you can take control, concentrate on cutting spending, and increase your savings percentage.

THE CREDIT CARD MENACE

Most people will not retire early because they cannot save the money necessary to do so. In other words, they do not have control of their spending. Why the big spending problem? Two words: credit cards. Many Americans are drowning in credit card debt. In fact, one recent statistic indicated that consumer debt has increased tenfold over the past 20 years. I also recently read that over 90 percent of all bankruptcies in this country are the result of credit card debt. Since that seemed a little hard to believe, my research took me to the American Bankruptcy Institute (www.abiworld.org) where I located a wealth of related information. Here are just five interesting facts from that site:

- Statistics from the Federal Reserve reveal that household debt is at record levels relative to disposable income.
- Over 97 percent of new bankruptcy filings in 2001 were non-business—that was a record high number of fillings, up 19 percent from the previous year. Personal bankruptcies are expected to increase in 2002 as a result of exces-

sive spending in the 1990s and the weakened economy today.

- In 1990 there were 718,000 non-business bankruptcy filings. In 2001, non-business filings totaled 1.5 million (more than double that of 1990).
- In a 1999 document the Federal Deposit Insurance Corporation (FDIC) cites figures indicating that personal bankruptcies increased almost 500 percent since the 1970s. A significant contributor to that increase has been consumer debt, particularly credit card debt.
- The Consumer Federation of America stated in a 1998 report that more than half of American households (55–60 percent) carry credit card balances averaging more than $7,000 and pay interest and fees exceeding $1,000 per year. (Wouldn't that $1,000 be better utilized in a tax-deferred retirement account earning you money?)

If you do not understand the problem with credit card debt and you are unable to manage your credit cards, then you probably don't need to spend a whole lot of time planning for early retirement. If you have some consumer debt but are eager to implement early retirement planning strategies, then there is a relatively easy way to start. **Cut up your credit cards, start paying cash for everything, and renew your relationship with money.**

When you have to physically count out the dollars you spend and think through what you buy (and how much you pay), especially if the dollars in your purse or wallet are limited, you will have a better appreciation of how much you spend. Plus, the inconvenience of having to get cash from the bank first, or having to carry around all that cash, will discourage many purchases.

There is nothing wrong with having a credit card; in fact, there are instances where you must have one for making purchases over the telephone or Internet, like airline tickets or motel reservations, and some cards allow you to build up points and receive discounts on future purchases. But the difference lies in whether you have control over that card or it has control over you. We have always had one or two credit cards. We also always pay off the balance each month within the 25-day grace period.

A credit card can be extremely handy in that you do not have to carry hundreds of dollars in cash with you. At the same time, you must have the self-discipline to buy only what you need (or want) and then to pay off the balance of that credit card each month. If you cannot do that, then you should not have a credit card. And keep this in mind: Except for your house and main vehicle, if you can't afford to pay with cash, you probably can't afford it.

Because revolving credit interest rates are often upward of 16 to 19 percent, paying the minimum per month results in that debt virtually never getting paid off. And if you continue to use those cards, you slowly start drowning in debt, just like you can drown in the ocean if you don't keep your head above water. If you already have charge card debt, the first thing you must do is pay it off. That may require cutting back on other expenses to save extra money, or borrowing money from elsewhere at a lower rate so that you can pay it off as quickly as possible. What doesn't make sense is to pay 16 percent or more on credit card debt while having money in a CD or savings account at 5 percent or less.

The intention of this book is not to be a credit counseling service, but to bring a major problem to the forefront and point out where more information can be obtained. Should debt be a problem for you, cut expenses and put yourself on a strict budget. If you cannot do that on your own, here are several options:

- If you are falling behind in your mortgage payments, you can go to the Web site of the U.S. Department of Housing and Urban Development (www.hud.gov) and click on **foreclosure** or **Talk to a Housing Counselor** to obtain a list of approved counseling agencies listed by state. These agencies provide free advice on home buying, renting, defaults, foreclosures, credit issues, and reverse mortgages. HUD also sponsors a National Servicing Center (888-297-8685) to help homeowners avoid foreclosure.

- For more information on credit card debt, start with the State Public Interest Research Group's Web site at www.truthaboutcredit.org.
- Turn to the Yellow Pages under "Credit & Debt Counseling Services" and inquire with the Better Business Bureau about any firm you choose. Several nonprofit credit-counseling agency Web sites are also listed in the appendix. The July 2001 issue of *Consumer Reports* magazine has a good article on credit-counseling agencies and lists questions to ask when seeking help.
- The American Bankruptcy Institute's Web site includes a **Consumer Corner** with a "Frequently Asked Questions" section where you can find numerous resources for debt and credit information. You can find those sources and their Web sites listed at www.abiworld.org/consumer/.

BORROWING YOUR WAY OUT OF DEBT

One potential solution for getting out of debt that you may want to consider is borrowing from friends or family. This strategy can be effective because you can possibly borrow money at a much lower interest rate than you could from a bank, which will allow you to pay off your debt quicker. We used this tactic on several occasions, both as borrowers and lenders. In our situation, credit card debt wasn't the problem; rather, we were building houses and needed money on a short-term basis so that we didn't have to cash in investments. But the principle is the same. We have loaned money for similar reasons.

In our case, when borrowing money we usually offered family members two percent above the rate they were getting wherever they had money stashed (normally CDs or money market accounts), which they always perceived to be a good deal for them.

This also allowed us to borrow at a reasonable rate without having to pay loan origination fees, which can amount to hundreds or even thousands of dollars. The only problem we've had is that no one wanted to be paid back!

If you are the borrower, you must be diligent in paying off your loan the way you would a bank or any other institution. This is important because otherwise you may not only lose a good deal now and potentially in the future, but it could also cause hard feelings between family members or friends. If you are the lender, you must be sure that the person borrowing money from you has a plan and the resources to pay you back.

Whether borrowing or lending, we always write up a promissory note so that if we were to die, the executor of our will would know about the loan. We have never gone to an attorney regarding loans to friends or family so I don't know what legal issues might arise under different scenarios. We have loaned to, and borrowed from, family members several times and never felt a need to involve an attorney. You will have to decide for yourself whether you believe that is advisable in your situation.

Borrowing money from family members has always been done on a strictly business basis—by presenting a proposal outlining why we need a short-term loan, how much we need, how much we are willing to pay to borrow the money, and how and when it will be paid back. No one is put on the spot and no whining is included. It's either a good deal for the other party or it isn't.

If a friend or relative asks to borrow money from you and you are not comfortable with it, how do you say no? I suggest you firmly state the reasons for your decision and remind the person that you are looking at it strictly on a business basis—that your money is more secure somewhere else. There is no guarantee that you won't demolish a relationship, but loaning someone money who doesn't pay you back could be worse; not only would your relationship suffer, but you would lose your money too.

In the right situation, borrowing from family can be effective in meeting short-term needs. There would be less of an inclination on my part to loan money to friends because it is too difficult to know the circumstances that could jeopardize getting your money back (a lesson we almost learned the hard way). However, you could consider borrowing from willing friends as long as you are absolutely sure you can make the payments as agreed.

CUTTING EXPENSES

Several years ago, while running our retirement projections (which we normally do every January to verify that we can remain in retirement the rest of our lives, and which I thoroughly discuss in chapter 9), we made an interesting observation. You gain more by cutting expenses than by increasing income. Why? Because for every extra dollar you earn, you lose some of it in taxes; however, for every extra dollar you save, you actually save a dollar.

Sit down and calculate how much you actually earn on your job. After deducting taxes and the costs related to earning that money—like business clothes, commuting, child care, eating out, make-up, and dry cleaning for example—you may be surprised at how little you earn, especially when you divide it by the number of hours worked (don't forget to include commuting time). It can be an eye-opening exercise that anyone can benefit from doing. It will also reinforce the advantage to be gained by cutting expenses and saving more versus working harder to earn more. Of course, if you do both, you will accelerate your net worth growth.

Taking control of your expenses and then cutting them is essential for most people to retire young. Your local library will have numerous resources devoted in part or in full to the topic of cutting expenses. Additionally, you will find a plethora of information on the Internet by using a search engine and entering a request such as "cut expenses," "frugality," or "saving." Many magazines also regularly feature sections or articles covering that topic. Why are there so many? Because generally speaking, financial self-discipline is not the American way of life. America is a country of spenders. If you want to retire young (or retire at all), you must become a saver, not a prodigious consumer.

Some of my readings in the past couple of years have included several books that address credit cards and cutting expenses. Many of the ideas in these books overlap; that is to be expected since Americans keep doing the same things over and over when it comes to spending beyond their means. I recommend these books for their coverage of the issue at hand, as well as because they provide other information beneficial to retiring young.

- *Die Broke* by Stephen M. Pollan is loaded with practical information relative to planning for retirement and functioning in your everyday life. (The author doesn't believe you should retire, however, so there is another perspective for you.) His chapter on paying cash was particularly interesting.
- Suze Orman's book *You've Earned It, Don't Lose It* has a chapter titled "Minimize Your Expenses/Maximize Your Income" with tables for figuring assets and debt.
- Let me tell you right up front, in *The New Rules of Money: 88 Simple Strategies For Financial Success Today* by Ric Edelman, one of those 88 rules is *not* "buy as much as you can with your credit card." In fact, rule #5 is, "If you want to avoid financial failure, watch the pennies you spend—not the dollars." Rule #8 should be useful for those who spend too much on Christmas presents.
- *The Simple Living Guide* by Janet Luhrs is a treasure of information. Chapter 2 is devoted to money and cutting expenses. Every chapter is followed by a list of resources for additional reading; the lists are comprehensive and could keep you reading for years. This book is dedicated to helping you simplify your life and it provides the philosophy and techniques to do that.

- For more advice on simplifying your life and cutting expenses, chapter 6 of *Your Money or Your Life,* "The American Dream—On A Shoestring," discusses frugality and lists over 100 ways to save money.
- For those who enjoy the "For Dummies" books, *Personal Finance for Dummies* is loaded with beneficial information on all aspects of personal finance. Chapter 6, "Putting Your Spending on a Diet," focuses on helping you cut expenses. And the best part is that I bought this excellent book at the thrift store for a dollar.
- *Financial Peace* by Dave Ramsey relates the experiences of a man who went from owning $4 million in real estate at age 26 to bankruptcy four years later. Since 1992, he has been teaching others how to not make the same mistakes he did. This book is full of practical advice and information and it includes several financial management forms at the end that could be utilized. His "snowball method" for reducing debt is a great idea and his "envelope cash system" could be particularly beneficial for those who have difficulty saving money.

If you want to retire early, you need to establish goals and work toward them. It is not that difficult, but it requires self-discipline and a true desire to succeed at those goals. You must eliminate debt and start saving aggressively; tracking expenses will be a necessary and beneficial first step in accomplishing the latter. The opposite approach is to spend as much or more than you earn. If you choose to do that, then you can continue toiling until you are 65 or older—maybe even for the rest of your life. That may work for some individuals too. It's your choice.

Chapter Nine

Take Control of Your Spending

After you start tracking income and expenses so that you have an accurate record of your finances, the next step is to establish a budget that will help you take control of your spending. (If you haven't yet started your income/expense tracking, don't let that delay your budget planning; you can implement them concurrently.) As beneficial as budgets can be, they are not endorsed by all financial planners. The main reason is that people do not stick with them anyway, so what's the point? The point is, they are not adhered to for generally two reasons:

- The budget is unrealistic—they cannot live within it.
- They are not committed to living within it regardless of how realistic it may be.

I firmly believe in budgets, which we'll also refer to as spending plans, as long as they are realistic. It doesn't matter what or how many tools you have to help you achieve something if you are not committed to accomplishing it in the first place. But given the desire and motivation to attain a spending/savings goal, a budget provides guidelines and focus.

If you were committed to digging a hole in the ground four feet deep, you would eventually complete that task digging with your hands. But if you used a tool, like a shovel, you could accomplish that goal easier and faster. If you want to save more of what you earn, you must cut spending. A budget represents the plan by which you decide where the money you earn is going to be spent. It is a tool that can help you accomplish your early retirement goal easier and faster. Without such a guide you could waste months or years before realizing that you are no closer to meeting your goal than you were before.

A budget establishes spending priorities in different categories so that if you meet those objectives, you have money left over at the end of the month (and year). Tracking your expenses tells you where your money *has* been going, while your budget establishes where your money *will* be going. The difference between those two can be your newfound savings. By developing a spending plan that is realistic for you, making a commitment to follow it, and applying financial self-discipline, you will have a useful tool for building net worth and retiring young.

We never had a formal budget until we retired in 1993, though it should be obvious by now that we are unusually disciplined savers. However, it was appropriate upon retiring in our early 40s because we wanted to be sure we would not outlast our money—and your level of spending is the critical factor in retiring early and not outlasting your net worth.

RETIREMENT PLANNING PROGRAMS/CALCULATORS

Future planning and budgeting can be more fun and inspiring with the assistance of a retirement planning program or retirement calculator. We purchased the Vanguard Retirement Planner (VRP) in 1995 and, without question, it was an exceptionally interesting and beneficial tool. After filling out forms, tables, and charts for years in an effort to confirm we were on target in meeting our goal of retiring at 50, we could not have found a more useful tool. That software program has been updated with the Vanguard Online Planner (or Navigator Plus, which can be downloaded onto your computer), both of which include interactive tools for college, retirement, investment, and estate planning. You can get them at no charge on Vanguard's Web site at www.vanguard.com.

Most financial firms and mutual fund companies offer free retirement calculators and/or planning programs on their Web sites, but they can differ considerably. Some calculators merely compute how much money you will have if you invest a given amount over a period of time, while others are full-featured planning instruments that can also help you devise your annual budget.

A good retirement planner will allow you to input multiple factors such as income, savings, current investments, rate of return you expect, amount of Social Security you anticipate receiving, and how much you are spending or intend to spend, and then vary those as you like. The program will calculate how much money you will have and how long it will last, and adjust the figures for the inflation scenarios you enter. It's easy to spend hours manipulating figures and entering different scenarios.

Every January after completing our year-end accounting and net worth calculations, we plug those numbers into our retirement planner and analyze how much more or less we can spend in the coming year and not outlive our money. Since the 2000/2001 (and now into 2002) bear market has had a minimal impact on our portfolio to date, the generally upward trend of the stock market in the past decade we've been investing has resulted in our long-term retirement projections being strengthened.

This continued growth of our net worth, even while retired, has given us two choices in future retirement planning: (1) increase spending and assume we will not live past a certain age, which was about 85 in our initial retirement plan, or (2) assume we are going to live beyond 85 and project our retirement to that age. We have now projected out to age 99 for both of us. As unlikely as that is, if we do live that long, our projections indicate that we will have the money to support us.

By assuming we will live longer and extending our retirement plan to age 99, a lower annual budget is necessary so that we will not outlive our money. To assume neither of us will live past 85 would allow us to increase our budget appreciably since our goal is to die broke. Each new year as we calculate our net worth we will have fewer years left to spend it—so we will adjust our budget accordingly. We are content with the amount of money we currently spend and easily live within our allocations. Our goal is to never work full-time again and our retirement planning program allows us to verify that we are on track.

Of the many retirement planner features, one of the most interesting allows you to manipulate your budget figures to see how increased spending will affect your future retirement plans. It can be fascinating to see the impact that increasing or decreasing your expenses, even a couple thousand per year, can have over the long term. But it is a simple concept. The less you spend, the more your money grows, and the longer it lasts.

If you fall short of money for the length of time you hope to be retired (in other words, how long you think you might live—a difficult projection for sure), the program should allow you to make adjustments in either your rate of return (which would generally mean investing more aggressively), the amount of money you spend, or how early you retire. There are so many variables you can manipulate to plan your early retirement that you can spend hours and enjoy every minute of it. You may also be able to print out graphs for each of your scenarios.

If you have a computer, you need to tap into a retirement planning program. If you are already involved with a financial firm, try their Web site. Otherwise, try the Web sites of large mutual fund companies and big brokerage firms (several are listed in the appendix). Most sites at least have some kind of retirement calculator. None of the programs I tried work exactly the same, so read the instructions carefully for each program you access to understand how it works and what assumptions have been utilized to derive the results. One Web site conveniently offering a variety of calculators covering four areas—Auto, Credit/Budget, Home, and Retirement—can be found at www.fool.com/calcs/calculators.htm (unfortunately, a full-featured retirement planner is not included).

INFLATION AND YOUR BUDGET

In chapter 5 you saw the significant impact that a 3.5 percent annual inflation rate can have on your savings and investments over 20 or 25 years. It can also impact your spending. Items you buy today will cost more in the future because inflation erodes the value of your dollars.

But as you will see from the two budgets detailed later in this chapter, although there have been increases and decreases within the various categories, once adjustments are made for rent expense, our 2002 budget is only 5.7 percent higher than the average of our 1994/1995 budgets; our actual expenses the past two years are only 6.6 percent higher than the average of our first two years. That reflects annual budget increases of a little over three-quarters of a percent on average, and part of that increase can be attributed to lifestyle changes. During that same time period, the government's Consumer Price Index (CPI) that measures inflation is up an average of 2.4 percent per year (or about 20 percent total).

We have had to make a concerted effort and some changes in our lives to keep expenses down the past eight years. But the point is, while the CPI may indicate inflation is going up 2, 4, or 8 percent per year, that does not necessarily mean it applies to your personal situation at that same level; it could impact you more or less. The Bureau of Labor Statistics (www.bls.gov) addresses that issue with the following:

> Because the CPI is a statistical average, it may not reflect your experience or that of specific families or individuals; particularly those whose expenditure patterns differ substantially from the "average" urban consumer.

Inflation, as measured by the CPI, may not impact your personal situation as much as indicated for another reason: The CPI measures price changes in specific items and not necessarily the increase in what people actually spend. If the price of a particular item increases, consumers may switch to a similar but different item. For example, if the price of bananas were to increase drastically, consumers would probably switch to other less-expensive fruits. Similarly with packaged goods, people will switch to other brand names or buy store brands if they are less expensive. Shoppers are also likely to stock up more when they see a sale. So although the cost of certain items has gone up according to the CPI, those increases can be moderated with adjustments in spending.

The impact of inflation may be seen in some categories more so than others. Although our overall budgets changed minimally the past eight years, our health insurance premiums increased a little over 10 percent per year on average—that's over 80 percent cumulatively compared to roughly 20 percent for the CPI. We kept premiums down only by increasing our deductible and rewriting our policy. Another example of inflation impacting some items more than others was seen in 2000, when petroleum-based-energy costs more than quadrupled the general inflation rate.

But one could also compile a list of items that have gotten less expensive over the years; clothing and shoes would be two categories and anything electronic another. Take televisions as an example. Our last 19-inch television was purchased in 1982 for roughly $600 and we bought a 13-inch TV in 1990 for $280. In the last few months I have seen name brand 19-inch TVs selling for as low as $130 and 13-inch sets for as low as $90. Computers have gone from thousands of dollars to hundreds, or even free (if you purchase a specific Internet service). Besides televisions, computers, and other electronic items being significantly less expensive, they have more features and generally better quality.

The impact of inflation on your life will depend in part on where you spend your money and how much you spend. While it may not be devastating to your personal situation some years, inflation may significantly impact your budget other years. Over time, it can erode your retirement funds. At the same time, over the past 76 years, the stock market has allowed investors to watch their money grow at a significantly higher rate than the CPI.

I should point out that the past decade we've been retired has been a period of relatively low inflation according to the CPI. But with history as our guide, it can be expected that there will be years in the future when we will confront high inflation while our mutual funds may decline in value on a short-term basis, rather than staying well ahead of the CPI as they have done this past decade. When those years come, the negative impact of inflation will become readily apparent.

BUDGETING BASICS

The first thing you need to do is set up a budget for this year, whether that is the beginning of a new year or the middle of a current year. Figure out how much you want to spend in each category (line item) and then make a commitment to live within that amount. Of course, if you have not yet started tracking your expenses, this is going to be a lot more difficult because you probably do not have a realistic idea of how much you spend.

Our budget is set up in January of each year after expenses for the previous year have been calculated. We look at how much we spent in each category that year and then decide whether we want to increase or decrease those expenses in the coming year. After now completing our eighth budget year, we have yet to spend the total allocated amount in any given year. That is not necessarily good or bad, but it feels better coming in below budget (in effect, allowing for additional money saved for the future), rather than above and knowing that the long-range plan is not being followed.

Establishing a budget so precise, and spending with such discipline, that you fall below every line item is difficult to do and it does not need to be your objective. Exceptional and unexpected expenditures can come up over a year's time that may require you to spend more than you allocated. There may be other categories where you can spend less to make up for it, or maybe those expenses are one-time exceptions (like some unexpected medical issue) that you can treat as a one-year extraordinary expense.

A budget should be flexible, but you must make a concerted effort to stay within the amount targeted for each category. Your goal is to plan expenditures so that you can cut your consumption, save/invest more, and increase your net worth to meet your early retirement goal (or to stay on target after you have already retired young). The further you live below your means—that is, below what you could based on your earnings—the more you save and the faster your net worth increases.

Retiring young and staying retired depends almost entirely on how much you spend. Your net worth is only so much and you can outlive that money if spending is excessive. Spend more than your net worth supports and you will begin eating away at your principal too quickly. Do that long enough and you can start planning your return to work. Spend less and you can continue saving even though you're no longer working. However, if your goal parallels ours (to die broke), then your long-range plan will incorporate spending your entire principal. You just don't want to spend too much of it in your first few years of early retirement.

As mentioned previously, we were willing to cut our standard of living some in order to retire early—smaller house, less large purchases, one vehicle instead of two, more use of coupons, finding less expensive activities to do, et cetera. Making similar adjustments while you are still working will allow you to save more and increase net worth faster.

Our budget has been kept fairly low because we have simplified our lives and have enough inexpensive interests to keep us entertained. We also have friends who could afford to retire now but who are choosing to work several more years because they want to have a higher standard of living than we have chosen. They want bigger and nicer houses, more luxurious autos, more assets in their homes, and frequent dinners at upscale restaurants. You'll have to decide what is most important to you.

Upon reading numerous books and magazine articles on early retirement, I observed that in some cases budgets containing only a few line items were used in illustrations. After plugging in our numbers, it looked like we were going to have a smaller budget than we ended up having. Some of those books and articles failed to list common expenses that could otherwise be easily overlooked, but which can add considerably to your bottom line: expenses like personal care items, various fees, household expenses, dental/eye care, contributions, and gifts. Of course, what each individual feels is an important expense will determine whether or not it will be included in his or her spending plan.

Historical data is immensely helpful in planning. Until you have collected your personal spending data, it is a matter of giving it your best guess. You may not spend as much as you allocate for each line item or you may spend more. Any semi-realistic spending plan will be better than nothing your first year. At least it is a focal point for planning your financial future—whether you want to eliminate unnecessary spending so that you can retire young, or whether you are ready now to exit full-time employment and begin your life of independence and freedom.

A PRELUDE TO DISCUSSING ACTUAL FIGURES

Some of you are undoubtedly going to look at our budget and specific line items and ask, "How can they live on that?" So let me preface the actual figures with these comments:

- We have been living within these budget figures for eight full years—they are realistic and feasible. However, it was also mentioned earlier that we average an additional $300 per month in off-budget "luxury or unnecessary" expenses which I'll fully explain later in this chapter. Even with the inclusion of the off-budget expenses though, our eight completed expense budgets through 2001 have only averaged $20,000 and our actual expenses have averaged about $18,000 per year total.
- Some areas of the country are less expensive than others (see chapter 14). Living costs are less in southern Utah than in many areas—but we could find parts of the country or world that are less expensive than here.
- Neither of us feels deprived or that we are making any major sacrifices by adhering to our budget. It would be fair to say that we have most of what we want.
- Since neither of us grew up in families with a lot of money, we learned to live on less and be happy without having to spend in excess.
- Our budget has worked well for us the past eight years, and it could work for others, but it's obviously not for everyone.

OUR EXPENSE BUDGETS: 1994 AND 2002

Prior to developing your budget, it may be helpful to examine two of ours detailed below (1994 and 2002); both are included so that we can look at the differences over the last several years. While we retired May 1993, our initial budget begins in 1994. The last half of 1993 saw extraordinary income and expenses due to the sale of our California home and the winding down of our businesses. By January of 1994 we had pretty much settled in as early retirees and that is reflected in our expense allocations. However, we still didn't have any experience living in a new geographic area as early retirees, so our first budget was not as accurate as those done after we had a track record of expenses to rely on.

The purpose of a budget is to categorize expenditures so that you can control where your money is being spent. The advantage to having a half-dozen expense items is that it is easier to categorize everything, especially if one of those categories is "miscellaneous." But is that realistic? Will you know where your money is going if a large portion of your spending is classified under miscellaneous? We added several line items over the years because we wanted to better define our spending. That probably comes from being meticulous, detailed-oriented people. The more detail you incorporate, the more accurate and useful your budget becomes, but also the more work it involves. You can make yours as simple or as complex as you like.

1994 and 2002 Expense Budgets

Budget Expense Item	**1994 Budget**	**2002 Budget**
Rent/Mortgage/HOA Dues	$ 560	$ 100
Property Taxes	0	80
Storage (Furniture)	50	0
Electricity	25	50
Natural Gas	75	35
Telephone	35	35
Water/Sewer/Garbage	20	70
Health Insurance	200	190
Auto Insurance	40	45
Home/Umbrella Insurance	35	25

Groceries	200	175
Dining Out	100	50
Gas (Auto)	50	35
Auto Repairs/Maintenance	50	30
Auto PP Tax/License	0	15
Travel	100	125
Rec/Entertainment/Hobbies	65	50
Clothes	50	25
Dental/Eye Care/Medical	100	210
Meds/Supplements	0	40
Gifts/Contributions	80	95
Personal Care	15	15
Office/Fees/ISP	25	45
Household	25	30
Total Per Month	**$1,900**	**$1,570**

The following discussion of each expense item along with its rationale will present the opportunity for you to assess whether it is suitable for your circumstances. Items that are not appropriate can be dropped and you may come up with specific items relevant to your situation that we do not have. Two of those may be life and disability insurance. We carried disability insurance until we retired, but we have not had life insurance for many years because we always believed that either of us was capable of taking care of ourselves financially should the other expire. That premium money was invested for retirement instead. Of course, if you have young children, you need to look at that differently.

To fairly compare our 1994 and 2002 expense budgets above, you need to subtract the rent and storage expenses in 1994 and add the property taxes and HOA dues included in the 2002 projection. With those adjustments, our latest and highest annual budget ($1,570) is $100 more than it was in 1994 and $70 more than in 1995. Although a line by line comparison below will reveal several category increases (and some decreases due to over-budgeting the first year after moving to a new geographic area), the biggest factor in our higher budget for 2002 over our first two is the dental/eye/medical category, which is $110 more than it was in 1994.

The increase in dental/eye/medical stems from our health insurance category. We had a $1,000 deductible policy in 1994 and budgeted $100 per month for dental/eye/medical to cover that deductible. Upon rewriting the policy in 2000 with a $2,500 deductible, we increased our dental/eye/medical line item to $210 per month to cover all out-of-pocket expenses up to our deductible; in essence, this line item reflects our level of self-insurance. If we don't spend our deductible in any year (and we haven't spent anywhere near $2,500 on dental/eye/medical in any of the past eight years), then this line item will come in under budget.

To get a better understanding of our budget categories and how they may or may not be applicable to your budget, let's look at each one along with the changes since 1994.

Rent/Mortgage/HOA Dues: This category includes your rent or mortgage payment. We own our home and have no monthly mortgage payment (and a noticeably lower monthly budget as a result). HOA stands for homeowners' association, the monthly dues we pay for living in a townhouse complex. Housing is generally an expensive budget item and often is not much cheaper for one person than two; of course, it could be higher for a family with children. The smaller the house you can comfortably live in, the greater the savings you can generally achieve in this category.

Property Taxes: We were renting in 1994 and did not have any property taxes to pay. We now own our home and anticipate paying approximately $950 this year.

Storage (Furniture): When we first moved to southern Utah in 1993 we were living in a 1,000-square-foot townhouse. Since our California house was twice that size, we had to store furniture temporarily after we sold the house. We eventually moved into a larger townhouse in St. George and brought the remaining furniture from

California. We have not needed to pay for storage since and your goal should also be to not have so much stuff that you have to pay to store it (either in a separate unit or by purchasing a larger-than-needed house to accommodate everything). If you see yourself in that position, then perhaps it makes sense to decide what you want/need, sell the rest, and add that money to your retirement fund. An old rule of thumb is that if you haven't used an item in three years, you don't need it. I'm not convinced that's always true, but it works for many things.

Electricity: We did not have air conditioning on the central coast of California and had no idea how much it would cost during the hot desert summers in southern Utah. That turned out to be one of the items we under-budgeted a little the first year. But electricity is cheaper than in California and for six years we averaged roughly $35 per month. Due to the California power shortage in 2000, Utah Power increased our rates some and we averaged $40 per month in 2001. We are planning for upward of $50 per month in 2002.

Natural Gas: What we knew about St. George upon moving here was that it was hotter in the summer and colder in the winter than where we lived in California the previous 14 years. Again having no idea what it would cost to heat our townhouse, we budgeted $75 per month. We were happy to learn we had over-budgeted appreciably and have been able to easily live within our $30 allocated amount for eight consecutive years, even though we moved from that 1,000-square-foot townhouse to one that is 1,500 square feet. We are planning for a small increase in 2002.

Telephone: We attribute our telephone expense item remaining the same over the last nine budgets to smart calling and use of e-mail. By smart calling, I mean we have been on some kind of discount calling plan for many years; our current plan allows us to call out-of-state (where our families live) any time, any day, for five cents per minute without a monthly fee. Several family members and many friends also have e-mail so that has been a great way to stay in touch without the long distance charges.

Water/Sewer/Garbage: At the end of 1998 we moved eight miles from our previous house and this line item more than doubled. Our previous HOA dues included water/sewer while our current dues do not, and the sewer charge is double what it was at the other house. As a result of a summer drought, our city implemented a significant water rate increase in the fall of 2000. In response, we raised this line item 50 percent in 2001 where it remains. This is getting to be a major monthly expense item for us.

Health Insurance: Next to Rent/Mortgage, this may be one of your most expensive items. We saw our premiums drop significantly upon moving from California to Utah. Although we budgeted $200 in 1994, we came in well under budget that year with the premiums at $135 per month. After escalating from $135 to $210 per month by 1999, we rewrote our policy and switched from a $1,000 to a $2,500 deductible (since we had only spent $1,000 once in a dozen years). That brought premiums back down to the 1994 level but, three budgets later, we are back to $190 per month (partially the result of my turning 50 years old and being bumped into a more expensive bracket). This is the one category where inflation has been a significant factor for eight consecutive years. If you are healthy and expect to stay that way, higher deductible insurance can save you a lot in premiums over the years.

If you currently work for an employer who provides insurance, this line item will not be the concern that it will be if you are: (1) not covered by your employer, (2) self-employed, or (3) soon to be early retirees (unless you are fortunate to have your premiums paid for the rest of your life, a benefit provided by some employers).

Auto Insurance: Considering that we were driving a 1984 vehicle in our first budget year and are now driving a 1997 vehicle, this item has changed surprisingly little. One factor helping to keep that cost down was a 23 percent discount we received in 2000 for being accident-free with the same insurance company for 20 years.

Home/Umbrella Insurance: Insurance protects what you cannot afford to lose. If you value your home and the valuables inside, then homeowners insurance is pretty much a necessity. Umbrella insurance protects your retirement nest egg. It provides one million dollars (or more) in coverage above your home and auto insurance limits in the event you would be sued—for example, the result of an auto accident or someone falling on your property.

Groceries: This could be a much bigger item for you than it is for us, especially if you have children. We overestimated in 1994 and actually only averaged $170 per month in both 1994 and 1995. After increasing about $30 per month over the next few years—partially the result of switching to a more healthy diet, which means more expensive foods—last year we saw that drop back down to the 1994/1995 level after Costco and the Wal-Mart Supercenter came to our area and we started shopping there regularly. We continue to eat the healthier diet, but without paying any more for groceries than we paid eight years ago. Since we are shareholders of both of those companies, shopping there regularly helps us in another way, too.

Dining Out: As explained in chapter 7, dining out is a minimal expense for us and it certainly costs less than we anticipated in 1994. We eat out once or twice a week, choose lunch rather than dinner, and either go where the specials are, use a discount coupon, use our two-for-one dining card, or occasionally pull out a gift certificate; that combination of choices allows us to keep this expense item surprisingly low.

Gas (Auto): St. George is relatively small and it doesn't take all that much gas to get where we go. Out-of-town trips for sightseeing or visiting friends are charged to the "Travel" category.

Auto Repairs/Maintenance: We always buy cars judged reliable by *Consumer Reports* and have never had significant repair problems. With our 1997 vehicle, we anticipate minimal repairs and maintenance for the next couple of years. This year we budgeted primarily for new tires and oil changes with a little left over.

Auto PP Tax/License: Utah has a personal property tax on autos in addition to a license fee. Nothing was budgeted in 1994 because we were not aware of the tax.

Travel: We are not big travelers and this line item has changed little in nine years. Our budget assumes flying or driving back to the Midwest every year or two to visit family, a trip to California to visit friends, and usually a couple of shorter trips in and around Utah. We plan to travel more once we hit our mid-50s and we won't mind increasing this category at that time.

Recreation/Entertainment/Hobbies: Every year it seems like this line item should be higher but we usually don't spend all that we budgeted. We find a lot of relatively inexpensive entertainment around St. George that keeps us content. This category includes such things as movie tickets (at the discount theater), live theater, concerts, tennis/racquetball supplies, our annual federal parks pass, hiking equipment, and cassette tapes/CDs/puzzles (all from the thrift store, of course). If we come up with more expensive things to do, we'll gladly increase this item. One way to see concerts and other entertainment events for free is to become a volunteer usher.

Clothes: Once you retire there may not be a big need for a closet full of new dress clothes. Casual-wear like T-shirts, shorts, sweatshirts, and jeans, is generally the norm for us—we do not go many places where dressing up is a necessity. When the occasion arises, however, we have what we need thanks to the great buys we get shopping the clearance sales. Tennis shoes and hiking boots are probably the most expensive items we buy in this category, as 75 percent discounts are hard to come by (though we occasionally find tennis shoes for 50 percent off). If you would like certain items that haven't been available on clearance and someone wants to buy you a gift for your birthday, Christmas, or some other holiday, clothes might be a welcome suggestion.

Dental/Eye/Medical: For seven years this category remained at $100; that changed two years ago when we increased our health insurance deductible. How much we spend depends on if either of us needs expensive dental work (like a crown) or if we both need eye glasses in the same year. Only once in the past eight years has this line item not come in under budget. Should one of us need unexpected medical treatment exceeding our budgeted amount, it will be written off as a temporary, extraordinary expense for that year. As early retirees, our goal is to stay active and healthy so that the need for expensive medical care is decreased.

Meds/Supplements: This category was added in 1999 after seeing enough research to convince us that we should be taking a few nutritional supplements. It also includes any over-the-counter and prescription drugs purchased.

Gifts/Contributions: This is our budgeted amount for gifts to friends and family and small contributions to charitable organizations. The bulk of our charitable contributions are off-budget expenses explained below. Once you retire you can spend time volunteering rather than giving cash to your favorite organizations.

Personal Care: Included here are haircuts and personal care items like toothpaste, shampoo, conditioner, bath soap, deodorant, razor blades, and the like.

Office/Fees/ISP: Because we work part-time out of our home, we budget for office supplies. Initially this category also included IRA fees. By consolidating accounts and transferring our IRAs from a full-service brokerage directly to the mutual fund companies in which we were invested, we were able to reduce IRA fees from $130 per year to $10. Go with a good no-load mutual fund firm from the beginning and you will pay nothing.

ISP stands for Internet Service Provider. We pay our local provider six months in advance and receive a $3.45 monthly discount in return. If you plan to stay with a specific provider for six months or longer, check to see if they offer a prepay discount.

Household: Laundry and dish soap, paper towels, facial tissue, toilet paper, tools, and other supplies are included in this category.

OFF-BUDGET EXPENSES

In addition to the expense items included above, we also have off-budget items. Our budget is set up to support our basic retirement needs—those considered necessary for remaining retired the rest of our lives assuming neither of us works. But we frequently seem to come up with things we want (but could get along without) that are not included in our basic plan, like new furniture, bicycles, treadmill, computer and software upgrades, newspaper subscription, solar window screens, specific charitable donations, and gifts. When that is the case, the house rule is that we pick up part-time jobs and establish a mad money fund to pay for those off-budget items. For most of the last eight years we have both done part-time work and we have had an ongoing mad money fund as a result.

While part-time jobs fund our off-budget expenses, they also allow us to continue funding our IRAs or SIMPLEs. Since we retired so young, we figured that earning and investing an additional $4,000 each year into our retirement accounts would further solidify our future retirement. We don't mind part-time work because we don't have to do it and we can quit any time; and it's a good reminder of why we worked so hard to retire young.

We could also not work at all and increase our annual budget by $3,500 to cover the items initially targeted as luxury or unnecessary expenses. That would still only put us at about $22,000 this year, which our net worth could easily support and could have supported for the past eight years. But for now, since we don't mind working part-time (especially Kris, who enjoys accounting), we have chosen to handle it in this manner. The day we no longer want to work at all, we will adjust our budget accordingly. Chapter 15 covers the rationale for working part-time early in your retirement and the significant impact it can have on your life later.

ESTABLISHING YOUR BUDGET

Now it's your turn. You can use your computer and a software program or you can photocopy the form below and easily do it by hand. Look at our 2002 budget categories and decide which line items are most appropriate for your situation. It is highly recommended that you track expenses for at least a couple months first, as you will have a better idea of how much you are spending in each category and your planning will be more accurate.

Assuming you have done that, look at what you spent over the last year (or months if you recently started) and then try to realistically estimate what you will spend in the coming year. Write those amounts in the "Current Year" column. Remember, your goal is to live within your budget so try to be as realistic as possible. The more you cut spending, the more you will begin saving for your early retirement. Set up your budget like the following example:

Budget Form

	Current Year	**Retirement**
Income:		
Wages/Salary		
Interest/Dividends		
Capital Gains		
Bonuses/Commissions		
Other		
TOTAL INCOME		
Expenses:		
Rent/Mortgage		
Property Taxes		
Storage (Furniture)		
Electricity		
Natural Gas		
Telephone		
Water/Sewer/Garbage		
Health Insurance		
Auto Insurance		

Home/Umbrella Ins.		
Groceries		
Dining Out		
Gas (Auto)		
Auto Repairs/Main.		
Auto PP Tax/License		
Travel		
Rec/Enter/Hobbies		
Clothing		
Dental/Eye/Medical		
Meds/Supplements		
Gifts/Contributions		
Personal Care		
Office/Fees/Stamps		
Household		
Savings		
Life Insurance		
Disability Insurance		
TOTAL EXPENSES		

One expense line item you might want to include that is not found on ours is "savings." This is especially important if you are in your net worth accumulation stage. Pay yourself first. Make sure you save at least something but go for as much as possible if your goal is to retire young. If you allocate a specific amount to savings each month, you will have a goal to meet and you will be more focused to achieve it.

If your savings are automatically deducted from your paycheck for direct deposit into your 401(k) or similar account, you may still want a savings line for additional money you want to put away; you can never save too much. If *all* of your savings are automatically deducted from your paycheck, then you might want to enter that amount as your line item for tracking and to reinforce your efforts. In either case, your **total monthly expenses (including savings) should equal your total monthly income.**

Notice that income taxes have not been included as one of our expense items. Initially we had it as a line item, but because our stock mutual funds distribute an unknown amount of capital gains at the end of each year, it was too difficult to estimate in January what we might be paying the following year in April. So we dropped taxes from our budget several years ago and starting covering each year's liability through our investment income. If we fall short on investment income any year, then we'll probably also have minimal tax liability.

If you work for an employer, income taxes are being taken out of your paycheck each pay period and you should not owe additional taxes at the end of the year for which you need to budget. Always try to set your exemptions so that you do not owe much at tax time and you do not get much of a refund; otherwise you are letting the government use your money all year when you could be investing the difference and making money on it. If you do get a refund, invest it for retirement.

It may be even more difficult for you to budget for income taxes if you are self-employed, because you may not know from one quarter to another what your income (and estimated tax payments) will be. But, as with all other aspects of your business, make your best projection and budget on that basis or use your prior year's tax liability as a guide.

If you are nearing early retirement and can realistically estimate your tax liability for the year, it is preferable to include taxes as an expense item. If your money is in CDs, bond mutual funds, or index funds where income from interest and dividends is fairly steady and there aren't wide variations in capital gains distributions from year to year, you should be able to estimate your future tax liability and adjust your budget accordingly. Since you have to pay taxes on your non-wage income, it makes sense to also include them as a planned expenditure so that your budget is inclusive.

FOCUSING ON THE FUTURE

Your budget allows you to focus on each line item and decide if you are spending more or less than you need to. The odds are that you are spending more in a given category, rather than less. This is the time to cut back. The less you spend the more you save and that is how you increase your net worth. You can look at our budget and see how much it is costing us to live. If you reside in a more expensive area of the country, obviously your expenses will be higher. On the other hand, your income should compensate. If it doesn't, then maybe it's time to move.

Now, to start focusing on early retirement, use the second column titled "Retirement" and go back over each line item, estimating how much you might spend if you weren't working. This can be fun—your first chance to start thinking about quitting work, or at least cutting back to part-time. Think about how much you would enjoy the freedom of not *having to work* and how great it would be to have control over your life from day to day. Then sit down and seriously consider where and how much you could cut expenses to make that a reality. Consider all the expenses required for work that you wouldn't otherwise have: commuting and travel costs, clothes/uniforms, make-up, child care, dry cleaning, eating lunches out, eating dinners out (because you don't have the time or you're too tired to cook), entertaining clients, tools of your trade, additional personal costs, seminars/conventions, and so forth. Enter your reduced expenses in the Retirement column.

Once you subtract all of those work-related and pared-down expenses, how much is it *really* costing you to live? It was this exercise that convinced us we could retire young. We realized that most of our income was being spent on our businesses or was being invested for retirement; a relatively small percentage (about 30 percent) was supporting our personal life. It became evident that if we didn't work, we didn't need all that much to live on.

The fun part about a budget is that it presents a genuine challenge: trying to live within your spending plan while still doing most of the things you want to do. It requires you to focus on your priorities and make decisions. The end of every month (and year) presents the opportunity to assess how well you met your budget goals and it provides reinforcement for your efforts. If you like challenges, this is a good one to initiate.

Chapter Ten

Investments for the Long Run

This chapter is not going to tell you specifically where to invest your money; that is a decision you must make for yourself based on individual circumstances. Rather, the following pages will provide a general introduction to investments for the long run that can help you increase your net worth to a level sufficient for retiring young. One caveat: neither Kris nor I were professional advisors or financial experts. We learned about investing through self-study, personal experience, and mistakes. There is no guarantee that what did and didn't work for us will necessarily do the same for you. Then again, maybe it will.

HISTORICAL PERSPECTIVE

You can read a multitude of books and magazine articles on investing and come up with the same general conclusion: Over the past 10, 25, 50, or 100 years, one couldn't do better than the stock market for return on investment and significantly beating inflation.

As risky as some people believe it is (and it can be on a short-term basis), the long-term payoff is compelling.

The following table presents average annual total return performance figures for the three major asset classes (cash, bonds, and stocks) from 1926 through year-end 2001; the returns are also adjusted for inflation, which averaged 3.1 percent over that same period. (Figures courtesy of The Vanguard Group.)

Average Annual Total Return
From 1926 Through Year-End 2001

Investment	Before Inflation	Inflation-Adjusted
Cash	4.0%	0.9%
LT Corp. Bonds	5.7%	2.6%
Stocks	10.7%	7.6%

To put those figures into hard numbers so that you can see the impact of such differences on investment return over time, assume you were around in 1926 and placed $1,000 into each of three tax-deferred investments: cash (like T-Bills or CDs), long-term corporate bonds, and stocks (in this case the S&P 500). What was the value of each of your accounts at year-end 2001 (rounded to the nearest $100), assuming you were still around to check them out?

Account Value at Year-End 2001

Investment	Before Inflation	Inflation-Adjusted
$1,000 in cash	$ 19,700	$ 1,900
$1,000 in bonds	$ 67,600	$ 6,600
$1,000 in stocks	$2,265,800	$222,600

The difference in the inflation-adjusted returns over the past 76 years of these asset classes is nothing short of startling. Parking your money in cash or bonds in an effort to build a retirement nest egg over that period of time would have you still working today.

However, each $1,000 invested in stocks would have meant a major step closer to early retirement.

At the time we retired in 1993, stocks had averaged 10.3 percent since 1926, bonds 5 percent, and cash 3.7 percent. It seemed obvious to us that, based on long-term performance, there was only one alternative that would allow us to remain in retirement for the next 35 to 45 years without running out of money. We assumed that, over time, the stock market would continue to perform at its roughly 10 percent historical average while our retirement projections indicated that we would do well with 9 percent and we would even do okay on 8.5 percent. Since then, the market has had five exceptionally good years, one break-even year, and two losing years. Overall, our emphasis on stock mutual funds has left us far ahead of where we would have been had mostly bonds or cash been our choice.

Another example of the long-term potential of mutual fund investing comes from the latest annual report received from one of our funds (Investment Company of America), which included a growth chart over its 68-year history. Assuming dividends and capital gains were reinvested, a one-time $1,000 investment in that fund on January 1, 1934 would have grown to $4.53 million on December 31, 2001 (not inflation-adjusted). Of course it was not a steady path upward from year to year like we would prefer to see, but the growth has been spectacular over the long term. What a shame we didn't buy in until 1990!

IT'S NOT ALL UPHILL

Although the stock market has a history going back to 1802, the period from 1926 to the present is considered the era of the modern stock market—a time in which the highly regarded Standard & Poor's (S&P 500) index has been in existence. Over the past 76 years the S&P 500 (generally referred to as the stock market in this chapter because of it's long history) has averaged a 10.7 percent gain per year, far exceeding the other major asset classes over that period, and returning well above the rate of inflation. But the ride was not all uphill. The key to earning that return is that you must have had your money invested over the entire time period so that you could ride out the short-term losses and take advantage of the longer upward trend.

For example, from 1926 through year-end 2001 the stock market gained as much as 54 percent and lost as much as 43 percent *in just one year.* Can you imagine investing your $500,000 retirement nest egg in equity (stock) funds and then watching it drop to $285,000 by the end of one year? On the other hand, how exhilarating would it be to watch that same $500,000 grow to $770,000 by the end of one year? Only those who can truly handle such volatility without panicking and selling when things look bleak should invest in the stock market for short periods of time.

Over longer periods, however, the story is different. The longer you leave your money in the market, the more that volatility levels out and the better your odds of averaging positive returns. For instance, whereas from 1926 through year-end 2001 you could have gained as much as 54 percent or lost as much as 43 percent in a one-year period, over any 20-year holding period your portfolio would have gained an average annual return of between 3 and 18 percent. Over the short-term, you definitely take risk, but over the long term, those risks are well rewarded, especially compared to how you could do with most other investments.

One must always be aware that past performance is no guarantee of future success, a disclaimer you will see on virtually every stock and bond chart, graph, and advertisement. While the odds of a positive average annual return are certainly with you over a period of 20-plus years, what if you entered the stock market at the beginning of one of the worst bear markets (commonly defined as a drop of 20 percent or more in stock prices over at least a two-month period) of all-time and there were no gains in the market for the next 10 or 15 years? Could it happen? It has in the past!

Looking at historical data once again, there have been several periods when investors lost a significant percentage of their stock market assets—either relatively quickly, or slowly over years—but only if they panicked and sold their holdings during the decline:

- Stock prices fells 86 percent from September of 1929 through July of 1932 and did not recover to their previous levels until 1954.
- The S&P 500 (large-company stocks) lost 48 percent of its value between January 1973 and October 1974 (small stocks lost over 70 percent) and didn't recover to its pre-collapse high for nearly eight years.
- From 1966 through year-end 1982 the Dow Jones Industrial Average made no progress while inflation skyrocketed as high as 13 percent.
- Black Monday (October 19, 1987) marks the largest one-day stock market drop in Wall Street history when the Dow Jones Industrial Average dropped 22.6 percent and the S&P 500 Index lost 20 percent. Between October 13 and the closing on October 19, the stock market lost nearly a third of its value.
- In 2000 the Nasdaq Composite Index had its worst calendar year since its creation in 1971, falling 39 percent. By year-end, it had plunged close to 50 percent from its all-time high in March. In 2001 it fell another 21 percent, giving it a cumulative two-year drop of 60 percent (71 percent off its March 2000 high).
- But the most intimidating example comes from across the ocean. After reaching an all-time high on December 29, 1989, the Japanese stock market (the Nikkei) plunged 63.5 percent by August of 1992. Nine years later, as I update this in January 2002, the Nikkei has not recovered; in

> fact, it is down even further, closing last year at 73 percent below its all-time high in 1989.

To give that last example some perspective, try to imagine how you would you feel if your $500,000 retirement fund dropped to $182,500 over a three-year period and then nine years later you only had $135,000? Japanese investors didn't believe it could happen to them either. But it did and one can never discount the possibility of that happening in the U.S. in the future. Bull and bear markets are common to every stock market in the world and that is not about to change.

What is important to remember about bear markets, however, is that the examples above mark the most extreme incidences. More often, bear markets are less dramatic, the recovery period is *usually less than two years,* and they are nearly always followed by extraordinary rebounds (called bull markets) in which investors recover that which was lost and soar well ahead of their position prior to the bear market. But in order to take advantage of those strong bull markets, one must be invested. That means not selling during the gloom and doom of the bear market and taking advantage of the reward that long-term investing in stocks provides.

The last two years have marked the most recent bear market. After five consecutive years of unprecedented growth, many experts argued that the stock market had reached a "new era" and couldn't go down. But it can, it did, and it will again. Although the Nasdaq slumped into a bear market in 2000 (plunging 50 percent from its all-time high in March and closing down 39 percent for the year), the other indexes did not fall nearly as much. The Dow Jones Industrial Average lost about 6 percent, the S&P 500 dropped about 10 percent, and the S&P Mid-Cap was actually *up* 17.5 percent.

Rather than turning back around in 2001, however, we saw all of the indexes slump further: the Dow Jones was down 7 percent (a two-year drop of 13 percent); the S&P 500 down 13 percent (two-year drop of 23 percent); the Nasdaq down 21 percent (two-year drop of 60 percent); and the S&P Mid-Cap, after rising 17.5 percent in 2000, closed down 1.6 percent in 2001. That's better than most of the indexes performed, but it still illustrates how the market sectors can turn. It is this unpredictability of the stock market that can make investors uncomfortable. It is for this same reason that diversification is essential. You will read about diversification as an important investment strategy in the next chapter.

When we retired in 1993, interest rates were below four percent. Although they moved up briefly to the seven percent range in the latter half of 2000, they have fallen again to the lowest levels in many years. Based on historical returns, there appeared to be no other logical place to invest our money in 1993 where we could earn enough to stay retired 35 or 40 years, or however long we live, than the stock market. We thought that was a risk worth taking then, and we still think so.

WHAT ABOUT BONDS AND CDS?

Short-term volatility in the stock market has prompted other potential strategies for those beginning early retirement. One approach is to invest in laddered certificates of deposit—CDs taken out for different periods of time or intervals such that one matures every month or two, giving the investor the option of withdrawing money for living expenses or rolling it over for another period. That might work if CDs were paying 8 percent or better and inflation wasn't equally high, but you can't count on that.

Here's an example of why this strategy will not work for most early retirees. A net worth of $500,000 invested in CDs at 7.0 percent—the highest rate we've seen in several years—would result in an income of $35,000 per year. Many early retirees could live on that. But then there's the issue of inflation. In order for your principal to not be eroded, you need to reinvest enough to compensate for the inflation rate each year.

> Note: The CPI has averaged 3.1 percent over the past 76 years, but 4.6 percent over the last 25 years due to a period of unusually high inflation from 1977–1981. As a compromise between those numbers, and since the trend has been lower inflation over the past 20 years, a 3.5 percent inflation rate is used for all illustrations in this book. (Be advised, that is not a prediction; it's just a reasonable number to use for our examples).

In this case then, you would need to put $17,500 back into another CD. ($500,000 x 3.5% = $17,500). That would only leave $17,500 for your retirement budget—minus federal and possibly state income taxes based on the entire $35,000—and probably not enough to live the lifestyle you'd prefer over the length of time you could potentially be retired. So what might be your options?

- Retire later with a larger net worth. For example, $700,000 invested at 7 percent would give you an annual income of $24,500 after a 3.5 percent inflation adjustment. A lot of people could retire comfortably on that.
- Start eating away at your principal and then possibly end up having to return to work if you live too long.
- Supplement your CD income with part-time work.
- Invest some of your money elsewhere (diversify) to get a higher return over time.

While CDs offer safe, dependable income from month-to-month, you may not be able to sustain early retirement because of the impact of inflation. CDs could be a viable strategy for many early retirees if, relative to the example above: rates were higher, inflation was lower, or there was a combination of the two. For risk-averse people, CDs are more comfortable because the income is stable, guaranteed, and you don't have to contend with the volatile stock market. But with interest rates having been relatively low for several years, the stock market, even with its increased risks, has been the better alternative.

Because of their income stability and safety (backed by the full faith and credit of the U.S. government), long-term U.S. Government Bonds have been another potential strategy for bypassing the stock market. Unfortunately, long-term bonds, similar to stocks, can be volatile and experience bear and bull markets. If you purchase individual bonds and hold them to maturity (like holding CDs), price fluctuations don't impact your portfolio. You collect regular dividends and get your principal back when the bond matures. That seems like the safe way to proceed.

But similar to CDs, the problem with bonds for the long term is evident through the 76-year performance table presented at the beginning of this chapter. While bonds outpaced inflation by 2.6 percentage points, after paying taxes on that income, you barely come out ahead. That may be all right if you are already retired, don't plan to live long, and merely want to hold your own. But if you are in the accumulation phase of your life, building net worth for early retirement, then you cannot afford to park your money in CDs or bonds for extended periods of time. Though bond returns have been better the past 10 and 20 years, stocks have still outpaced them by a wide margin over the past 10, 20, and 50 years.

Whereas the long-term results of the stock market are compelling for anyone serious about retiring young, there is no guarantee that its performance will be the same over the next 76 years. For those seeking returns that will grow net worth appreciably, but who are also risk-averse, there needs to be a compromise. And there is. It involves diversifying your accounts among at least stocks, bonds, and cash (called asset allocation); real estate is often a fourth component. This is probably the most practical alternative for those investing for early retirement, as well as for those who are already enjoying it—more on that in the next chapter.

INDIVIDUAL STOCKS

Rather than reiterate information easily found elsewhere, I will share some of our investing experiences in an effort to help you make future investment decisions. For starters, if we make the assumption that stocks are a viable place to be for the long run, then there are two types of investments for most potential early retirees: individual stocks and stock mutual funds.

Our first venture into the stock market involved buying, holding for the long term, and occasionally selling individual stocks. But over several years, I found it too frustrating. Part of the reason for that may be my own weaknesses—lack of patience and intolerance for losing money. Although our stockbroker's advice and recommendations were usually followed, we always had more losers or minimal-gainers than winners. Of course one major winner can make up for numerous losing stocks (as long as you sell them before they lose too much); the opposite is also true. After realizing that individual stocks were incompatible with my personality, the easy answer was to sell all but the true winners and try something else; and that's what we did.

Prior to describing what we did next, let me clarify and quantify our experience with individual stocks. I pulled our Gain/Loss Worksheet for the period we owned stocks and ran the numbers. We were never prolific stock traders because our initial goal was to hold most of them for the long term. But between 1988 and 1998, we bought 49 stocks and sold 46 (all of them were purchased between 1988 and 1994). By the time we had sold those 46 stocks, 19 were losers and 27 made us a profit (though for many it was small). In all, those 46 stocks had cost us $143,000. Subtracting the losers from the winners, our total profit on those 46 stocks sold was $13,800. On a percentage basis, our profit over 10 years averaged 1 percent per year. Wow!

Of course, in all fairness, we still own three stocks (and a few spin-offs) that were purchased near the beginning and we have held onto them because they have been winners from the get-go.

Though having had their ups and downs, all three have done well to this point and we plan to continue holding them indefinitely.

If we add in the current value of those held stocks (and spin-offs) plus a few hundred shares of those we previously sold, the total profit comes to roughly $126,000 as of year-end 2001. Adding that to our profit from all the other sold stocks increases our 13-year return (1988–2001) to approximately 7.5 percent per year. That's better than CDs would have done over the same period, but it was clearly not worth it considering how well our mutual funds did in comparison over that same time period.

Though individual stocks aren't compatible with my personality, believe me, it can be exciting picking winning stocks and watching them move up at a rapid pace; of course, they can fall pretty fast, too. Of our 49 stocks, three made us $126,000 (on paper at least) while the other 46 stocks netted us a combined profit of $13,800. Pick the right stocks and you can do very well. Pick the wrong ones and you can lose your money or, at a minimum, become quite frustrated.

If you like the challenge that trading individual stocks can bring, if you trade through a discount broker so that your trades cost a fraction of the $100 or so each that we generally paid to buy and sell, if you cut your losses early so that you don't lose as much, and if you have more patience than I had, then you may actually enjoy buying and selling individual stocks. One of the advantages is the control you have over your portfolio. That is, you decide when to buy and sell and you do not realize capital gains, and the taxes that go with those gains, until you sell. If all that sounds good to you, then buying and selling stocks may be appropriate for your portfolio (at least for a portion of your money). Experience can truly be the best teacher and it taught us that *we* could do much better with less stress by turning to mutual funds.

MUTUAL FUNDS

In 1992, after seeing the pattern in our individual stock portfolio where three or four were making a good profit and most of the rest were borderline profitable or in the red, we started investing in no-load mutual funds (no-load meaning there's no sales commission to a broker). We found them much more suited to us. One advantage is diversification; the portfolio manager buys stocks in different industries to spread out the risk so that if one stock goes down significantly, it doesn't drag down the entire portfolio.

Our funds have done well since 1990 when we bought our first one through our broker. Don't think it's not possible to buy losing funds, because it is; different categories and styles of funds have good and bad periods. So a wise investor builds a diversified portfolio of mutual funds, just like you should diversify a portfolio of individual stocks. If you want the long-term success of stocks, but also need or want income and a little more stability, look at balanced funds, which combine both stocks and bonds.

There are hundreds of books and magazine articles to guide you when buying appropriate funds to meet your future goals. *Consumer Reports* magazine publishes one or two articles on mutual funds every March—the 2000 issue included seven steps for portfolio management and March 2001 rated the largest fund families. The 2000 issue also recommends several Web sites for investors. *Mutual Funds* magazine and other personal finance and business magazines publish similar types of articles. You can also type "mutual fund basics" into a search engine and be busy for hours. When searching for information over the Internet, I look for articles from credible, objective sites like *Bloomberg*, *Forbes*, *Kiplinger's*, *Money*, *Smart Money*, or any of the other business or personal finance magazines.

Another good resource is Morningstar. They are known for a five-star rating system that reflects risk-adjusted performance for over 1,700 mutual funds (though that is merely a starting point in choosing funds). You should be able to find Morningstar reports at your library or go to their Web site at www.morningstar.com. There you will find abbreviated information but also the opportunity to conduct searches to narrow down funds that may be good choices for your situation. Morningstar offers free investing courses on its Web site and, as a bonus, you can earn points towards free merchandise while learning what you need to know. Click on the **University** tab and then on the **Investing Classroom**.

If you want to take control of your portfolio and buy no-load funds so that you do not pay more in fees than necessary, then focus on finding funds that have good long-term track records (preferably with the same managers still at the helm) and low fees. You can find good funds in all categories with expense ratios of less than 1 percent. Don't buy funds that have 12b-1 fees, which are marketing expenses that can cost you a lot over time but gain you nothing. Fees for index funds run as low as 0.2 percent and nothing else comes close. Buy funds that meet your needs for the future. In other words, don't buy a fund for a goal that is six months off, because a downturn in the stock market during that period could leave you without the money you need.

HIRING HELP

If you are too busy to do the research necessary for investing on your own, whether you choose to pursue individual stocks or mutual funds, or if you simply are not interested and don't mind paying someone else, your next step is to contact a financial advisor (also commonly referred to as a financial planner). But be aware that financial advisors operate under different titles and do not provide the same services. And like any profession, some are more competent than others. A good financial advisor can save you time and make you money; a bad advisor can cost you money. You must sort through your options and choose an advisor that you believe can best meet your needs.

One thing you should be cognizant of is compensation. Financial planners are compensated through either commissions or fees, sometimes both. Many securities brokers, and insurance representatives who call themselves financial planners but basically sell their company's insurance and annuity products, are compensated solely through the commissions derived from the investments they buy for you. Be aware of a potential conflict of interest any time commissions are an advisor's sole compensation.

Fee-only financial advisors charge an hourly rate to develop an investment plan for you. Because their income is not dependent on the commissions received from the products recommended, their investment choices can be more varied—such as index funds and other good no-load actively-managed funds instead of only load funds. Their focus should be more on your financial success. How much their advice will cost you will depend on the amount and type of assistance you need. But you can expect it to cost significantly less than the $5,750 (a 5.75 percent load) you might pay a commissioned advisor to primarily help you invest your $100,000 retirement nest egg into mutual funds. (Be advised that some fee-only planners are really fee-based and charge commissions in addition to an hourly fee. Be sure you understand how any advisor you plan to work with is actually being compensated.)

Before hiring any financial planner, determine what kind of assistance you need—investments, taxes, estate planning—and then look at your options. Ask friends about their experiences and, unless an advisor has been highly recommended by someone you know and respect, don't choose the first one you talk to. Do not hesitate to interview several before deciding which one to work with, just like you would any employee. Your future retirement may depend on this person's recommendations so you want to feel comfortable. Get references of clients each advisor has assisted for several years and check them out. We have seen first-hand examples of financial planners being more interested in the money they could make off their clients' investments than they were in meeting their clients' needs and long-term goals. Every financial planner is not necessarily interested in *your* financial well-being. Try to weed out those who aren't, or do without an advisor.

For help on choosing a financial advisor (as well as on many other investing topics), I have found Vanguard's "Education Center" and "Plain Talk Library" to be easy to access and understand. The latter currently has 19 publications that you can find at www.vanguard.com. From their home page, click on "**Personal Investors**," and then the tab for "**Education, Planning, and Advice**" where numerous helpful links are found. Click the "**Plain Talk Library**" tab to see those specific publications (which you can read online or have sent to you by mail). In this case, look for "**How to Select a Financial Advisor**." If you don't have a computer or Internet access, telephone Vanguard at 800-871-3879.

A helpful magazine article on choosing a financial planner, "The Right Advice" by Lynn Brenner, was published in the September 2001 issue of *Bloomberg Personal Finance*. Another article worth reading, "Ten Things Your Financial Planner Won't Tell You" by Nkiru Asika Oluwasanmi, appeared in the January 2002 issue of *Smart Money*.

The financial advisors you interview should be registered with the SEC (U.S. Securities and Exchange Commission) and/or with state securities regulators. To find out if the person you are going to entrust your money to is properly registered, ask for his/her Form ADV, Parts 1 and 2. These two forms provide information on the advisor's proper registration, background, education, services and fees, as well as any problems he or she has had with regulatory agencies or clients. You should be able to get copies of Form ADV from either the investment advisor or the regulatory agency in the state that person does business. If the advisor is registered with the SEC, write the address found at their Web site at www.sec.gov, call the SEC at 202-942-8090, or e-mail them at publicinfo@sec.gov. For more information, go to the SEC's Web site where they also provide a number of publications of interest.

And here's some final advice. Even though you may elect to turn your portfolio management over to a professional, the more knowledgeable you are about investing, the better off you will be.

ADVANTAGES/DISADVANTAGES

There are advantages and disadvantages to both individual stocks and mutual funds. You have more control over individual stocks (and the taxes that accompany their sale). If you are lucky or good enough to pick profitable stocks, you can make a lot of money in a short period of time; if you aren't so lucky or good, you can lose a lot.

Mutual funds have the advantage of diversification and professional management. If you buy good funds with low expenses, you have less need to worry about your investments. The main disadvantage we have seen is the lack of control over the buying and selling that the fund manager does throughout the year. That can result in large and generally unexpected capital gains distributions at the end of each year for which you have to pay taxes; with index funds that is less of a problem. In fact, it is not impossible for a fund to lose money in any given year and still distribute capital gains for which you have to pay year-end taxes.

Buying mutual funds works much the same way as stocks. If you buy through a broker you pay a load (commission) one way or another. With stocks, you pay up front when buying and selling. That was usually the case with mutual funds too. But now different "classes" of shares are more common so that you pay up front when you buy, at the time you sell, or through higher fund expenses. You get advice buying through a broker but there is no guarantee that it will get you where you want to go, or that it will necessarily even be in your best interest. Conversely, it may be excellent advice for meeting your short and long-term goals.

No-load mutual funds are generally purchased directly from a fund company, but they can be purchased through other sources, usually for a fee. If funds are purchased directly from a fund company, you still pay annual fund expenses, but you do not pay a commission to a broker and you don't have to try to decide whether to buy Class A, B, C, X, Y, Z, or whatever shares. We own funds through Janus, T. Rowe Price, Vanguard, and the American Funds Group. The latter were purchased through our broker when we first got started in stock market investing and didn't have a clue as to what we were doing. We had a broker we liked, respected, and believed was working in our best interest—unfortunately, that is not always the case.

Like individual stocks, if you invest on your own and buy no-load mutual finds, do your research and diversify within different categories (large, mid-size, and small companies) to reduce risk. Just like there are different types of stocks that fluctuate in price, there are different styles (growth, value, and blend) of mutual funds that invest in those stocks. There are also international, global, and sector funds.

In addition to equity funds, you have the option of bond mutual funds. Over time, bond funds tend to be more stable (though history proves that they can be quite volatile) and investors buy them for that reason, as well as the fact that they provide steady income through periodic dividend payments. But the return on bond funds is generally lower than stock funds. Over long periods of time, as the tables at the beginning of this chapter illustrate, you will not make the money in bond funds that you will in stock funds.

Bond funds are divided into high, medium, and low quality, and are categorized by their maturity (short, intermediate, or long). You can choose corporate bonds, or purchase federal, state, and/or local government bonds. There are relatively safe bonds, such as U.S. Treasuries, and riskier high-yield bonds. Foreign bonds often offer a higher return accompanied by even more risk.

Whatever your investment goals, you can find appropriate mutual funds. But even choosing good funds does not exempt you from losing money. If the stock market has a bad year, you can lose money regardless of its category or style. If the stock market should experience a prolonged bear market, which could last several years, you could find your portfolio losing money (or at least not making any) over an extended period.

That is always the risk you take in the stock market. But it is because of that risk that you also earn higher returns on your investment. And that is the difference between "investing" versus "saving." You can save money via CDs, savings bonds, Treasury Bills, or other instruments and collect a fixed amount of interest while also having your principal guaranteed. But the return on those savings is generally low, and if it isn't low, then inflation is probably high and eating away at your increased return anyway. When you risk your money in the stock market, whether through individual stocks or mutual funds, history shows that you are amply rewarded over time.

INDEX VERSUS ACTIVELY-MANAGED FUNDS

Assuming you are convinced of the merits of mutual fund investing to build and maintain your net worth, it is important to discuss index funds versus actively-managed funds (also referred to as non-index funds). We will briefly look at some of the arguments for and against each. Based on our experience, you would be wise to choose a direction early and stay with it so you do not get caught in the situation we have found ourselves. We bought all actively-managed funds (load and no-load) and have since come to believe that a core holding of index funds may have made sense for us. It's not that we don't have good managed funds, because we do. But index funds have advantages we didn't adequately research.

Understanding Indexes

We chose actively-managed funds with good track records and relatively low expenses, and all have performed well within their categories. How do we know? That's where indexes come in. In brief, indexes are groups of stocks or bonds that represent some portion of the stock or bond market and serve as a benchmark for measuring performance. They can be broad-based (like the entire stock or bond market) or target specific market sectors in order to track the performance of a select group of stocks or bonds (like small-cap stocks or short-term bonds).

There are too many indexes to discuss them all, but a few of the most commonly referred to for mutual funds include the S&P 500, which tracks 500 large-company stocks (commonly referred to as large-cap stocks) currently representing about 70 percent of the value of the stock market; the Wilshire 5000 Total Market Index, which represents the overall U.S. stock market; and the Russell 2000, which tracks relatively small companies (small-caps). There are also indexes for mid-cap, value versus growth, international, and global stocks, and a whole series for bonds.

John Bogle, founder of The Vanguard Group, started the first index fund for individual investors (designed to track the S&P 500 Index) in 1976. The rationale behind index funds is rather simple: If a lot of time is not spent researching and trading companies because the stocks of a given index are merely bought and held, the fund can be run far less expensively and it should do as well as the market index, less the annual fund expenses. Of course, the argument against index funds is that, since they only mirror a certain index, an investor can never do better than that index—and we all want to do better than the average.

Is Average Good Enough?

We started our investment program under the premise that merely matching the overall stock market wasn't good enough. We wanted to beat the market. In retrospect, that appears to not have been the best philosophy under which to initiate an investment program. We started buying mutual funds through a broker (choosing those with low expense ratios) and paid a 5.75 percent load. Because that commission was deducted up front when the funds were purchased, we had less money invested from the beginning. For example, if we purchased $10,000 of fund shares, our net amount invested was $9,425 after the 5.75 percent load. Once we realized the impact of starting out behind, we switched to no-load actively-managed funds with relatively low expense ratios wherein all $10,000 went into buying shares. What we didn't realize at the time were all the advantages of no-load index funds.

A compelling case for index funds is found in the book *Earn More (Sleep Better): The Index Fund Solution* by Richard E. Evans and Burton G. Malkiel. One chart illustrates the number of stock mutual funds that have failed to match the returns of the Wilshire 5000 Stock Index (representing the overall U.S. stock market) from 1972 through June of 1998. Of the 26 full years represented, the Wilshire 5000 Stock Index topped the majority of actively-managed funds 18 of those years—that's over two-thirds of the time. The Index *outperformed 66 percent* of the actively-managed funds in a typical year and it topped them by about two percentage points. A performance edge of one or two percentage points per year can mean a difference of thousands of dollars in your retirement portfolio over a 15- to 20-year period, or even hundreds of thousands of dollars over a 40- to 50-year period. As an update, Vanguard reports that the Wilshire 5000 has outperformed 61 percent of all general equity funds in the ten-year period ending December 31, 2001 (figures were not available for 1972–2001).

The various categories of mutual funds have different objectives and each type of fund (like large-cap, mid-cap, small-cap, growth, value, international, and world, as well as all the different types of bond funds) needs to be compared to its respective benchmark index to fairly gauge performance. Most categories of index funds do well compared to actively-managed funds because their rock-bottom expense ratios give them a competitive edge.

For updated information on mutual funds, ask your librarian for the Morningstar binder. This mutual fund information company provides data, analysis, and commentary on over 1,700 funds; its ongoing updates are excellent tools for choosing and tracking funds appropriate to your needs. To see how index funds are faring against their actively-managed counterparts, I checked the latest reports from Morningstar. Since Vanguard has the largest selection of index funds, I chose a variety of their funds for comparison.

For large-cap stocks, and short and intermediate-term bonds, outperforming Vanguard's index funds by choosing an actively-managed fund would be difficult. In fact, for the following funds, the chance you will outperform them by choosing a non-index fund pencils out to 30 percent at best.

- Morningstar's July 2001 analysis revealed that, since its inception in 1992, Vanguard's **Balanced Index Fund** (which holds roughly 60 percent large-cap stocks and 40 percent bonds) has topped its competitors by 1.5 percentage points per year. Over the past five years, it has *surpassed 87 percent* of its peers on an after-tax basis; on a pretax basis it outperformed 78 percent.
- According to an October 2001 analysis, the Vanguard **500 Index Fund** (which replicates the S&P 500 index—a combination of large-cap growth and value stocks) has *surpassed 80 percent* of its peer group over the past 10 years on a pretax basis; it did even better after taxes. The past 15 years it has *topped 75 percent* of its peers.
- A November 2001 analysis of the Vanguard **Total Bond Market Index Fund** (which represents the overall U.S. bond market) revealed that it *outperformed at least 70 percent* of its peers over the past 1, 3, 5, and 10-year periods—and it did that with below-average volatility.
- As of November 29, 2001, Vanguard's **Short-Term Bond Index Fund** has *beaten more than 85 percent* of its peers for the past 1, 3, and 5-year periods—without assuming more risk than the funds it surpassed.

Other Vanguard index funds surpassing 60 percent or more of their peers over investment periods of three years or longer were:

the **European Stock Index** (over the past 5 and 10-year periods), the **Growth Index** (the past 5-year period), the **Mid-Cap Index** (the past 3-year period), the **Value Index** (the past 5-year period), and the **Pacific Stock Index** (the past 10-year period). But not all index funds are topping their competitors. The small-cap and foreign index funds have turned in the weakest performances. In those categories, you may be better off with non-index funds.

The primary concern some people might have about index funds is their relatively short track record. Only Vanguard's 500 Index Fund (started in 1976) has a track record longer than 20 years. The Total Bond Market Index Fund began in 1986, the Extended Market Index in 1987, and the Small-Cap Index Fund at the end of 1989. That means most of Vanguard's index funds have been around less than 10 years, with several less than 5 years.

Because of the cost advantage of index funds, Vanguard predicts they will outperform two-thirds to three-fourths of all actively-managed funds in a given market segment over extended investing periods. So far, Morningstar's statistics support that projection for many of Vanguard's funds, especially their large-cap blend (500 Index) and total bond market (intermediate-term bonds) index funds, which have been topping a majority of their peers for at least 10 years. Several of their other index funds have solid records over the past 3- and 5-year periods. If those funds can beat their competition over relatively short investment periods, then perhaps they will continue to do so over longer periods.

Whereas we started with all actively-managed funds, we now have two index funds. As we rebalance our portfolio the first quarter of each year, we are transferring money from other accounts to those funds. But be aware that in non-retirement accounts, there are tax consequences when selling one fund to buy another, so you want to determine whether you will gain more by moving your money and paying the taxes, or leaving it where it is. Calculate any moves you make based on the long-term ramifications.

Should you own actively-managed funds? Sure, if you believe you are capable of selecting funds that will outperform the indexes over time. The odds are not in your favor for many categories; however, some non-index funds and certain fund categories do outpace the indexes. Several of our funds have surpassed their respective indexes over the past 10 years and/or over the lifetime of the funds, and a couple beat their benchmarks by wide margins.

Take Janus Fund for example. According to our latest Annual Report, had you invested $10,000 in that fund on its February 5, 1970 inception date, reinvested all dividends and capital gains and held on through October 31, 2001, you would have amassed $901,960. The same investment in its benchmark, the S&P 500 Index, would have been worth $373,573. That's a remarkable difference. But be advised that Janus Fund lost 43.4 percent in its fiscal year ending October 31, 2001. This is a good example of how investing short-term in the stock market can be devastating and long term can pay off big—whether you choose individual stocks or mutual funds.

The ongoing argument for buying index funds versus non-index funds has become, why buy non-index funds and pay higher expenses if we can buy an index fund and maybe not beat the market (the index, in other words), but beat the majority of actively-managed funds? If you are currently in your net worth accumulation stage and will be investing for years to come, read arguments both in favor of and against index funds before deciding how much money you want to invest in them.

To learn more about the case for index funds, read *Earn More (Sleep Better): The Index Fund Solution,* as well as Rule 7, "Take Prudent Risks," from *Getting Rich in America.* Of course, Vanguard's Web site has loads of information, as do some of the other books and sites listed in the appendix. Morningstar is a particularly valuable resource for additional research on index and non-index fund performance.

Index funds can be purchased to track a wide variety of stock and bond benchmarks, so your investment alternatives are not limited. But there are some very good non-index funds, too. Many experts today suggest using index funds for the core of your portfolio while supplementing them with actively-managed funds that you hope to use to outperform some segment of the market. That seems a prudent strategy. With index funds you won't beat the market, but you won't under-perform it either. And you will probably beat the returns of most professional money managers.

Portfolio Turnover

One other point about index funds that I alluded to earlier and now wish we had considered prior to choosing all of our funds, is portfolio turnover. Non-index fund managers have a tendency to buy and sell stocks throughout the year; some managers in aggressive portfolios will buy and sell their entire portfolio two or three times. What that means to you as a shareholder is that, every time a manager buys and sells a stock in the portfolio, it costs you money in trading costs and having to pay the manager to do that. Since index funds buy and sell stocks only when the stocks in an index are changed, there is minimal turnover throughout the year. The result is less cost to operate the fund (a lower annual expense ratio for you to pay) and fewer capital gains at the end of the year.

And therein is where we have some regrets. In an actively-managed fund, even if you choose not to sell any of your fund shares, you may still have to pay taxes on capital gains because the fund manager bought and sold stocks in the portfolio during the year. A couple of our funds have distributed thousands of dollars a year in dividends and capital gains for which we had to pay taxes. The amount of capital gains we receive changes each year, depending on how much the managers bought and sold during the year and how those stocks performed. On the positive side, when you choose to sell shares of that managed fund in the future, you will owe less taxes because you will have already paid each year on the capital gains. But you have no control from year to year.

Index funds have minimal portfolio turnover so less capital gains are generally distributed each year and you pay less taxes. Now understand that eventually you will pay taxes if the stocks in the portfolio increase in value. When you do sell shares, you could have an even higher profit per share because you have not been paying from year to year. But at least it's your choice as to when and how much of your index fund you sell and, subsequently, on how much capital gains income you will pay taxes that year.

What to Choose

So are index funds the only way to go? Not necessarily. It can be fun owning funds that do better than their respective indexes. We have a couple of equity funds that beat their indexes by wide margins for several years, and that was both profitable and exciting to watch. Those funds cost us significantly from year to year due to the capital gains distributions from those profits. But the logical argument is that if the fund significantly beat the index and made us more money than we could have made investing in an index fund, we can afford to pay the taxes on those capital gains. There isn't a right or wrong between these choices and probably a combination of index funds and non-index funds makes the most sense.

Should you choose individual stocks or mutual funds, index funds or actively-managed funds? For all of the reasons discussed in this chapter, we have become big supporters of mutual funds over individual stocks and we are impressed with the performances of many index funds, especially those involving large-cap stocks and bonds. Do your research and choose whichever you believe will best meet your short- and long-term needs. You will find considerable support for mutual funds if you read some of the resources recommended in the supplemental reading section at the end of this book. For starters, you might try *Bogle on Mutual*

Funds, Getting Rich in America, Personal Finance for Dummies, and *The Only Investment Guide You Will Ever Need.*

INVESTING MADE EASY

If reading all of the above has left you in a quandary, consider the following simplified investing technique. Rather than having to choose mutual fund styles, categories, and managers, and then compare expense ratios, portfolio turnover, and return after taxes, you might pursue one of the following strategies:

- Purchase a balanced index fund. This gives you an exposure of about 60 to 65 percent stocks, which represent the total U.S. stock market, and 35 to 40 percent bonds, which represent the total U.S. bond market. Though their share price still moves up and down, balanced portfolios tend to be less volatile, which is important for many investors.
- If you want more exposure to stocks than you get from a balanced index fund, then purchase a total stock market index fund; this would give you a portfolio of 100 percent stocks comprised of the entire U.S. stock market. Based on past performance, you could expect this portfolio to outpace most actively-managed funds in a bull market, while it may or may not do worse in a bear market because of the total exposure to stocks.
- If you want more exposure to bonds than you get from a balanced index fund, purchase a total bond market index fund, which gives you 100 percent bonds. The problem with this strategy, based on historical returns, is that you cannot grow your net worth sufficiently to retire young. It might be more conducive to those already retired, although some stock market exposure is recommended by experts to keep your net worth outpacing inflation.
- Combine these last two in whatever proportions you want. For example, if you want 80 percent stocks and 20 percent

bonds, commit 80 percent of your money to a total stock market index fund and 20 percent to a total bond market index fund.

One advantage of pursuing the above is *simplicity* with minimal cost; you should be able to buy an index fund with an expense ratio of about 0.2 percent. There is no reason to pay a load for a fund that is going to track an index. Vanguard has the widest selection of index funds with low costs and good service (they also offer a wide variety of actively-managed funds, so your choices are not limited if you decide to invest with this fund family). A second advantage of this simplified investing approach is reduced paperwork (prospectuses, semi-annual and annual reports for each fund, plus newsletters from each fund family you invest with) for the rest of your investing life—a much bigger advantage than what you may realize at this time.

Check out business and personal finance magazines like *Forbes*, *Kiplinger's*, and *Money,* as well as *Consumer Reports*, for their annual or semi-annual mutual fund reports. These magazines present beneficial information about funds and rank them based on past performance—which, again, is no guarantee of future performance but can be an indicator of consistency. Purchasing one or two index funds would serve as a good core holding that could be supplemented with a few actively-managed funds for variety. For better portfolio diversification, you may want to include some foreign or world funds as you become more knowledgeable about investing. Active managers tend to do better than index funds in the small-cap and foreign fund categories.

LEARNING FROM OUR MISTAKES

Previously it was mentioned that you could profit by not making the same investing mistakes we did, and we made several rather expensive ones. You just read that we jumped into actively-managed mutual funds without adequately researching index funds. In our defense, there were few index funds available when we bought most of our mutual funds between 1992 and 1994. Now there are many choices and track records that can provide guidance. Fortunately, at least we bought good non-index funds. Outside of paying thousands of dollars in commissions and a lot more in taxes each year than we should have, things could have been a lot worse. As the following examples will confirm, we weren't as lucky on some of our other investments.

Real Estate Limited Partnerships

Our first and most notable investing disaster was real estate limited partnerships. The concept behind them seems a good one: pool investors' money, buy different types of real estate, and then either develop the properties or otherwise make them more attractive for resale. We (and millions of other investors) bought the argument that "there's only so much land" and it certainly appeared that we couldn't lose. One of the companies we invested with had never lost money in a limited partnership in 30 years.

Our first four years of Individual Retirement Account (IRA) investments went into these can't-lose partnerships, and all the slick materials we received in the mail sucked us in further. We were so impressed, in fact, at how easy it was going to be to make money that we bought into four more. Most of these partnerships were invested in land located on the West Coast, primarily in California. All eight partnerships had the same goal: buy, build, sell, and liquidate within seven years. Unfortunately and unexpectedly, the California real estate market began a long, steep decline starting about 1988. We had gotten into all of our limited partnerships between 1984 and 1987. Timing is everything.

When the real estate market fell precipitously, the land values depreciated below the loans outstanding and our first four partnerships went bankrupt—that was $16,000 of our IRAs down the drain. Another partnership we entered outside of our IRAs also went bankrupt for the same reason and we lost that $5,000. That's

$21,000 and counting. We have three remaining partnerships, all of which are currently still marketing their properties for sale. We hope to get our $8,000 investment back on one and half of our $10,000 investment back on the other two. With any kind of luck, we hope to recover $13,000 of $39,000 invested. What great investments these turned out to be! Imagine what that $39,000 invested 17 years ago in good mutual funds would be worth today. We feel better not thinking about it.

Lesson: There may be only so much land, but you cannot necessarily count on making money on it.

Should real estate investing interest you, do your research and talk to others who own the types of real estate you are interested in—whether that is raw land, houses, apartments, or commercial buildings. There is no guarantee you will be profitable, but other people have been making money in real estate for years. Learning from our experience over the past 17 years, however, real estate limited partnerships are not the way. An Internet search revealed that limited partnerships have not disappeared. Before you invest in one, research alternatives, especially REITs (Real Estate Investment Trusts). They are similar in concept but operate like mutual funds and can be easily bought and sold—unlike limited partnerships, which as you saw above, you could be stuck with for many more years than you prefer.

Like stocks, bonds, rare metals, and cash, real estate falls in and out of favor over time. There have been periods in the past when the stock market declined in value for several consecutive years while real estate flourished. That is why real estate is often one part of a well-diversified portfolio. But like all other investments, if you choose real estate, do your research first.

Soybean Futures

This investment story is as bad as the one you just read, except that we didn't lose as much money. In 1986 a friend and I were playing tennis on a regular basis. Each week he would comment that there should be a law against making money as easily as he was making it in soybean futures. That is how we got involved. Futures are extremely risky and I would not recommend that budding early retirees who want to grow or keep their money get involved. In essence, you leverage your money to bet on what might happen to some commodity in the future.

Our commodities broker was convinced that it was going to be an unusually dry year in the Midwest and the soybean crop would suffer, subsequently causing a shortage of soybeans and an increase in prices. (We later found out that he based his prediction on astrological signs.) So, given the fact that my tennis friend was earning—no, "stealing," he said—so much money in soybean futures, we gave the broker $5,000 to make us some big bucks too.

To make a long story short, there was an initial drought that summer in the Midwest, soybean prices rose, the prices of our futures rose, and we were up thousands of dollars in profit. But rather than take the money and run, our broker convinced us that there was more money to be made if we held on longer. Then it rained, the price of soybean futures dropped, and we ended up losing all of our profits plus our original $5,000 investment. My friend, who joked that there should be a law against making money so easily in soybean futures (and who, as I recall, was up something like $70,000 at the peak), lost all of that plus his $10,000 investment.

Lesson #1: Futures are risky—whether soybeans, pork bellies, precious metals, or anything else. Unless you have money to throw away or you thrive on taking big risks, stay with something more secure, stable, and dependable—like mutual funds.

Lesson #2: If you do go this route (and you can also apply this to individual stocks), don't get greedy.

Rentals

In 1982 we bought a condo to rent out. What we learned from this investment is that it takes a certain temperament to be a landlord and a meticulous, conscientious, perfectionist personality may not be the best match. Mistakes made:

- We paid too much for the condo because we trusted the realtor and didn't do our own research.
- We wanted our condo to be in the same condition as we would want it were we living there.
- We expected it to stay that way.
- If a problem developed, we expected the tenants to notify us before the problem got more expensive to repair.
- And the last mistake was clearly mine—trying to be something I wasn't: a landlord.

People have made money in rentals for decades, and for some, it provides their retirement incomes. They buy a rental each year for several consecutive years, taking out 15-year mortgages. The rents cover the cost of the mortgages plus taxes. By the time they retire in 15 years or so, the first mortgage is paid, the rental is owned free and clear, and the rents thereafter start funding retirement. Each year another mortgage is paid off and the rent from that house adds to retirement income. Or another strategy is to sell a house every couple of years and take the profits. Under current tax laws, the owner could live in the rental two of the last five years prior to its sale and owe no taxes on the profits (limited to a gain of $250,000 for a single person and $500,000 for a married couple). The real advantage to this strategy is that someone else pays the mortgage and you reap the benefits at the end.

Should that be an investment area in which you are interested, do your research and, by all means, talk with other people first who have been landlords or who have successfully used property management firms. Similar to any other investment, learn as much as possible about the advantages and disadvantages before jumping into something unfamiliar. Our experience suggests that it takes a certain temperament and knowledge gained from experience to be effective and profitable in rental real estate. For those to whom it is well suited, it can be a great investment/retirement strategy.

Lesson: Know your strengths and weaknesses and go with your strengths.

Although the above investments did not work for us, that does not mean they won't work for you. But if you choose to pursue any of the previous examples, prepare yourself better than we did. Thoroughly research any potential investment and consult with others who have hands-on experience to learn what you can. If you then decide to pursue that investment, at least you will start with the knowledge you need to make informed decisions.

Chapter Eleven

Growing Your Net Worth

Investment alternatives range from relatively simple and low-risk, to complex and high-risk. From the perspective of retiring young, there is little reason to risk your money more than is absolutely necessary to achieve net worth growth. From a historical perspective, one need look no further than a combination of stocks, bonds, cash, and perhaps real estate, to achieve the desired results.

THE $6,000 BOOK

If you could earn $6,000 reading a book, would you read it? Of course you would. In essence, that is what you can earn by reading a book on investing. Consider this example. By learning how to purchase $100,000 worth of appropriate no-load mutual funds, you save the load or commission (say 6 percent) that you would have been charged to buy similar funds through a broker. In other words, you earn $6,000 by doing your own research—by reading that book. The same math applies to all other dollars invested, too.

While our experiences with individual stocks, mutual funds, and other investments discussed in the previous chapter may have been helpful, you should not base your investing decisions on that information alone. At a minimum, you need to understand:

- Asset allocation—probably the most important factor in growing your net worth.
- The various asset classes and what combination will likely pull the return over time that you need to reach your goals.
- If you choose mutual funds for your portfolio, which categories and styles of funds will best fulfill your future objectives?
- If you choose index funds, which make the most sense for your situation?

You need some basic investing knowledge to successfully plan your early retirement. You can either educate yourself or hire someone else and pay out thousands of dollars that could otherwise be going into your retirement accounts and compounding tax-deferred for many years (refer back to the tables in chapter 5 for a reminder of how your money can grow over time).

We have no regrets about purchasing our first mutual funds through a broker. They are excellent funds. At the same time, had we made the effort to do what I am recommending to you (and what we ended up doing later anyway), we could have saved ourselves several thousand dollars in commissions and still bought into comparable funds. Load funds do not perform any better or worse than no-load funds; in fact, the load is a sales commission and has nothing to do with underlying fund performance. Once we took the initiative and did some research, we discovered no-load funds with low expenses and performances as good as or better than our load funds, and they cost us nothing to buy.

So here is some good advice for building your net worth for early retirement. **Take the time to go to the library, or get on the Internet, and read about investing.** Type "basic investing" into any search engine and the resources available will overwhelm you. All of the major investment firms and mutual fund companies I looked up have basic investing sections (or entire courses) on their Web sites. If you don't have a computer, try your library. Check out the no-load mutual fund companies, as well as sites like www.fool.com (which tends to be entertaining as well as informative), www.morningstar.com, and www.money.com (see the appendix for more). This may not be the most exciting reading you will do in your lifetime, but stay with the basics if you are new to investing. Don't try to learn it all in one sitting or you will probably become more confused than knowledgeable. It will get easier as you take your time and read different sources.

The free online retirement planning programs and some of the Web sites recommended in this book, should help you determine an asset allocation (discussed later in this chapter) based on your tolerance for risk. If you're utilizing a mutual fund site to learn about investing, they may also recommend specific funds within their family appropriate to your needs. Assuming it is a good fund family, this can be an easy and helpful way to get started. You will later have the option of changing your asset allocation as you become more knowledgeable about investing.

As a regular reader of personal finance books and magazines, I consistently find mutual funds to be the most recommended choice for building wealth, especially for novice investors. There are funds appropriate for virtually everyone and every situation. If you are in your net worth accumulation phase, you may want to invest more aggressively than if you are about to retire. In the latter case, you may need income derived from dividends, or you may not want to risk a prolonged downturn in the stock market.

MANAGING RISK /SLEEPING BETTER

We have reached a phase in our lives of becoming more averse to risk; perhaps you are in a similar position or you will be in the future. It is the 64 percent drop in the Japanese Nikkei between 1990 and 1992 (which is now down 73 percent nine years later at year-end 2001) that most influenced our thinking. While that may or may not happen in the U.S., we are less willing to take the risk. A well-diversified portfolio is regarded as the best defense for whatever may happen in the future.

Our first six retirement years we were top-heavy in equity funds and light on bonds. As our portfolio grew through the exceptionally strong years of 1995–1999, we began to get a little nervous; the higher the stock indexes went, the more nervous we got. Although it looked like the market could only go up (and many "experts" were predicting the same), we looked at the historical pattern and became concerned that the bubble would break and a bear market would ensue—statistically, bear markets occur about every five years and the U.S. hadn't experienced one since 1990. Since no one can accurately predict bear markets, the wise move is to take a defensive stance and prepare in advance. When stocks decline, the steady income from bonds and cash can cushion the blow to one's portfolio, and bonds may even increase in value.

In the first quarters of 1998, 1999, and 2000, we began taking profits and moving our money out of large-cap growth funds and into primarily bonds; we also added some small-cap value funds and REITs. Our goal was to adjust our asset allocation and rebalance our portfolio to reduce our volatility—not on a short-term basis, but for the long term.

One thing we learned from this experience is how difficult it is to sell investments when they are going up, especially when most experts are predicting a continued rise in the stock market. But the more we considered the historical pattern of the stock market, the more we were compelled to sell. As it turned out, our shift of assets for better long-term diversification turned out to be a prudent move. The stock market peaked in March of 2000 and it has been downhill since for most of the indexes. In contrast, bonds, small-cap value funds, and REITs have had positive returns.

So far, we have weathered this two-year (going on year three) bear market well. The 2.8 percent drop in our net worth over the past two years includes paying income taxes and taking money out for living expenses (up and above some earned income). Compare that to the 23 percent loss for the S&P 500 and the Wilshire 5000 indexes over that same period or, worse yet, the 47.5 percent average drop in the three growth funds from which we transferred most of our money in 1998–2000.

We were fortunate to have taken advantage of the unprecedented bull market from 1995–1999, but we were similarly fortunate to have lost little of what we'd gained when the market started its two-year decline in March 2000. It wasn't a case of being brilliant, it was a matter of feeling uneasy enough to rebalance our portfolio to better match our risk tolerance, and betting against the experts who were saying the market couldn't go down.

No one knows how long this bear market will last, but we are not worrying about it. As many others stressed out in the gloom of the falling stock market the past two years, we have been comfortable with our position. We are diversified among stocks, bonds, cash, and real estate and we are prepared to ride out whatever happens. You also need to build a diversified portfolio based on *your future goals and risk tolerance* so that you are comfortable with your investment portfolio regardless of the day-to-day fluctuations in the market—or even if there is a two-year or longer bear market.

We calculated last year via our retirement planning program that, even if we average a return as low as 7.5 percent per year for the next 30 or 40 years (which should be attainable with our combination of stocks, bonds, cash, and real estate), we will never have to work again—as long as we continue to follow the 3 Keys, and something totally unexpected doesn't happen—like one of us having a prolonged illness or severe accident. If our portfolio does better than 7.5 percent based on our asset allocation (and it should), it will give us more discretionary income.

If we already have enough, then how much more do we need? We can afford to invest more conservatively and take less risk at this stage in our lives. At the same time, we'll still retain a good share of our money in stock mutual funds to: (1) benefit from additional long-term gains in the market, and (2) protect our portfolio against inflation over time. We believe that is a prudent strategy we can comfortably live with over the long term.

DOLLAR-COST AVERAGING

Market timing—an attempt to buy or sell shares based on when you believe the market is going to rise or fall—has not proven to be a reliable investment strategy. What is more commonly recommended for deriving the best returns over the long run is a *buy-and-hold strategy,* where you buy good stocks or mutual funds and hold onto them for years. Another recommended investment strategy known as *dollar-cost averaging* entails consistently investing the same amount of money each month, whether the market is up or down. You will end up buying fewer shares when the market is up and more when it is down and, over time, you should end up paying less per share than if you invest haphazardly.

Let's assume you invest $500 per month into your mutual funds. If the market is on the rise, you will buy fewer shares because the share price is higher. You feel good because, as the market continues to rise, you immediately make money on those shares. If the market falls, however, investors are inclined to not contribute to their funds because they are afraid they will immediately lose money if the market continues to drop. But in a declining market, you will be buying more shares with that $500 because the share prices are cheaper. It is like buying your funds on sale. In the long run, through a consistent program of dollar-cost averaging, you will pay less per share and you will do better over time than if you try to outguess the market by buying shares only when you think the market will rise.

Try this example. The first month you invest $500 into a fund that is priced at $20 per share. You get 25 shares. The next month you invest $500 but the market is moving upward and your share price has risen to $30 per share. This time you get 17 shares (rounded). The following month the stock market falls significantly and your fund drops to $10 per share. You invest $500 as usual, but this time you get 50 shares. After 3 months, how much did you pay per share on average?

$20 + $30 + $10 = $60 ÷ 3 = $20. Right? Wrong.

As illustrated below, the average cost of your shares was $16, not the $20 as it first appears. This is because you bought so many more shares at $10 per share when the market dropped than what you bought at $30 when the market rose. As the market begins its next ascent, you will own more shares increasing in price.

Dollar-Cost Averaging – Average Cost of Shares

Cost	Shares Purchased
1st Shares: $ 500 @ $20 per share	25
2nd Shares: $ 500 @ $30 per share	17
3rd Shares: $ 500 @ $10 per share	50
Total $1,500	**92**
$1,500 ÷ 92 shares = $16 per share	

Dollar-cost averaging takes the emotion out of investing. It eliminates the temptation to not purchase shares in a down market, which may be the best time to buy because it may start rising the next day and you were able to buy more shares for the same money. This technique keeps you on a steady and consistent investing program. Start using it as early as possible in your investment program and stay with it for the long term.

ASSET ALLOCATION

The best strategy overall, whether you are building net worth for later retirement or you are already retired and want to stay that way, is to diversify your portfolio among at least stocks, bonds, and cash (cash includes equivalents like Treasury Bills, CDs, and savings/checking/money market accounts); real estate is often a fourth component. This is known as asset allocation. The amount you position in each of those asset classes will generally depend on your age, risk tolerance, future goals, and length of time you have to reach those goals.

Although we have been referring to the stock market so far primarily based on the 76-year results of the S&P 500 (large companies), investing in the stock market via mutual funds should entail buying shares in medium and small company funds, as well as foreign funds, because investments tend to rotate in popularity. Over given time periods, small-caps, mid-caps, and foreign stocks can be expected to outperform large-company stocks; that is why diversification among a variety of investments is important. (For a comprehensive look at diversification, non-correlated asset classes, and asset allocation strategies, read *How to Retire Early and Live Well With Less Than a Million Dollars* by Gillette Edmunds.)

A good illustration of the impact diversification can have on portfolio volatility is seen in a chart on Vanguard's Web site. It features seven asset-allocation model portfolios and their performances over the period 1926–2000 (you can find the chart by going to www.vanguard.com and clicking on **Personal Investors**, ***Plain Talk Library***, and then the **Bear Markets** link, or calling Vanguard to have the booklet sent by mail). Here are two representative portfolios updated for average annual return through 2001:

- A portfolio of 100 percent large-cap stocks—the S&P 500—returned an average annual 10.7 percent over the years 1926–2001. It declined 22 of those 76 years with an average loss of 12.3 percent. (Technically, 12.3 percent is the average loss through 2000; but because the 2001 decline in the S&P 500 Index was the same as its average, this figure should not change). The worst one-year loss for this all-stock portfolio was *43.1 percent.*
- A portfolio of 50 percent stocks/50 percent bonds on the other hand, returned an average annual 8.7 percent over the years 1926–2001. (Through 2000, this portfolio declined in value 16 of 75 years with an average loss of only 7 percent. While those figures should change minimally as of year-end 2001, no official update was available at the time of this writing). The worst one-year loss was about half of the all-stock portfolio at *22.5 percent.*

If an 8.7 percent average annual return would have been sufficient to meet your long-term needs between 1926–2001, you could have invested in a balanced fund and not had to ride out quite so much volatility in the stock market—the part that makes many investors uncomfortable or keeps them out of the market altogether. (Note: It's not the bull markets that are the problem, it's the bear markets that stress people out; losing money seems to have more of a psychological impact on people than making money.)

And what about the current bear market? Another chart on Vanguard's Web site, Plain Talk's "Bear Market Survival Guide," includes the period March 31, 2000 through March 31, 2001 (no update was yet available for this chart as of this writing in January 2002). A mutual fund comprised of all growth stocks would have lost *42.5 percent* over that one-year period; a more diversified mutual fund, such as a total stock market fund (which includes large-cap, mid-cap, and small-cap stocks), would have lost about half that, or *24.8 percent*. But a balanced fund of 60 percent stocks/40 percent bonds would have declined only *11.2 percent*.

If you don't like losing money, even on a short-term basis, it should be obvious that a diversified portfolio of at least stocks and bonds can better meet your needs. You must realize that your portfolio will not grow as quickly during the bull market periods. But a lot of people are willing to give on the upside to not lose so much on the downside. That's the point we reached in 1998 and where our thinking remains today.

Retirement planning programs, mutual fund firms, investing-related Web sites, and personal finance books and magazines often have asset allocation guides to help you decide how much money invested in cash, bonds, and stocks is generally appropriate for your age and risk tolerance. Use them as a starting point and then make adjustments based on your personal situation and comfort level. You should be able to find a few interactive Web sites by typing "asset allocation" into a search engine.

One rule of thumb is that the percentage of bonds in your portfolio should equal your age. So if you were 30 years old, you would have 30 percent of your money in bonds (or maybe 20 percent bonds and 10 percent cash) and 70 percent in stocks. However, if you want to invest more aggressively, then go with a higher percentage of stocks, regardless of your age. As life expectancy increases and people remain in retirement longer, many experts recommend that retirees keep a higher percentage of their portfolios invested in stocks, and less in bonds, than age suggests. This is especially true if you retire young and expect to have 30 or 40 years of retirement ahead.

THREE INVESTMENT MOVES YOU MUST MAKE

Here are three investment moves I believe are critical to growing net worth and achieving your early retirement goal:

- Maximize your tax-deductible, tax-deferred contributions.
- Start investing as early as possible.
- Save the highest percentage of your annual household income that you possibly can.

Maximize Your Tax-Deductible, Tax-Deferred Contributions

There are several important advantages to maximizing contributions to your 401(k), 403(b), 457, SEP, IRA or any other tax-deductible, tax-deferred plan that is available to you. Since your contributions are tax-deductible (except for IRAs if you earn too much income), your overall tax liability is lower each year you contribute. Because annual dividends and capital gains are not being reduced annually by taxes, your account grows faster (you saw in chapter 5 the huge advantage of tax-deferred over taxable investing). And large capital gains distributions at year-end do not cost you anything in taxes in these accounts, so you can afford to invest more aggressively if you choose.

The primary advantage of a 401(k) or some other employer-sponsored retirement plan is that there is often some kind of employer match. That is free money to you. When we first moved to California, the nonprofit organization where I worked had a 403(b) plan available to employees. They matched the first $15 per month that an employee contributed. Now that may not sound like much, and it wasn't, but it was still free money to the employees. Regardless of salary, it meant that the first $15 any employee contributed monthly immediately doubled in value. Where can you invest money and be assured of a 100 percent return as soon as you invest it? And yet, amazingly, not all of the staff were contributing even $15 a month because they said they couldn't afford it. The question is: How could they *not* afford it?

The authors of *The Millionaire Next Door* present an interesting example of a couple who were of modest means and supposedly did not have any money to invest. But they each smoked three packs of cigarettes per day. The authors calculated that they spent approximately $33,190 on cigarettes over 46 years. Had that money been invested all along in a stock index fund, they figured it would have grown to $100,000 over the same time period rather than going up in smoke. Even more impressive, the authors calculated that if the couple had invested in the stock of their cigarette manufacturer, Philip Morris, and reinvested all dividends over those 46 years, they would have amassed over $2 million in their investment portfolio. Who could imagine such small change being transformed into such wealth?

It could be argued that most everyone spends money in areas where they could cut back if they wanted to save more (like smoking, drinking, eating out, and convenience items). In the "2001 Retirement Confidence Survey" cosponsored by the Employee Benefit Research Institute, the American Savings Education Council, and Mathew Greenwald & Associates, 65 percent of workers already saving for retirement indicated that it would be possible for them to save an extra $20 per week. Nearly half (47 percent) of the surveyed workers who *were not* currently saving for retirement reported that they could also save $20 per week for retirement.

While that may not sound like a lot, it can accumulate faster than you think. Investing $20 per week for 25 years in a tax-deferred mutual fund returning an average annual 10 percent per year will total a little over $102,000; over 30 years it will total $171,000. You won't be able to retire solely on that, but it will certainly contribute to a better retirement than if you hadn't saved anything. For numerous examples of how the little things can add up, read Rule 3 "Resist Temptation" in *Getting Rich in America.*

If saving is a problem for you, one of the most effective strategies for putting money away for any future goal is to utilize automatic savings plans that take money from your paycheck before you ever see it. That is how contributions to a 401(k) or other employer-sponsored retirement plans are handled. But you can also set up accounts to have money automatically sent to mutual fund companies by your employer or bank. Money that never gets into your hands in the first place is rarely missed. If you have difficulty saving, these forced-savings plans might be your answer.

It continues to baffle me why all employees who have the opportunity to participate in employer-sponsored retirement plans do not contribute as much as they can afford in order to at least get as much of their employer's match as possible. The employer is offering free money, not unlike giving you a raise. But many are too busy spending their money to worry about saving and investing for the future; and some of them will never be able to afford to retire. The question is: Will that be you? If you want to retire young, you must maximize your tax-deferred retirement accounts.

Start Investing as Early as Possible

The power of tax-deferred compounding cannot be overemphasized. Let's say you intend to retire at age 45 and are currently 25 years old with no dependents and an annual household income of $50,000. Because you are focused on early retirement, you invest $15,000 per year (30 percent of your income) in a tax-deferred mutual fund retirement account that earns 10 percent per year. Twenty years later, at age 45, you will have $960,000.

Now let's assume that you are not focused on early retirement until age 30. You still plan to retire at age 45, are still investing $15,000 per year at an average 10 percent return in a tax-deferred mutual fund retirement account, but now you only have 15 years until retirement. What will be your net worth at age 45 when you plan to retire? Try $539,000. Perhaps you can still retire on that, but by not starting your investment program a mere five years earlier, you have sacrificed $421,000 in net worth. Do not underestimate the need to start investing as early as possible.

Save as Much as Possible of Your Annual Household Income

As previously explained, we saved and invested an average 30 to 60 percent of our annual income, which is extraordinarily high compared to the 1.6 percent savings rate for Americans in 2001 and 1.0 percent in 2000. The authors of *The Millionaire Next Door* comment that most people want to be wealthy, but they are not willing to do what it takes to reach that goal. Growing net worth requires discipline, lifestyle trade-offs, and diligent effort, which most people fail to apply to their lives. That's why there are a lot less wealthy people, and less early retirees, than there could be.

If you recognize all the advantages of financial independence, then the answer for achieving that goal is not difficult. What we did, and what you must do, is spend less and save more, especially as your household income increases. Your goal can be to take control of your life and retire in your 40s or 50s (or as young as possible). But to achieve that goal, you must set aside a much higher percentage of your income than what most people do.

Let's say your two-person household earns $50,000 per year after taxes and you save the 2001 average of 1.6 percent for retirement—that's $800 per year. After 20 years, you will have contributed $16,000 toward retirement, which will have compounded to $45,800 tax-deferred, given a 10 percent average annual return; after 25 years, it will have compounded to a mere $78,700. You won't retire early on that unless you plan to inherit a lot of money or have a substantial employer-funded pension to supplement it!

At $800 per year set-aside for retirement, it will take you 44 years to accumulate over $500,000 (actually $522,100) on a tax-deferred basis. If you started saving at age 25, you still will not have enough money to retire at age 69 because inflation will have eroded the purchasing power of your money to $173,100 in today's dollars. If you did not start saving until you were 30, which would make you 74 at retirement after working 44 years, you better hope Social Security is still around doling out enough for you to survive.

But what if you save 30 percent of your $50,000 after-tax annual income—the minimum we saved over our first 10 years on an average annual income of $27,700 after taxes?

Save 30% of Your $50,000 Income	Total	3.5% Inflation-Adjusted
After 20 years	$ 859,100	$568,700
After 25 years	$1.5 million	$856,200

After 20 years you will have contributed $300,000 to your retirement accounts which, growing tax-deferred at an average 10 percent return, will have reached $859,100. Even inflation-adjusted that would be enough for many people to retire. If you are 25 years old reading this book, you can potentially retire at 45 with well over three-quarters of a million dollars (over a half-million inflation-adjusted). In fact, you can probably retire younger than that, depending on the lifestyle you want to live. But if you wait another five years and retire at the grand old age of 50, your account will be worth $1.5 million ($856,200 inflation-adjusted). Other factors that can dictate how young you retire under this scenario include:

- You save more than 30 percent of your income.
- Your household income exceeds $50,000 per year after taxes.
- Inflation averages less than 3.5 percent.
- Your rate of return averages more than 10 percent.
- You choose to work part-time in retirement.

As clearly illustrated in the table before, if you have an above-average income, start investing early, and set aside a significant percentage of your income, it is not impossible that you could retire as young as your late 30s, but surely in your 40s or 50s. You can choose to continue working full-time and prepare for a more luxurious retirement lifestyle later, you can work part-time, or you can choose to retire altogether. But the only way you can give yourself those options is if you have a sufficient net worth.

Anyone earning less than the $50,000 per year in these examples should not be discouraged. If you are a prodigious saver, start early, and contribute as much as possible to your tax-deferred retirement accounts, you will accelerate your retirement date. It is not that difficult to save a higher percentage of your household income once you convince yourself that the end justifies the means. Establish spending priorities with a goal of saving money to retire young, and you will be on your way to achieving that goal.

LIVING OFF YOUR NET WORTH

The day has come when you decide to retire. Now, where do you get the money to survive? You have probably heard or read that you need 70 to 80 percent of your pre-retirement income to retire with the same lifestyle you had while you were working. But will you? We were grossing nearly $100,000 per year our last few working years. Are we living on $70,000 to $80,000 now? Not even close. In fact, we are doing just fine on about $20,000—that's only 20 percent. How can that be?

Because we simplified our lives and embraced financial self-discipline while employed full-time, we were not spending anywhere near what we were earning. Because most people spend a large percentage of what they earn, it is assumed that they will continue to do so in retirement. From that standpoint, it is understandable that most retirees will need 70 to 80 percent of their pre-retirement income to enjoy the same lifestyle in retirement.

But most young retirees have gotten where they are because they lived below their means. They lived on a lower percentage of their income and saved/invested a higher percentage than is common to most employed people. Therefore when they retire, they continue to live on a lower percentage of their pre-retirement income than most retirees do.

The lower your annual income, the higher the percentage you will necessarily spend on basic living expenses like food, housing, insurance, and clothing. But as your income grows, the percentage spent on living expenses should decrease and the proportion set aside for retirement should increase. When we averaged less than $28,000 per year after-tax our first ten years, we *spent about 65 percent* of our income on living expenses. The last few years prior to retiring, as our income increased appreciably, we *decreased our spending to less than 40 percent* of after-tax income and invested the rest to meet our goal of retiring when I turned 50. Once retired, and after eliminating expenses related to working, we were able to cut annual expenses even more. That should also hold true for most early retirees. If you were disciplined enough to retire early, you have control over your spending and you will probably continue to live more simply than most people do. From that standpoint, 70 to 80 percent of your pre-retirement income will not be necessary.

Once you retire young you will need income. Provision 72(t) of the tax code allows penalty-free withdrawals from retirement accounts prior to age 59½ using substantially equal periodic payments. While that may work for some, there are pitfalls that must be clearly understood before any early retiree chooses that option; most will likely wait. But not tapping those funds will require income from non-retirement accounts, an employer-funded pension, and/or part-time employment during the intervening years.

If you are retiring with an employer-funded pension that comprises a good share of your income, you have a distinct advantage. Assuming that is not the case, though, the following five potential options for deriving retirement income apply to your taxable (non-retirement) accounts, as well as to your tax-deferred accounts once you can start withdrawing from them without penalty:

- Live off your interest, dividends, and capital gains distributions.
- Sell some of your investments when you need money.
- Work part-time.

- Derive other income.
- Employ a combination of these.

Live Off Your Interest, Dividends, And Capital Gains

Assuming you have a diversified portfolio of at least stocks, bonds, and cash, you will get monthly interest and dividend payments from the bonds and cash. You should also receive quarterly dividends—if your funds invest in dividend-paying stocks—and quarterly, semi-annual, or annual capital gains distributions from your equity funds. Rather than having those dividends and capital gains distributions reinvested into your funds as you did throughout your accumulation phase, you will now start taking them.

Your portfolio will not grow as quickly because you do not have the benefit of adding that dividend and capital gains money to your funds. But, based on historical performance, your equity funds will still grow over time through price appreciation and should continue to outpace inflation. If you don't need as much money to live on as you receive from your total distributions, you can elect to receive some of them while continuing to reinvest the rest. It would be best to take the interest and dividends derived from bond and cash investments prior to your stock dividends and capital gains, because the latter will continue to grow your net worth at a faster pace over time if reinvested.

Sell Some Of Your Investments When You Need Money

Another option is to sell shares of whichever fund has gained the most that year and sell only as much as you will need to live on for the next couple of months. Or you might sell an equal percentage of each fund you own so that your asset allocation remains the same. The idea is to let your money grow until you need it, but when you need some, take it. If your goal is to die broke, you will be drawing on your principal for the rest of your life—you just don't want to draw it down too quickly if you are young and have many more years of retirement ahead of you.

So how much of your portfolio can you take annually and not run out of money? As a general guide, you can safely withdraw 3 to 4 percent of your portfolio per year. Taking out significantly more than that in your early retirement years might deplete your net worth too quickly. Of course, as you grow older, you will reassess annually, based on your net worth and best estimate of how long you might live.

Another critical factor is the return being generated on your investments. Mutual fund firm T. Rowe Price recently added the interactive Retirement Income Calculator to its Web site. The RIC can help determine how much of your portfolio you can withdraw based on how it is invested (your stock/bond mix). For example, if your $500,000 portfolio is invested in 60 percent stocks, 30 percent bonds, and 10 percent cash, there is an 80 percent probability it will last 30 years if you withdraw $1,800 per month, a 90 percent probability if you withdraw $1,600 per month, and a 99 percent probability if you take $1,350 per month. The RIC can be found at www.troweprice.com (click the menu under **Investment Tools** and select **Retirement Income Calculator**).

Withdraw your taxable account money first and allow your tax-deferred accounts to continue growing until you turn 70½ and are required to take money out. You will probably always have some income from cash, bonds, and capital gains, so you may only have to sell a small amount of your funds in any year.

Work Part-Time

Unless you are so busy that you have no time for work, you have the option of taking on a part-time job that will bring in additional income and allow you to keep your retirement accounts growing longer. Surveys reveal that most people want a paid part-time job during retirement, even if they can afford not to work. If you have that same interest, then you may be able to either retire earlier with less net worth, or you can let your retirement funds grow larger so that you will have more income at the time you decide you no longer want to work at all. Part-time work has definite benefits for early retirees, but only if that is what you want to do.

Derive Other Income

Another source of income can be derived from reverse mortgaging your home. A reverse mortgage is a loan on your house, only the bank pays you! Of course, when you sell the house or die (whichever comes first), the loan must be repaid and it could comprise the total equity in the house. If your goal is to die broke, that's not an issue; if your house is supposed to be someone's inheritance, then it could be a problem. Another option is to sell your house when you get older and use the cash to pay rent and fund your retirement activities. You could end up with a nice chunk of money while no longer having to worry about house repairs.

Employ a Combination of These

Where the money will come from to support early retirement will depend on several factors: how much net worth you have, where it is invested, how much is available in dividends and capital gains, whether or not you want to work part-time, how comfortable you are with selling or reverse mortgaging your home, and your age (specifically, whether you are over or under 59½). Taking dividends and some or all capital gains, occasionally selling some investments, and working part-time (which most people indicate they would like to do), would be a good combination for many early retirees. If you don't want to work, you'll need a sufficient net worth to live off a combination of dividends, capital gains, and occasional equity sales.

Of course, an employer-funded pension could provide a good share of your retirement income. Supplemented by interest, dividends, capital gains or, again, part-time work, you could find yourself retiring young in a comfortable financial position.

Chapter Twelve

The Social Security Pension Myths

One question you may be wondering about is: How will retiring young affect my Social Security pension? If that is your first question, then perhaps your second should be: Will I even get a Social Security pension? The younger you are upon reading this book, the more concerned you need to be. This chapter will tell you why and help you to understand the Social Security pension myths.

MYTH #1: IT'S IN THE CONSTITUTION

Contrary to what some believe, Social Security is not included in the United States Constitution. It was a part of the Great Depression New Deal package of programs that President Franklin D. Roosevelt and his advisors conceived and presented to Congress to give America's hardworking people "something to live on when they are old and have stopped working," and Congress passed it in 1935. It was initially a simple plan that has since grown in complexity (not unlike most government social programs).

Upon its implementation, the Social Security Act levied a 1 percent tax, which then incrementally rose to 3 percent. According to the original document, workers would be taxed "3 cents on each dollar you earn, up to $3,000 a year. That is the most you will ever pay." Obviously, nothing lasts forever. The tax increased from that 3 percent to 7.65 percent for both the employee and employer for a total of 15.3 percent. (Actually, the Social Security Act comprises 12.4 percent of that figure while the remaining 2.9 percent—split between employee and employer—is credited to the Medicare program which was signed into law in 1965.) In addition to increased tax rates, the amount of wages subject to Social Security taxes has also continued to increase.

So what happened to 3 percent and $3,000 being "the most you will ever pay?" Program expansion has a lot to do with it. What started out as a relatively simple program to cover the risks of old age grew considerably after 1935 with the addition of numerous costly amendments, most notably the following:

- Amendments in 1939 changed the Social Security Act from a program that covered only workers, to a family-based economic security program. Payments were added to the spouse and minor children of a retired worker (called dependents benefits), as well as survivor's benefits to the family in the event of the premature death of a worker.
- In 1950 and 1952, cost-of-living increases were granted which "almost doubled the value of Social Security benefits for existing beneficiaries." (Initially, such increases were not automatic like they are now.)
- In 1956, Disability Insurance was added to cover severely disabled workers ages 50 to 64 and disabled adult children; that was amended in 1960 to include disabled workers of any age and their dependents.

- Amendments in 1961 lowered eligibility for Social Security to age 62 with reduced benefits; that doubled the number of beneficiaries between 1961 and 1969.
- One of the most significant, and not inexpensive, expansions came in 1965. President Johnson signed into law the social insurance program known as Medicare, which provided for the medical needs of persons aged 65 or older, regardless of income. Created at the same time were federal grants to states for Medicaid, which provided medical assistance to those with low incomes.
- In 1967, disability benefits which provided for widows and widowers 50 years of age or older were added to the Social Security program.
- Automatic annual cost-of-living increases tied to the Consumer Price Index (CPI) were added beginning in 1975, together with the start-up of the Supplemental Security Income (SSI) program which replaced and broadened the previous state-administered cash assistance programs for the aged, blind, and disabled.

Other amendments to the Social Security Act have been added since the 1970s, but none as significant as those listed. However, the continued growth in the number of program recipients is significant. According to the Social Security Administration (SSA), 222,000 people received monthly benefits in 1940; today it is over 45 million. Beginning about 2010, some 76 million baby boomers will begin retiring and it is projected that the number of older Americans will double within about 30 years. At the same time, there will be fewer people paying FICA (Federal Insurance Contributions Act) taxes to fund the Social Security benefits of that growing retiree population.

At the time the Social Security Act was passed, average life expectancy at birth in this country was 58 for men and 62 for women; benefits were not paid until covered workers turned 65, or older if they elected to continue working. That would lead one to believe that the program wasn't really set up to pay much in benefits.

In response to that criticism, the SSA explains that life expectancy figures were low due to high infant mortality rates, whereas the majority of Americans lived into adulthood. After paying into Social Security during their adult years, those who reached age 65 could look forward to collecting benefits for at least 12 years. (However, less than 54 percent of men lived to age 65.) According to the SSA's September 2001 "Basic Social Security FactSheet," medical advances have extended the average life expectancy of a 65-year-old from 12½ years in 1940 to 17½ years today; subsequently, a lot more is being paid out in benefits.

Social Security is a "pay-as-you-go" system, meaning that the workers of today support the generation preceding them (those currently in retirement). That system can be effective because several workers paying FICA taxes can support a retiree, called the worker-to-beneficiary ratio, without the percentage of taxes paid completely strapping the workers—although some would argue that's the case now. According to a chart on the SSA Web site, which is summarized below, the number of workers paying FICA taxes for each beneficiary has dropped dramatically since 1945 and it will continue to drop for the next 75 years.

Worker-to-Beneficiary Ratio

Year	Workers Paying FICA For Each Beneficiary
1945	41.9
1950	16.5
2000	3.4
2025 (projected)	2.3
2050 (projected)	2.0
2075	1.9

Considering the taxes now paid to support the number of retirees we have—at a ratio of 3.4 workers per beneficiary—imagine what will happen when the ratio drops to 2.3 within 25 years, or less than two workers-per-beneficiary after 2050. How much will each of those working Americans have to pay to support all those retirees at the inflation-adjusted benefit level everyone is receiving now and expecting in the future?

And therein lies the problem: something is going to have to change. Either FICA taxes will need to be increased appreciably, the retirement age will need to be raised again, benefits to the baby boom generation will have to decrease significantly, or there will need to be a combination of those. It is the decrease in the worker-to-beneficiary ratio that is going to have the greatest impact on Social Security's pending insolvency unless significant changes are implemented.

According to "Status of the Social Security and Medicare Programs: A Summary of the 2001 Annual Reports" (March 2001) published on the SSA's Web site (www.ssa.gov), annual tax income from those 3.4 workers per beneficiary is expected to equal or exceed benefit expenditures until 2015. As of 2016, expenditures will exceed income—in essence, Social Security will be insolvent. That is a "best estimate" scenario. In a worst-case scenario, it will be earlier. There will not be enough money to pay full benefits to the baby-boom generation unless changes are made in the program. So your next question has to be: "But what about the trust funds?" You will have to wait a bit, because that is Myth #3.

MYTH #2: AN ACCOUNT WITH YOUR NAME ON IT

Many people believe that the money taken from their paychecks for Social Security taxes is placed in an account with their name on it, from which their future benefits will come (like an IRA or other genuine retirement account). Sorry, but that is a myth. This issue is addressed by the SSA in their publication "The Future of Social Security":

> Many people think that their Social Security tax contributions are held in interest-bearing accounts earmarked for their own future retirement needs. Social Security is actually an intergenerational compact—the Social Security taxes paid by today's workers and employers go mostly to fund benefit payments for today's retirees.

In other words, there is no account with your name on it collecting real interest, and no guarantee that when you reach retirement age the generation under you will be contributing enough to support your retirement benefits.

MYTH #3: THE TRUST FUNDS

Another common belief is that all of the money you and I and the rest of the workforce have been paying into Social Security is being placed in a trust fund for our future use. *We wish.* The Social Security taxes we pay today are funding the benefits of today's retirees. Currently, more money is coming into the system than what is being paid out: there is a surplus. The logical person would think that, since there is a surplus, that money is being saved for the future (in those trust funds we keep hearing about). But is it?

According to SSA documents, the surplus FICA contributions (the trust funds) are invested in "special Treasury bonds" and then borrowed by the federal government who is paying the trust funds back with interest. That sounds like a prudent strategy—collect excess tax funds, invest that money in bonds that will accumulate significant amounts of interest, and then have that money available to pay the benefits of future retirees. It would be great if that were the case. But here is another side to the story.

The Social Security program has drawn a lot of attention the past few years because expenses will exceed income in an estimated 14 years. That projected date has prompted an increased number of articles in newspapers, magazines, and books telling a different story about the trust funds. *The Retirement Myth* by Craig

S. Karpel describes the SSA's "special Treasury bonds" as worthless pieces of paper—in essence, IOUs that the government gives to the SSA in return for taking the excess trust monies. The author points out that the problem is: Where is the federal government going to get the money to pay the interest *and* pay back the trust funds themselves when the surplus contributions end? If it had money, what was the reason for borrowing the trust funds and leaving IOUs all of these years?

Another thought-provoking book on Social Security, *Let's Get Rid of Social Security: How Americans Can Take Charge of Their Own Future* by E. J. Myers, includes a chapter titled "The Amazing, Vanishing Trust Fund Surplus." Among the many interesting points brought out in this book, this chapter states that the trust funds could have adequately funded the baby boomers' retirements if our legislators had actually saved the annual surpluses in investments that pay real interest, instead of using that money to make it appear as if the national debt was smaller than it was.

Syndicated columnist Thomas Sowell wrote in February 1999 that Social Security functions on the same basic principle as illegal pyramid schemes. Initial contributors get their money back and much more because of the many who join after them. But after the pyramid stops expanding, which is already the case as the worker-to-beneficiary-ratio continues to drop, the last contributors end up with nothing.

In the September 2000 issue of *Smart Money*, New York's Democratic Senator Daniel Patrick Moynihan commented that since the IOUs in the trust fund have no stored value, the government will need to use general revenue funds in the future to pay Social Security benefits. He added that instead of a social insurance program, it will become another welfare program—and that is not what President Roosevelt and Congress had in mind when the Social Security Act was passed in 1935.

Over the past few years numerous other articles exposing these mythical trust funds and written by different journalists have been seen in a variety of magazines: Clifton Leaf, *Smart Money* (February, 1999); Andrew Tobias, *Money* (Forecast, 1998); Deb Riechmann, The Associated Press, (April 1998); Norman Fosback, editor-in-chief at *Mutual Funds* magazine (March 1997); Steve Forbes, editor-in-chief, *Forbes* magazine (June, 1997); Roger Lowenstein, *Wall Street Journal* (April 1996); and the list goes on. They all wrote about the borrowing of the trust funds to reduce the federal deficit and the ultimate necessity of raising taxes or decreasing benefits, or both, when those IOUs come due as of 2016 and there is no money to pay them back.

That argument is even supported by the Social Security Administration in their "2001 Summary Report" in which they comment about 2016 and beyond:

> Social Security and Medicare will begin to be in direct competition with other Federal programs for the resources of the Treasury, requiring either growing tax increases or debt financing (or some combination of the two) to pay the benefits promised under current law and provide for the continuation of other Federal expenditures.

Concerning the trust funds, there appear three undeniable facts:

- There are currently Social Security surpluses because FICA taxes are exceeding expenditures; so there are theoretical trust funds.
- The federal government has been borrowing those surpluses (the trust funds) to decrease the size of our annual budget deficit (or more recently, to show a surplus).
- The federal government is replacing those borrowed surpluses with IOUs that will need to be redeemed (interest first, then principal) starting in an estimated 14 years.

The big question is: Where is the money going to come from to pay the interest on these IOUs and then to eventually redeem them? Congress and the president have been debating how to "save" Social Security for years. However, as of this writing, no agreement has been reached. The debate started to heat up last year and, currently, four different "solutions" are gaining support:

- Create private investment accounts that would allow workers to invest all or part of their FICA taxes in private capital investments like stocks and bonds.
- Tweak the current system: increase FICA taxes, decrease benefits, change the retirement age, eliminate cost-of-living increases, et cetera, as discussed in this chapter and the next.
- Combine aspects of the above two approaches.
- Do nothing, but maintain solid economic policies to keep the U.S. economy strong and healthy.

There is much controversy and little agreement concerning the nature of the problem and how it should be resolved. Expect the debate to go on for a long time.

MYTH #4: FULL BENEFITS AT 65

A fourth myth is that you will be able to retire and collect full Social Security retirement benefits at age 65. In the "2001 Retirement Confidence Survey" conducted by the Employee Benefit Research Institute and American Savings Education Council, most people surveyed were unaware that the retirement age had been changed from 65 to 67. Only 15 percent were able to correctly identify the age at which they would receive full retirement benefits. Clearly, most people are not aware that the rules have changed, even though they did so in 1983.

Besides significantly raising FICA taxes and making numerous other revisions, the 1983 changes resulted in development of a comprehensive schedule (abbreviated below) of ages at which you can collect full retirement benefits, and the amount of reduction if you choose to retire at 62. Most of you reading this book were probably born in the 1950s or later. You can see that your retirement age to receive full benefits is already either 66 or 67, and if you decide to retire at 62, the amount of reduction in those benefits increases (that is, you'll get less money). There is a chance Congress will increase the full retirement age to 70 for those in their 20s today, and the age at which you can retire early and collect reduced benefits will likely be moved up or eliminated altogether.

Full Retirement Benefits Schedule

Year of Birth	Full Retirement Age	Age 62 Percent Reduction In Benefits
1937 or earlier	65	20.00
1940	65 and 6 months	22.50
1943 to 1954	66	25.00
1955	66 and 2 months	25.84
1956	66 and 4 months	26.66
1957	66 and 6 months	27.50
1958	66 and 8 months	28.33
1959	66 and 10 months	29.17
1960 & later	67	30.00

For more information on the myths exposed in this chapter, as well as for a wealth of other information on Social Security, visit the SSA's Web site at www.ssa.gov. The National Center for Policy Analysis, a nonprofit, nonpartisan public policy research institute that "seeks innovative private sector solutions to public policy problems" sponsors an interesting independent site. Look for the sections titled "Quick Facts" and "Social Security Q&A." You can find their site at www.mysocialsecurity.org. Other Web sites that present different viewpoints and solutions on resolving Social Security's long-term financial problems include:

- Campaign for America's Future—www.ourfuture.org
- The Cato Institute—www.socialsecurity.org
- The Heritage Foundation—www.heritage.org
- National Council of Women's Organizations—www.women4socialsecurity.org

Chapter Thirteen

Retire Young and Still Get Paid!

Based on the facts presented in the previous chapter, early retiree hopefuls would be wise not to peg their retirement security on future Social Security benefits. You can expect to get something, but it won't be enough to support you, much less allow you to live an enviable lifestyle. In fact, for workers earning "average" wages, even under the most optimistic scenario the Social Security Administration advises that your benefits will only replace about 40 percent of your pre-retirement income. And as you read in the last chapter and will read again in this one, you may not want to plan on the most optimistic scenario!

Follow the strategies in this book to plan your early retirement without having to rely on Social Security and it won't matter one way or another what happens to that program in the future. As long as you don't have unrealistic expectations, any additional monthly benefits you receive will give you more financial flexibility and improve your standard of living a little. But if things don't pan out the way some are projecting today, your retirement will still be secure. Either way, you can't lose.

THE IMPACT OF RETIRING YOUNG

For purposes of illustration over the next few pages, we need to make two assumptions: (1) that I have a Social Security account with my name on it and FICA taxes going into it, and (2) that Social Security stays solvent without any changes from its present form. With those in mind, the question to be answered is this: How will retiring early impact my (or ultimately your) future benefits?

Like most people, you are probably under the assumption that you have to work until age 65 or older to get full benefits, but that you can retire with partial benefits when you turn 62. But do you realize that you can quit work almost any time (once you have worked 40 quarters or about 10 years cumulatively) and still collect partial benefits at 62 or full benefits at 65, 66, 67, or whatever it increases to in the future?

In order to determine the impact that retiring young would have on my potential Social Security retirement benefits, I ordered a Personal Earnings and Estimated Benefits Statement (now simply titled Social Security Statement) in the summer of 1993. The form requested basic personal information, my prior year's income, estimated current-year income, and the age I planned to retire. It also asked me to estimate an average wage for the years between now and the time I plan to retire.

> Note: As of October 1999, the SSA began mailing all working Americans a Social Security Statement about three months prior to their birthday. These statements are important for confirming that the SSA correctly recorded your earnings and tax payments. If there is any discrepancy, you can call a toll-free number to correct errors. Obviously, doing this every year will make corrections easier than if you wait until retirement to try and do so.

Rather than fill out one Social Security Statement, however, I submitted two, using different scenarios. The first stated that I earned $30,000 in 1993 and was retiring that same year. My estimated future average yearly earnings were $0. The second stated that I earned $30,000 in 1993 and would continue earning an average of $30,000 per year (which the SSA would adjust annually for inflation until retirement at 62). The purpose for submitting the two scenarios was to determine what the difference would be in my future estimated Social Security pension benefits if I:

- Retired at 42 and never paid another dollar in FICA.
- Worked until retirement at 62 and paid "x" amount more in FICA taxes over those 20 additional years.

The expectation was that I would get a significantly higher monthly Social Security benefit for working and paying additional FICA taxes another 20 years. But the question was: Would the higher benefit be worth it relative to the amount of taxes I would pay in over all those years? A few weeks later the results were back and are charted below in 1993 dollars:

Social Security Benefits Paid

Retire at 42, Start Benefits at Age	Monthly Social Security Benefit	Retire at 62, Start Benefits at Age	Monthly Social Security Benefit	Diff.
62	$ 680	62	$ 955	+ $275
66	900	66	1,275	+ 375
70	1,190	70	1,685	+ 495

MORE THAN JUST A RETIREMENT PROGRAM

Social Security covers more than retirement; it is also a disability and survivors insurance protection program for younger workers and their families. According to "Status of the Social Security and Medicare Programs" (March 2001) published on the SSA's Web site, out of the 12.4 percent FICA taxes that workers pay (self-employed individuals pay it all, employers and employees split it), the Old Age and Survivors Insurance program is allocated 10.6 percentage points (85 percent) while the Disability Insurance program is allocated 1.8 percentage points (15 percent).

In the next few pages we will look at Social Security relative to other retirement programs to see how good of a deal it is for you and me. Because a small portion of our FICA taxes are funding the Disability Insurance program, the following computations will necessarily include only the percentage of FICA that is allocated to retirement—approximately 85 percent or 10.6 percentage points of the 12.4 percent we pay.

RETIRE AT 42—COLLECT SOCIAL SECURITY AT 62

From the first year I worked and started paying Social Security (FICA) taxes until retirement in 1993, my Social Security Statement confirms that $44,600 was paid in FICA taxes (and $11,500 more in Medicare taxes). To determine how good of a retirement plan Social Security will be for me, we'll assume that 85 percent of that figure ($37,900 rounded) was allocated for my future retirement. Had that $37,900 been paid into any legitimate tax-deferred retirement plan available today—like a 401(k), 403(b), 457, SEP, SIMPLE, or IRA—it would have earned compound interest or dividends from the day of my first FICA tax payment at age 17 until all the money was paid back to me via retirement, or until I died and the remainder went to my heirs.

To what amount then should my $37,900 have compounded were the Social Security trust funds earning compound interest like any legitimate retirement plan would? If the SSA had invested the trust funds in negotiable bonds paying 6.4 percent interest (the average annual return on intermediate-term Government Bonds over the past 50 years), my FICA taxes would have compounded to $65,400 by the time I retired at 42. That $65,400 would continue to compound for another 20 years, even though I was no longer contributing to it, until the SSA began paying me benefits at age 62.

Question: How much should my FICA taxes compound to by the time I start collecting benefits at age 62?
Answer: $226,200
Computation:
$65,400 x 6.4% compounded for 20 years = $226,200

Based on those initial 26 years of FICA taxes (from age 17 to 42), if I never have any other earned income, my 1993 Social Security Statement (see the chart at the beginning of the chapter) verifies that I am eligible to begin collecting estimated Social Security retirement benefits beginning at age 62 of $680 per month.

Note: Keep in mind that all of the figures in this section and the next date back to 1993 dollars, whereas the SSA adjusts benefit amounts each year based on the CPI. To update the chart figures (the second column) to 2001 dollars for comparison, last year's Social Security Statement projected that I will receive $859 per month if I start collecting at age 62, $1,139 if I wait until 66, and $1,504 if I wait until 70. (Updated benefit figures for the fourth column of the chart—working until age 62 and then collecting benefits—are not available because I have not been earning the $30,000 per year that was projected in 1993 when this comparative analysis was conducted.)

With monthly benefits of $680 coming from the SSA, will I get back all the money I paid in? NO. Will I even get a fair share of my money back? NO. And here's why.

All the while Social Security is paying me $680 per month ($8,160 per year), my theoretical $226,200 should continue to draw interest from those intermediate-term Government Bonds at the rate of 6.4 percent ($14,500 per year), as it would in any legitimate retirement plan. In other words, the longer I live and continue to draw Social Security, the larger my account theoretically grows. In actuality, I will collect only 56 percent of the interest my account should be earning per year and none of the $226,200 principal—which would significantly increase my monthly payments if it could also be withdrawn.

To illustrate that point, I ran two calculations. Let's assume that my theoretical Social Security account principal and interest could be withdrawn and amortized over my life expectancy—similar to what we could do if those funds had accumulated in any legitimate retirement account like a 401(k), 403(b), SEP, or IRA, and similar to how annuities are paid out. If that were the case, my $226,200 amortized on the basis of a life expectancy age of 76 would pay me almost $2,000 per month rather than a paltry $680. That's more than Kris and I live on now! But you're probably wondering what would happen if I lived longer than 76 years.

In reality, that would not be a concern because a life-expectancy payout schedule would be based on a financially-balanced actuarial table that factors in the off-setting costs of some people living longer and some dying earlier. However, if a real actuarial table were constructed, there's no guarantee that 76 would be my projected life expectancy age; it could be a few years later. Absent that information, and to compensate for possibly living longer, I calculated what my monthly benefits would be assuming a Social Security payout amortized over my current life expectancy plus ten years.

On that basis I would receive $1,500 per month rather than the token $680. Right now, $1,500 is about what Kris and I live on. We would have it made! Not only that, but, under this scenario, Kris would also receive a Social Security check for almost that much. What would we do with all the extra money?

It should already be painfully obvious that, because Social Security does not operate like other legitimate retirement plans, it will be paying all of us baby boomers—and those younger—far lower benefits in the future than it should or could be providing. But as depressing as that may sound, it's not even the worst news. For that, we have to return to the issue of the trust funds.

As you read in the previous chapter, the trust funds are actually invested in non-negotiable government bonds earning *no* tangible interest. Only if the federal government comes up with some way to pay the interest owed on the trust funds when the annual Social Security surpluses run out and the benefits being paid begin exceeding the revenues coming in (beginning in an estimated 14 years), will there be any tangible interest earned. What kind of a retirement program is that?

The bottom line and point of my calculations is this: If you are depending on Social Security for your retirement security, you better come up with another plan. You will only get back a fraction of what you would get back from a 401(k), SEP, IRA, or any other genuine retirement plan, especially relative to what you pay into it.

RETIRE AT 62—COLLECT SOCIAL SECURITY AT 62

If what you just read doesn't seem right, you are definitely not going to like the rest of the story. If Social Security isn't a good deal for me working only until age 42—because I'll never get all the annual interest theoretically being generated, much less the principal back—what will I gain by continuing to work another 20 years and retiring instead at age 62? The answer to that question came after submitting my second Social Security Statement, which stated I would work another 20 years earning $30,000 per year.

(The SSA would annually adjust that for inflation but, for simplicity's sake, I use a straight $30,000 per year in this example. As my income is adjusted for inflation, the FICA taxes paid would increase beyond the figure calculated below.)

Question: How much *more* would I pay in FICA taxes working another 20 years from age 42 until age 62?
Answer: $63,600
Computation:
$30,000 per year x 10.6% FICA = $3,180 per year
$3,180 per year x 20 years = $63,600

Question: Had that $63,600 been invested into any tax-deferred, interest-bearing retirement account, or had the SSA actually held those FICA taxes in a trust fund account earning 6.4 percent annual compound interest, how much would the account be worth after working 20 more years?
Answer: $122,100
Computation:
$3,180 per year compounded for 20 years = $122,100

Add that $122,100 to the $226,200 compounded amount from FICA taxes paid between ages 17 and 42, and by the time I retire at age 62 and start collecting Social Security benefits, my account should total $348,300. (In actuality it will be worth more because of the increased taxes paid on the annual inflation-adjusted earnings.) According to the chart at the beginning of this chapter, the SSA says it will give me $955 per month—$275 more per month than if I had not worked those additional 20 years. But my $348,300 should be compounding at 6.4 percent per year yielding $22,300 in interest alone; the SSA is sending me $11,460 per year. That's only 51 percent of the interest earned and, on a percentage basis, less than I would be paid had I not worked that additional 20 years. And I'll also never get back any of the $348,300 principal!

Let's assume again that my FICA taxes are invested like other retirement accounts available today, and after retiring I will get all of the interest each year plus a portion of the principal. What is the difference this time? If the $348,300 were amortized over my life expectancy plus ten years, the SSA would send me almost $2,400 per month instead of $955. But if my principal and interest were paid back based on my life expectancy age of 76, I could go to the mailbox every month and collect *$3,100* rather than that measly $955. That's over three times as much retirement income!

Imagine having been able to invest all of the FICA taxes you have paid (and for most of you, what you will continue to pay) into a legitimate tax-deferred retirement plan that would return all of your interest and principal over a reasonable life-expectancy payout period. Were that the case, we would all have a far more secure retirement—whether we retired at 40 or 70, or any time in between. Unfortunately, that's not the way it will be for you and me.

According to the chart at the beginning of this chapter, the longer I delay starting to collect benefits (and this will apply to everyone else as well), the higher my monthly benefit will be when I do collect, whether I retire at 42 or 62. But numerous calculations were run to see if there were any circumstances wherein working longer and paying more FICA would end up being a better deal for me in terms of the amount of money I would recover relative to what I paid in. There were none.

And the worst part is that there isn't anything we can do about it since, currently, we cannot opt out of Social Security. There's always the slim hope that changes will one day be implemented that will correct some of these deficiencies. But the wise person won't base his or her future on it.

THE WAY IT IS

According to all of the computations involving the two scenarios above (retiring at 42 and receiving benefits at 62, 66, or 70, versus working until age 62 and then collecting benefits at 62, 66, or 70), working past age 42 does not make good fiscal sense. Even though the average life expectancy of about 76 today is projected to edge up into the mid-to-late 80s over the next 70 years, future retirees will still collect none of the FICA taxes they paid into the system (their principal) and only a portion of the interest income that *should be* generated on their accounts each year. Worse yet, in reality, there are no individual accounts and the trust funds are earning phantom interest. And keep in mind that all of the computations above make two assumptions:

- That FICA taxes don't increase even more during those 20 additional years I theoretically could have worked (they probably will increase).
- That the revisions Congress and the president must make to keep Social Security from going broke do not result in benefit cuts, which would decrease the amount of money received from what was estimated in my 1993 Social Security Statement (you should plan on benefit cuts).

It seems crystal clear that continuing to work beyond age 42 would have been a loser's game for me as concerns Social Security. And that will be true for you, too. Sure, you will be paid a higher monthly benefit the later you retire. But the benefits you receive will only be a fraction of what you would get if that money was invested in a legitimate tax-deferred retirement plan earning compound interest that is being totally distributed to you and which also provides for tapping the principal.

From a monetary standpoint, then, the question once again arises: What is the incentive for me (or you) to continue working and paying Social Security taxes? Has retiring young adversely affected my future Social Security retirement benefits? It certainly hasn't, based on my computations. In fact, it appears that I have saved a lot of money by retiring young—money that would have been paid in FICA taxes and never recovered by me in future Social Security pension benefits.

Now the scenarios presented above would work out differently if you are an employee rather than self-employed. As an employee, your employer pays half of your Social Security taxes, leaving you 6.2 percent to pay rather than the 12.4 percent that self-employed individuals pay. However, experts argue that were employers not required to pay 6.2 percent into FICA for each employee, most workers would earn higher wages. So, in essence, you paid it anyway, and that would then put your calculations in line with mine.

The longer you continue to work and pay FICA taxes, the less you can expect to get back on a percentage basis when you finally retire (relative, of course, to what you would receive if Social Security were operated like any real retirement plan). There is no justifiable reason to work any longer than you have to from the standpoint of your future Social Security pension. If you want to retire young (or maybe retire at all), you need to invest as much as possible into your 401(k), 403(b), 457, SEP, IRA, or any other legitimate retirement plan available to you.

LESS THAN A TOTAL RETURN

My personal scenarios detailed above—which will apply to most baby boomers and younger generations—illustrate how we will get back none of our principal and only a fraction of what our FICA taxes should be earning in interest. In contrast, senior citizens over the past two decades (and probably continuing for another decade) have gotten back their principal plus interest and a whole lot more. Below are five statistics illustrating that dichotomy. The first two come from *The Only Investment Guide You Will Ever Need* (copyrighted 1996), wherein Andrew Tobias writes:

> The truth is that the average person retiring today at 65 gets back all the money he or she paid into Social Security, with interest, by age 71.... According to the Congressional Re-

search Service, the average person who retired in 1980 got back all he—and his employer—paid into Social Security (including an adjustment for interest!) in under three years.

The three other statistics come from a July 1998 document "Study #217—Privatizing Social Security" found on the National Center for Policy Analysis Web site (www.ncpa.org):

- Babies born in 1998 will receive only 29 cents in Social Security benefits for every dollar paid in FICA taxes.
- Today's average 20-year-old male will pay $182,000 more in FICA taxes than what he can expect to receive in Social Security benefits.
- In contrast, 70-year-old males in 1998 will receive over $89,000 more than they paid in FICA taxes and females will get $101,000 more than they paid.

Today's retirees get back far more than they paid in because their benefits are so high relative to the amount of FICA taxes they paid. That is quite a contrast from the other examples above and from my personal scenarios, which will likewise apply to you. As the outlook for Social Security grows dimmer, benefit cuts, higher FICA taxes, and a retirement age of 70 are likely. That will further reduce the amount of money recovered by future retirees compared to what they will pay in FICA taxes. It should be clear by now that continuing to work if you don't have to for the purpose of increasing your future Social Security pension would be foolish.

Obviously the examples above are necessarily simple and cannot take into consideration all potential factors that could change those figures. Social Security tax rates could increase and tax laws could change (and they did regarding self-employed individuals who can at this time partially deduct their FICA taxes on their tax return). Continued medical advances will likely increase the average life expectancy beyond that projected as of 1993. Over the past

70 years, life expectancy at birth has increased from 58 to 76. Over the next 70 years, based on current declining mortality rates, a study by the Employee Benefit Research Institute indicated that life expectancy at birth will rise to the age range of 85 to 89. But even if you live to be 110, the monetary benefits derived from Social Security as currently operated will only be a fraction of the retirement benefits your FICA taxes would provide if they could be invested in a legitimate tax-deferred retirement plan.

ANTICIPATING THE FUTURE

Will Social Security be there for you? You can count on the program being around for many more decades; but don't expect it to be the same as it is today. Rather than running annual surpluses as the program has done since 1983, there will be deficits; rather than getting back far more than they paid in like today's seniors, future retirees will get back only a fraction of what they've paid in.

In fact, the Social Security Administration addresses this issue in its March 2001 publication, "Status of the Social Security and Medicare Programs." The SSA Trustees project that once expenses exceed income and the trust funds are exhausted (and remember, the trust funds are comprised entirely of IOUs), there will only be enough income through FICA taxes, in addition to the taxes paid on benefits by Social Security recipients, to pay 73 percent of program costs; and that is projected to slowly decrease to 67 percent.

In other words, unless changes are forthcoming, most baby boomers and younger generations can optimistically anticipate receiving less than three-fourths—and possibly as little as two-thirds—of the monthly benefit amount shown on the Social Security Statement they receive each year from the SSA. And, as pointed out above, your Social Security Statement already reflects only a fraction of what you would be getting if Social Security were operated like other legitimate retirement plans available today. Anything you get in the future will be better than nothing, but

Social Security isn't a retirement program upon which any of us should stake our future financial independence.

According to a projection by the National Center for Policy Analysis, once the trust funds are exhausted, in order for the SSA to continue paying recipients benefit levels comparable to what seniors receive today, FICA taxes will need to increase 50 percent (from the current 12.4 percent to 18.6 percent). And that doesn't include additional tax increases necessary to save Medicare. There is simply no way our future workers will be able to afford that. Other possible remedies indicated by the NCPA include raising the retirement age, reducing annual cost-of-living adjustments, changing benefit formulas so that you get less back relative to what you pay in, and increasing the tax on Social Security benefits. Already up to 85 percent of those benefits are subject to income taxes for retirees with incomes over certain limits. Look for that to increase to 100 percent in the future.

And that is the position in which many early retirees will find themselves. Because we simplified our lives, embraced financial self-discipline, and saved/invested wisely, we will have accumulated enough income to retire young and live the remainder of our lives on our net worth (and employer-funded pensions for those who will get them). For that reason, we will likely have enough income to be fully taxed on whatever Social Security benefits we receive so we won't end up with much anyway.

On the other hand, for those who spend most of their money in their younger years and fail to save for retirement, it is unlikely that the federal government is going to let them live in poverty. That was the goal in establishing the Social Security Act and it has been effective to this point in meeting that objective. So if you live for today rather than tomorrow, you may be one of those whom Social Security bails out when you retire at 67 or maybe 70. But is it your goal to live out your retirement (which could total 15, 20 or even 30 years) on the brink of poverty?

Our retirement plan assumes no monthly Social Security benefits in the future. With that approach, we won't be dependent on the income or disappointed if things don't go as planned. Once we see what portion of our projected benefits we actually receive, we'll increase our standard of living some. However, after reading these last two chapters, if you have a more optimistic outlook for Social Security than I do, then factor all or part of your anticipated benefits into your long-range retirement plan.

Frankly, we should all be upset at our future prospects for Social Security. Given the amount of FICA taxes we pay, we should expect to get all of the principal back plus compound interest. That is obviously not going to happen. Look at Social Security as an example of the necessity to rely on ourselves, not the government, to meet our future needs. Not planning to receive Social Security in the future forces us to save more now. We can do that.

WHAT COULD HAVE BEEN

There could have been Social Security benefits for all of us for many decades to come with those benefits at the same levels as our current retirees enjoy, adjusted for inflation. How? By our elected representatives doing two things: (1) saving the Social Security surpluses starting in 1983 when FICA taxes were increased significantly to keep Social Security from future insolvency, and (2) investing that money in negotiable bonds that paid real interest. Since they didn't do either of those, the Social Security program is now facing potential insolvency in 14 years.

And how about this for an example of what could have been? In his book *Let's Get Rid of Social Security*, E.J. Myers points out that if Social Security benefits had increased at the same rate as FICA taxes since the start of the program, recipients would have been receiving $10,120 per month in 1995 instead of the $1,248 maximum they were getting. Who couldn't retire well on that?

One other point on Social Security that you may not be aware of is that, at the time the Social Security Act was passed, government agencies were given the opportunity to opt out of the program. And they did. Most state and many county governments set up retirement programs that far exceed the benefits Social Security will ever provide anyone. You can read all about these alternate programs in Myers's book. Had we all been able to opt out and invest our FICA taxes into some other program that has been generating tangible interest all of these years and was actually being credited to accounts with our names on them, the future retirement of all baby boomers and those younger would be far more secure.

TAKE CONTROL OF YOUR LIFE

Take control of your future now by simplifying your life, embracing financial self-discipline, and investing wisely so you can achieve a goal of financial independence; then it will not matter one way or the other what happens to Social Security in the future. With an adequate net worth and a retirement plan that will allow you to never work again unless you choose to, you can retire young and enjoy the rest of your life without relying on the government to take care of you.

Consider the FICA taxes you have paid, and will continue to pay, as your contribution to today's elderly—which may include your parents and/or grandparents—many of whom would be living poorly without it (and many who are living well with it). But do not plan on your children or grandchildren doing the same for you. There will be too many of us and too few of them for us to receive the same level of benefits today's retirees receive. Take any Social Security benefits you get in the future and treat yourself to something special. In the meantime, future retirees would be wise to look out for themselves and plan accordingly.

Chapter Fourteen

Where to Live When You Retire

Where you choose to live when you retire will depend on your retirement income and personal preference. This chapter will point out some factors to consider when making that decision.

COST OF LIVING

If you retire young with enough money that you can reside wherever you want without giving it a second thought, then this chapter may be less relevant to your needs. On the other hand, if you retire early but the vault is not overflowing with money, then give sufficient consideration to where you will establish roots.

This book focuses on retiring within the United States. However, many books cover retirement in other countries. (Try your local library or bookstore, or an online bookstore such as www.amazon.com or www.bn.com and type "retirement places" into their search engine.) The main argument in favor of retiring abroad is cost of living. The same retirement income will allow you to live better in a country with lower living costs. But then there are many other considerations, too, such as standard of living, politics, laws (or lack of), cultural differences, and language.

If you have entertained the thought of retiring outside the U.S., thoroughly research your options and travel to those countries before making any decisions. Paul and Vicki Terhorst (*Cashing In on the American Dream)* have lived in numerous countries and write about some of their experiences in their book. They also have a home page describing their travel and living experiences in various countries since the book was published in 1988. You can find them at: www.geocities.com/TheTropics/Shores/5315/.

Upon retiring young it is generally advantageous to relocate from an area with higher costs to one with lower costs. But there are other factors that need to be considered, too. We chose to relocate to St. George, Utah because it was about the perfect size for us, it's below the snowbelt, there were lots of activities available, and it had a reputation for being a desirable area for retirees.

St. George is a snowbird/vacation home area for people primarily from northern Utah, with a cost of living below most of the better-known resort areas like Palm Springs, California; Santa Fe, New Mexico; and Scottsdale, Arizona. We could have found a city in the United States that was less expensive than here—one that didn't have ten golf courses, two well-known resort/spas, thousands of seasonal residents (snowbirds), and thousands of tourists due to our proximity to three popular national parks—Zion, Bryce Canyon, and the north rim of the Grand Canyon.

Although it is a more expensive area than we could have found elsewhere, we are attracted to small, growing cities. We like the vibrant feel of a growing area and the newness of the buildings and neighborhoods. It's exciting to see new development and to watch new businesses come to town. Because we enjoy that aspect of a community, we are willing to pay a little more to live in one. And on the positive side, as long as that city continues to grow, you can buy a house and likely turn a profit when you later sell. On the negative side, a growing town (especially if it is growing too fast) can escalate rent and housing prices beyond an early retiree's reach if the income stream is limited.

Prior to relocating, we read several books providing information on favorable areas in which to retire. We like living in the western U.S., so we selected cities for consideration within our preferred population range. When the opportunity arose while winding down our businesses, we visited each of our target cities. On that basis we ended up in St. George and have found this to be a great place to live.

The cost of living in an area you relocate to is important and you don't want to be negatively surprised *after* moving there. Check your library or any bookstore for a list of books that might provide the information you seek. As a starting point, you might try reading the most recent editions of:

- *America's 100 Best Places to Retire: The Only Guide You Need to Today's Top Retirement Towns*
- *50 Fabulous Places to Retire in America*
- *Retirement Places Rated*
- *Where to Retire: America's Best and Most Affordable Places*

Although we researched St. George and visited several times prior to moving here, we still discovered after relocating that some aspects of the cost of living were higher than anticipated. We knew the sales tax was 6 percent compared to 7.75 percent where we lived in California, but we failed to recognize that the 6 percent tax applies to everything, including food. Although we did not believe our retirement income would be high enough to pay any significant state income taxes, we did learn the first year that state income taxes are higher in Utah than California at the lower income levels. In fact, whereas Utah seemed to have a reputation for being a less expensive state to live in, certainly compared to California, it was more expensive than we expected. But several significant items that were less costly were gasoline, electricity, insurance, housing (but the latter was climbing rapidly), and property taxes.

The American Chamber of Commerce Researchers Association (ACCRA) publishes quarterly cost-of-living indexes for cities throughout the United States. The average for all cities, metropolitan and non-metropolitan, is a composite score of 100, with each city's index reflecting a percentage of that average. In addition to an overall score, the index provides a rating for the relative cost of groceries, housing, utilities, transportation, health care, and miscellaneous expenses. A dollar figure is also given for the cost to rent and purchase an average home.

You can compare the cost-of-living indexes for a few metropolitan areas in the United States on the ACCRA Web site at www.accra.org (click on the **Cost of Living Index** or **COLI** button and then the **Sample Comparisons**). Cost of living indexes for other metropolitan and non-metropolitan areas can be obtained on their Web site for a fee of $5 each. You may be able to access the latest report for free through your Chamber of Commerce or Department of Economic Development. (For a quick, easy, and free—though less detailed—comparison of differences in cost of living from among a long list of large and small cities, go to www.bankrate.com/ndo/movecalc.asp.)

After reviewing ACCRA's latest report (third quarter 2001), here are the cost of living index numbers for several cities covering the East, South, Midwest, and West:

- New York (Manhattan) — 237.3
- Los Angeles – Long Beach — 142.2
- San Diego — 127.5
- Las Vegas — 107.0
- Salt Lake City — 99.6
- St. Louis — 99.4
- Dallas — 98.5

- St. George, UT — 97.1
- Mobile, AL — 93.6
- Joplin, MO — 88.2
- Douglas, GA — 88.0
- Paris, TX — 87.4

According to the ACCRA cost of living index, a family needs 137.3 percent more after-tax income to maintain the same standard of living in New York (Manhattan), as they need in the average American city—a significant factor to consider if one is retiring early and relocating with a limited income. To put that in perspective, a couple earning an after-tax income of $50,000 in the average city needs $118,650 in New York. Similarly, Los Angeles residents need 42.2 percent more after-tax income to maintain the same standard of living than they need in the average American city ($71,100 as opposed to $50,000). A Manhattan or Los Angeles couple retiring early should do a lot better on the income derived from their net worth by moving to Dallas, Mobile, or Joplin, or to one of the many non-metropolitan areas like Douglas (Georgia) or Paris (Texas) that score significantly lower on the index.

One way to get the most for your retirement dollars is to move to a low-demand area. The lower the demand for housing, for example, and the greater the supply, the lower the costs (whether you rent or purchase); the reverse is also true. Since we all need to live somewhere, housing is one of the primary cost-of-living factors on a limited income and it should be an important consideration in choosing a retirement spot. Of course, the type of dwelling you want to own or rent is also important. If you are content to live in a tar-paper shack next to the city dump, your housing costs will be much lower than the person who wants to live in an upscale house in the most expensive neighborhood in the city.

Most of the books we read prior to relocating gave this sage piece of advice: Rent for at least six months in the area you choose prior to purchasing a house. We definitely concur with that advice. An advantage of renting prior to purchasing, if you choose to purchase at all, is so you can determine in which neighborhood of the city or county you want to live and in what type of dwelling: apartment, condo, townhouse, single family home, or maybe country farmhouse. We rented almost two years before purchasing our first house in St. George.

Whereas we initially rented in a 16-unit attached townhouse complex close in and could walk to virtually everything we did, we later leased in a quieter detached townhouse complex (comprised largely of retirees) outside the main activity of the city. We then purchased a similar-type townhouse in that area. Though these latter two townhouses were less convenient to the types of activities we had previously enjoyed, both complexes had tennis courts, indoor/outdoor pools, spas, exercise machines, table tennis, and a library (one also had a billiards table and horseshoes), so there were plenty of activities to keep us entertained without having to drive all over the city to do them.

Other noteworthy expenses to consider in retirement are food costs, insurance, property taxes (if you plan to buy a home), and possibly state income taxes. While your income will likely be lower than when you worked full-time, you will still find yourself paying some taxes on your interest, dividends, capital gains, pension, and earned income if you choose to work part-time. Prior to any relocation, you might want to research sales and income tax rates, and fees for services you intend to use.

Seven states currently have no income tax and five have no sales tax. But the lack of revenue generated from those sources has to come from somewhere. Find out where and how changes in that alternate revenue source might affect you later. Taxes can impact your early retirement, so check them out for any state and/or city that attracts your interest. Pulling up income and sales taxes for every state was easy on the Internet by typing "state taxes" into a search engine. Many cities also have Web sites you can research.

DESIRED ACTIVITIES

What kinds of activities are you retiring to do? That, in part, can influence where you choose to live. If you are retiring to sit in the house and watch television all day, then you can live pretty much anywhere in the country with low housing costs—whether you buy or rent. On the other hand, if you want to regularly participate in recreational, social, and cultural events, then you will want to live in a community that offers those activities.

We decided prior to retiring and relocating that we wanted to live in a city of approximately 35,000 to 50,000 people with clean air, low crime, minimal or no snow, a decent public library, discount movie theaters, bowling, tennis, hiking areas, cultural activities, and preferably beautiful scenery surrounding the city. We wanted to live within an hour or two of a large city so we'd have access to a major airport. A quiet neighborhood, someone else doing the lawn maintenance, and a number of recreational activities within or close to our neighborhood were also preferred.

Ultimately, those criteria led us to St. George and a detached townhouse complex with a host of amenities. We currently pay $100 per month in homeowners' association dues. For that fee our HOA takes responsibility for: maintenance of front yards; cable TV; exterior home insurance; cleaning and maintenance of the clubhouse, swimming pools, and exercise machines; watering and landscape maintenance of the common areas; repair of streets and sidewalks; and bookkeeping. We feel the dues are fair for what we get and we enjoy not having to take care of all those things. You can partially compensate for the cost of HOA dues in your budget by shifting money from the travel and recreation categories; after all, if you have recreational facilities on the premises, you don't need to pay to go outside your complex to do those same things.

You need to make similar decisions about the kinds of activities you want to do in your retirement and the type of city, geographic area, and neighborhood you desire. Then choose where you want to live on the basis of your answers to questions like these:

- Do you like living where you are now and is it affordable? If so, then you don't need to pay to relocate (which can cost thousands of dollars), unless you want to try something different.
- Would you like to live closer to family and friends, or farther away? (Yes, we have met people who didn't want to be perpetual babysitters for their grandchildren so they moved away from their kids.)
- If you are living in a cold/snowy northern climate, would you like to try moving to where the sun shines most of the time and snow is something you see on TV or atop the surrounding mountains?
- How about moving to the mountains if you've always lived in the plains, to the country if you've always lived in a metropolitan area, or to a city if you've always lived in a rural area? A change of pace can be fun.

You need to balance living in a low-demand area with whether it offers the types of activities that will contribute to an enjoyable early retirement. If a low-demand area does not offer what you want, and you cannot afford to live elsewhere, then you may need to continue working to increase your net worth prior to retiring so that you have better relocation options. Another alternative might be to take on a part-time job during early retirement or make some other trade-off so you can afford the more expensive area.

We could return to Wisconsin where we grew up and buy a house or rent for less than in St. George. From the standpoint of getting to see our families more often, that would be great. But the downside is that neither of us gets excited about snow, cold, or high humidity. After living in the western United States for 22 years, we find the drier climate and the variability of scenery more to our liking. Relocating to another part of the country has new challenges and opportunities. For us, the change in scenery, climate, and experiences from Wisconsin, to Kansas, to California, and now Utah, has been enjoyable. We would not have the same appreciation of the country around us were we to have stayed in the same city, state, or geographic area our entire lives.

BUYING VERSUS RENTING

What are some considerations for buying versus renting a house? The biggest factor in buying a home is the permanency issue. That is, should you decide to relocate at a later date, you may have difficulty selling your house—and it can get expensive and be a hassle owning two homes concurrently, or owning one and renting another. If you are renting, you need only wait until the end of your lease and then you are free to go. Sometimes you can even sublet or get out of a lease earlier if the owner can find another tenant. You have more flexibility.

But in terms of buying, home ownership continues to be the American dream. It is almost a universal goal and one that is attainable for most. The monthly payment is seen as an investment rather than money thrown away in rent to pay off someone else's mortgage. And for many people, their home is the only major investment they will ever have. Home ownership represents security and it provides for control—to make improvements at will and do whatever one wants to do with it.

Not knowing how long we might stay in St. George, we initially intended to rent for the duration. But rentals were hard to come by, and though we felt fortunate to get the townhouse we settled into the second year we lived in the city, we moved in knowing it would be put up for sale at the end of our lease. That meant either buying it or being displaced 10 months later.

The problem with renting is that you are at the mercy of your landlord; it could be put up for sale any time or the rent increased beyond what you want to pay. If you want or need to move, you have to be lucky enough to find another rental you like (and that you will be able to move into) at the same time your lease expires; otherwise you can find yourself paying double rent. Moving can get expensive, and if you do it yourself to save money, it can be physically taxing and you risk injury. Moving isn't so much fun that most people want to do it every few months.

Upon relocating to a new geographic area, renting initially provides the time and opportunity to decide if you are compatible with the city, climate, and people, and if it is an area in which you want to stay. It's not impossible that you could find your new location entirely different from what you expected. Give yourself at least six months and be sure you utilize that time to get to know the community. If you find it is not what you expected, you can easily pack up and move at the end of your lease, or you might rent month-to-month until you can find a new area in which to relocate.

Once you feel comfortable with the community and decide to stay awhile, then you can debate the issue of renting versus buying. Should you reach that point, here are some factors to consider:

- Is there a surplus of rentals in the area? If so, renting may be advantageous, as rents will generally be lower and you will have better choices. Of course, the opposite is true if it is a tight rental market.
- Do you know where in the city or area you want to live? If so, you have made one decision easier. If not, you may find yourself moving once or twice until you find the right area for you. It took us several months to find the part of St. George that was more compatible with our desires (and what we were willing to pay) and we did not purchase a home for almost two years—after living in two rentals first.
- Do you need the security of owning your own home? Some people do. If you fall into that category, then buying may be right for you. Again, it will depend on your retirement finances and/or your ability to secure a loan (if you choose that option). Although it was our initial belief that we could not get a loan because we did not

have sufficient income, a banker advised us that if our down payment was 50 percent or more so the bank felt secure that we wouldn't just walk away, virtually any bank would loan the balance.

- How sure are you that you are going to remain in that area for a long period of time? One long-standing argument for buying versus renting is that houses often appreciate in value. If you buy in a rising housing market, you can make money on your home over the years should you later decide to sell. However, the past few years have seen some housing markets throughout the country undergo significant losses.
- Another factor to consider is that real estate commissions generally run 6 percent. You can lose considerable money on the sale of your home if you do not remain in the house long enough for it to appreciate (or if it has depreciated) and you sell through a realtor. Again, renting provides more flexibility for future moves.

Analyze different scenarios for buying versus renting. For example, if you have $100,000 invested in mutual funds earning an average of 10 percent per year, in essence, you are deriving $10,000 per year income (which would support $833 per month rent). If your money is returning 8 percent, then you will have $8,000 income, which would support less than $700 per month rent. Now if you take that $100,000 out of your investments to buy a house, your retirement budget will have less income per year (in this example either $8,000 or $10,000) but your expenses per month will decrease because you will no longer be paying rent. You will have property taxes to pay but they should be considerably less than rent, especially if you move to a state that has low taxes. Of course, you now own a major asset and have decreased your flexibility, which may or may not be a big concern.

Consider this, too. While your investments in the stock market should average 10 percent per year based on historical performance, you could earn much less or even lose money over any given period of time, such as in a prolonged bear market. In that scenario, your money might be better invested in a house. But recent history has also demonstrated that you cannot depend on housing appreciation, either. Nationwide or regional recessions can significantly impact housing appreciation. Should you choose to buy in a slow housing market, you need to contemplate whether taking so much money out of your investments while getting minimal, if any, price appreciation (or maybe even depreciation) makes sense for you. In contrast, buying in an area undergoing a housing boom could result in a profitable real estate investment.

The first two years we lived in St. George, housing prices increased upward of 16 percent. That translated to an $18,000 increase in two years on a house in the $110,000 range. At the same time, rents climbed to the $900 range for a townhouse or single family home. Given that a large part of our retirement budget was being consumed by rent, we calculated several options and concluded that continuing to rent made sense if our investments would earn more than what we were spending on rent. But if our rent exceeded the money we were earning on our investments, and assuming we planned to stay in the city a few years, then buying would make more sense.

Once we made the decision to stay for awhile, we reasoned that the fast-growing housing market would result in appreciation over several years that would compensate for pulling money out of our investments. We also assumed that we would earn less than 10 percent on our investments over the next few years because the stock market was so high already—of course, that didn't turn out to be the case! Again, it is speculation, and regardless of which decision you make, there is no way to know how any housing market will perform. That same speculation also applies to stock market investments, especially over the short-term.

In our 25 years of marriage, we have moved nine times and owned five houses. Each time we buy or build a home, we try to do so with an eye on resale. We choose a neighborhood and either buy or build in features we think will appeal to future buyers. We keep our furnishings simple and our houses in salable condition. Of the four houses previously sold, the first took a couple of months to sell, the second 3 hours, the most expensive one 17 days, and the last one sold in 6 months during a slow market. That last house made us a small profit after paying the realtor while each of the other three earned us a good profit after commissions.

We followed that same strategy for our current house—a desirable location with a good floor plan and several unique features relative to the other houses in the neighborhood. We built this house speculating that, largely due to its location, it will also appreciate in value over the next few years and will turn out to be another profitable investment. But one never knows for sure. In the meantime, it's a great place to live and we do not have to be concerned about someone selling it from under us or raising the rent. We own it free and clear.

HOME SWEET (MORTGAGE-FREE) HOME

If you decide that purchasing a home best meets your needs, then your next decision is whether you should pay cash or assume a mortgage. Your ultimate goal in retiring young is to be debt-free and that includes your house. However, this is a controversial issue among financial advisors.

One side of the argument is that a house without a mortgage means a large sum of money tied up without getting a return on it, other than maybe it is increasing in value with inflation. Were that money invested in the stock market at a 10 percent average annual return while your home mortgage was at an 8 percent interest rate, for example, you could be earning 2 percent on that relatively large amount of money (e.g., $125,000 mortgage x 2.0% = $2,500 per year income, less taxes). You can also take the mortgage interest as a tax write-off, saving you even more money. And all the while your house will still be appreciating with inflation. Another argument is that you are paying off your loan with inflated dollars.

Of course, the opposing argument is that there is no guarantee you will earn a 10 percent return in the stock market over the period of time you own your house. Historically, the odds are with you the longer you stay invested. But there are no guarantees and most people do not keep their houses 30 years. Over shorter periods of time, you could lose money via this strategy. If you choose an asset allocation that decreases your portfolio volatility, such as a balanced fund or some other combination of stocks, bonds, and cash, your total return will be lower. An average annual return of 8 percent or so may not be much more than your mortgage.

One reason we, as well as many other early retirees, have elected to not have a mortgage is the immense peace of mind knowing our home is truly ours. We do not have to make monthly mortgage payments and it allows us to live on a budget of less than $1,600 per month. Should something happen to one of us, such as an accident or illness, we do not have to be concerned about losing our house because we cannot make our monthly payments.

The stock market has averaged a 10.7 percent annual return over the past 76 years. But what if stocks would experience a prolonged bear market and lose money for the next 5 or 10 years, which is always a possibility, based on the historical ups and downs of the stock market? Psychologically, it would be more difficult for us to be burdened with house payments of several hundred dollars per month while our mutual funds were losing money for 5 to 10 years, than it would be to pass up the extra income that could be generated through additional investments in a rising stock market while having to maintain a mortgage.

Once you have enough money to retire early, why gamble it in the stock market trying to earn more than you pay on your mortgage? You could make money short-term, but you could also lose money. Why take such an unnecessary risk? Whatever happens in the stock market, you can be secure in knowing your home is paid for and your budget is lower as a result. Besides, you will probably have enough other long-term retirement account money already invested in the stock market riding the ups and downs.

If you need money, you can take out a home equity loan; later you can reverse mortgage or sell the house to garner additional retirement income. So although the house is not generating income, other than possibly increasing in value with inflation or market conditions, it is not a useless asset, either. You can always borrow against the equity and raise any short-term cash you need.

PERSONAL PREFERENCE

If you can live without the security of owning your own home, and if rentals are reasonable in the location you choose for your retirement, then renting is less risky and provides flexibility—one never knows when unexpected events can turn plans upside down. An illness or accident in the immediate family could change things in a moment. But barring a major catastrophic event, buying versus renting seems more a matter of personal preference.

You can rent and have more retirement income, or buy with cash and have lower expenses. I doubt that most early retirees will want to take out a large mortgage to purchase a house, though it may appeal to some (especially if there are tax issues from having sold a business, for example). Should you be leaning toward purchasing a home, plan to stay in it long enough to recover the costs of moving and to hopefully gain some appreciation. If your circumstances were less sure, renting would be my recommendation because of the flexibility it allows.

Chapter Fifteen

What's Wrong with Part-Time Work?

What if you have the desire to retire early but you don't have an employer-funded pension and your net worth alone does not quite support quitting your full-time job? Do you strap on the ball and chain and keep plugging away at something you would rather not be doing? Absolutely not; you have options. And one option that might work for you is part-time employment. But you might also look at part-time work from another perspective. Although we have had a sufficient net worth since retiring in 1993 to not work at all, we have elected to work part-time nonetheless. Why might you choose to do the same? Try these five reasons:

- The longer you work, even if only a few hours per week, the more money you can accumulate for your future retirement. Any income supplementing your retirement leaves your investments growing to provide for a higher income later when you decide the time has come to fully retire. In addition, you can add to your retirement accounts through an IRA or other retirement plan.

- If you are like us, it is difficult turning down what we perceive to be a good deal for earning a little extra spending money. Look for flexible part-time or temporary jobs that allow you to earn supplemental income while also not tying you down. We quit working full-time so that we could get away from having to do things we did not want to do on a daily or even weekly basis. With flexible part-time jobs, that is not a problem.
- Because you don't have to work and you can quit any time, a job doesn't seem quite so much like "work." And quitting whenever you feel like it poses no undue hardship on your financial situation.
- From the onset of retirement, Kris, especially, has been uncomfortable with the concept of living off our investments. It is a concept that takes some getting used to. We have always lived off what we earned while saving and investing a large percentage for future retirement. How could we suddenly start spending the money we saved? Had we retired at 62 or 65, it might have been a different story. But at 42 (and Kris 40) it was hard to fathom living off investments for the rest of our lives, even though our retirement plan assured us we could.
- If you do not have enough money in taxable accounts to survive until age 59½ when you can start withdrawing from your retirement accounts penalty-free, part-time work can provide supplemental income. You may still be working, but you will have a lot more freedom and flexibility than full-time employment affords you.

Kris has continued to utilize her accounting skills in several part-time jobs. For a couple of years we also contracted with another couple to clean the clubhouse once per week for our homeowners' association. I have worked occasional jobs doing apartment maintenance, painting for our homeowners' association, and other small handyman jobs, as well as occasionally filling in as a courier—all being quite a contrast from my primarily deskwork career. You might find that you enjoy doing work that is different from your past career, although it probably won't pay as well.

My primary interest upon retiring was writing this book. It was started in January of 1994 and is getting a last-minute update in January 2002. Bits and pieces were written over the first six years; there wasn't any rush to finish it, because I figured the longer we were retired the more credibility it would have. Writing a little here and there was fun and it has improved the accuracy over trying to write it all now based on recollections of things that happened years ago. But it has also entailed hundreds of hours these past two years as I progressed through researching, final writing, editing, updating, and copy editing. And promotion is just starting.

WORKING TO STAY ACTIVE

An article in the February 1999 issue of *Kiplinger's Personal Finance* magazine revealed a figure of 80 percent of baby boomers expecting to work during retirement—some will choose part-time work, some full-time, and some self-employment. A surprisingly low 16 percent planned to fully retire to travel or do other retirement-related leisure activities. Consistent with that was a survey conducted in 1998 for AARP (formerly known as the American Association of Retired Persons) wherein 80 percent of baby boomers planned to continue working in retirement; only 23 percent of those planned to do so out of financial need.

The 2-Minute Survey on Work, developed for this book, also confirmed the above findings. Even if they could afford not to work, 77 percent of respondents indicated they would. Of those, 71 percent would choose part-time paid, 39 percent would volunteer, and 16 percent would continue in some full-time capacity—either extending their current career or pursuing self-employment ventures as opposed to working for someone else. (The numbers do not add up to 100 percent because some respondents chose both part-time paid and volunteer work).

Although respondents to our survey were not asked why they would choose part-time paid work over volunteering, the answer is most likely found in the first survey question, which asked why people work. They primarily work for money and benefits, but also for the opportunity to socialize with coworkers, to maintain or build self-esteem, for the challenge that work can bring, and for the opportunity to help others, among other reasons. Since all of those, except money, can be achieved through volunteer work, it would still appear that money continues to be the main incentive to work, whether it is a necessity for survival or not.

If you start applying the 3 Keys to retiring young now, continued employment during retirement should be a matter of choice, not necessity. However, as mentioned earlier, working part-time during early retirement may be the means by which some people will be able to retire younger. For a couple with $300,000 of net worth (rather than the $400,000 to $500,000 net worth or $2,000 to $3,000 per month that still appears reasonable for many people today), working part-time could compensate for the difference between what they have and what income they need to enjoy early retirement.

IT'S SIMPLE

Assuming you have a sufficient net worth to fully retire but you choose to work part-time anyway, a great investment vehicle you may be able to take advantage of is the SIMPLE (Savings Incentive Match Plan for Employees). This is applicable if your employer has 100 or fewer employees or if you are self-employed (wherein you are both the employer and the employee). Effective January 1, 2002 you can contribute up to $7,000 of your income to this tax-deductible, tax-deferred retirement plan and that will increase annually until it peaks at $10,000 in 2005. Thereafter, it will be indexed to inflation and increase in $500 increments—at least until the law expires at year-end 2010 or it is extended.

Self-employed individuals can choose where they want to invest their SIMPLE and select the type of mutual fund (or whatever choice) they want it to go into. Those employed by someone else will have the options provided by their employer. One limitation to the SIMPLE is that an employer may require a minimum earned income of $5,000. Anyone who doesn't want to work that much may find an IRA the better choice. Of course, an employer may have a 401(k) or other retirement plan available rather than a SIMPLE. Self-employed individuals can choose to not have a minimum earnings requirement for their SIMPLE.

Assume you and your spouse retire at age 50 but decide to work self-employed part-time, earn $5,000 each, and invest it into SIMPLE plans. After paying FICA taxes, you can contribute roughly $9,200 per year into your SIMPLEs. If you then decide to fully retire after five years, you will have contributed about $46,000 additional dollars to accounts that are growing tax-deferred and compounding over the next 10, 15, or 20 years of your full retirement (or until you need the money).

Invested in a more conservative balanced fund with an average annual return of 8.5 percent, that $46,000 investment (which has compounded to $54,500 at the end of those five years of contributions) would accumulate to $123,200 after an additional 10 years when you are both 65, and $185,300 when you are 70 years old—an admirable, and might we say sizable, addition to your net worth. And all five years you were earning that money you were concurrently retired—at least most of the time. That is how we chose to approach early retirement while in our 40s and we hope to at least live into our 70s, or even 80s if we're healthy. Because of a few years of part-time employment now, we should be in much better financial condition later when we fully retire. Our retirement accounts are growing appreciably as they accumulate tax-deferred and as we continue to contribute to them.

WHERE TO WORK

How much your part-time jobs pays, who you work for, and how much you work, will determine whether an IRA, SIMPLE, 401(k), or other retirement plan, (or maybe just some extra spending money), will be appropriate. In any case, seasonal or part-time temporary jobs provide potential opportunities. Take tax season as an example. Tax preparation firms hire seasonal employees for January through mid-April. That could fund a good share of your retirement or mad money account and then you would have the rest of the year off to do whatever you retired to do. If you live in a tourist area, a seasonal retail store might provide the perfect opportunity to work part of the year and have the rest of the year off.

Painting for our homeowners' association provided me flexibility in a part-time job; I had a list of exterior door casings that needed to be painted and I could do them on my schedule. A job like interior or exterior house painting for people who do not want to do their own, or who are too busy working full-time to do it, could be temporary work. Anyone with talents to work freelance, like artists or writers, could also work when they wanted to and take off the rest of the time. The population growth of senior citizens, many of whom are doing quite well financially, could be a potential source of part-time work (like handyman, companion, or errand runner) for many early retirees in the next few decades.

Your first choice may be to work part-time at your present job. Some employers will do that, especially if you have skills that are not easily replaced. But if that cannot be arranged, or if you would just as soon leave your current employer and try something different, then you might search out short-term, temporary jobs in some new field you think you might enjoy. Another option might be a temp agency. They have grown increasingly popular over the past several years as more people choose to work part-time. Look in the Yellow Pages under "Employment Contractor—Temporary Help."

WORKING UNDER YOUR TERMS

As an early retiree, you should establish criteria under which working is acceptable so that, as much as possible, you are working under *your terms*; you can be as flexible or inflexible as you want. Perhaps you don't want to clean, paint, or fix stuff. What kind of work would you find tolerable, or preferably fun? Give some thought to jobs you would probably enjoy and then seek out employment opportunities.

Kris had some flexibility in her work criteria. She enjoys accounting and was willing to work full days, part-days, weekends, holidays, or whatever needed to be done, as long as the work was part-time and could generally be done between the first and fifteenth of each month (although for a few months she was even willing to work full-time). That left the last two weeks of each month open. My criteria was more stringent:

- No having to get up early.
- No dressing up.
- No extensive driving.
- No heavy labor.
- Outside work only when the weather is nice.
- At least $10 per hour.

You might think my criteria would have been limiting, but that has not been a problem. On the contrary, both of us have had more work offers than we have wanted or accepted. Many temporary jobs we have undertaken have been done together. We figure we are more efficient, dependable, and motivated when we work together. It is also easier to coordinate with one vehicle.

Dependable, competent, and reasonably intelligent part-time workers can be hard to find. If that description matches you, then you probably will not have much difficulty finding work. It has been our experience that once people find out you are an early retiree with flexibility to fill in as needed, you become a valuable resource. Of course, that assumes you live in a city that has jobs available. It may be more difficult if you chose a rural town in Wyoming with a population of 100. And it might help not to set up criteria quite as strict as I have; but remember, if you're going to work, do it on your terms.

Whereas our initial plan was to retire in 1993 and never work again (and according to our retirement plan and projections we could have done that), we have since chosen to work part-time for the first few years. Because we don't have to, and because we work on our own terms, there's no comparison to how it used to be. What it has done for us in addition to contributing more money into our retirement and mad money funds is provide the opportunity to meet a lot of people, develop new friendships, and help people who genuinely need it. But most important, it has served as a continual reminder of why we closed our office doors and walked away from full-time employment nearly nine years ago.

This time we get to stand back and observe the daily grind that businesses face—deadlines, office politics, never-ending employee issues, too many meetings, business-to-business politics, legal issues, computer problems, the marketing game, and so on—issues for which we once had the responsibility. Needless to say, it is more fun watching from the sidelines. We have "been there, done that" and are now exceedingly happy to not be directly involved. And we can even leave the sidelines any time we want to.

Of course, you could observe most of the same things via part-time volunteer work. Most charitable organizations exist only because of volunteers. The work can be fun and challenging and we have also done plenty of that. But unless you have retired early with so much money you don't know what to do with it all, there can be a huge advantage to earning additional dollars for your future full-time retirement, or to spend on off-budget items.

So what's wrong with part-time work in your early retirement? Nothing. It can allow you to retire early when you are a little short of the net worth to otherwise do so, it can cover part of your expenses so that your retirement accounts can continue to grow, or it can provide the opportunity to live off your taxable accounts and invest your part-time earnings into retirement funds that are tax-deductible and tax-deferred. So unless you want to totally get away from work (and there will be early retirees in that position, too), part-time employment can have definite advantages for young retirees. And the best thing about it is, it's your choice.

Chapter Sixteen

Those First Few Weeks (and Months)

After being used to 40-, 50-, or even 60-plus-hour workweeks, you may find the first few weeks of early retirement the most difficult. You are used to having your time filled, whether you want it to be or not, for a good part of the week by your job or business. Suddenly having 24 hours per day of unstructured time to fill may seem a bit overwhelming. Although you have a multitude of activities you want to pursue when you retire, at first it may be hard to get started—you may find yourself trying to decide which to do first or thinking you might run out if you start right away. Dive in. Your interests will change and expand as you have more time and flexibility. If you retired young to do things *you* want to do, chances are slim you will run out.

On the contrary, you may find that there isn't enough time to do everything you want. There are many days I get so involved in projects that it's hard to go to bed; then I look forward to getting up and starting again the next day. There weren't an overwhelming number of days like that when I was working full-time, especially the last few years. Since retiring in May 1993, I have enjoyed getting up each morning with the option of being able to do whatever I want and there hasn't been a day yet that I've been bored. That's what early retirement should be—something you look forward to each and every day.

MAKE A LIST AND CHECK IT TWICE

Long before you begin early retirement, sit down and compile a list of things you want to do in your retirement. List as many activities as you can think of that interest you; remember every day is yours to fill however you want. By drawing up a list, it will help you focus on whether you have enough hobbies and interests to fill the time you otherwise spent at work. Let me stress once more: the purpose for retiring early is so that you can do what you want to do, not just to quit working. Looking forward to each successive day is what it's all about.

Get A Life: You Don't Need A Million to Retire Well is based on the premise that you need to develop interests and friendships long before you retire. From that standpoint, it was an interesting book, well worth reading if you would like to retire but are not sure you have sufficient interests to fill 24 hours a day. Remember that you are retiring young, when you are healthy and physically able to pursue activities that you could maybe not do if you waited until you were older. Perhaps you have been too busy in your career to develop a wide variety of interests but you still believe it would be fun to retire while you are young and healthy. If so, then it is never too late to start expanding your interests and looking at the endless variety of activities you could do if you had the time.

Below is the list I drew up before we retired. Some of these activities I was doing while working full-time, but not as much as desired. For others, there was never enough free time. Once the decision was made to hang up my clipboard, stopwatch, and pen, I was eager to tackle my list and retirement could not come fast enough. A wide range of potential retirement activities was listed in chapter 1; realistically, the possibilities are endless. But here was my list at the time of retirement:

- Tennis
- Fishing
- Bowling
- Walk/hike for exercise
- Bike for fun
- Read books from the best-seller list
- Read various magazines monthly
- Trade stocks
- Learn to play the keyboard
- Tape music with my guitars and keyboard
- Learn to play the guitar better
- Play board games
- Go to movies
- Attend concerts and plays
- Travel
- Write a book on how to retire young
- Write magazines articles (hopefully for profit)
- Canoe
- Volunteer a few hours a week
- Join a fitness center
- Learn electronics repair
- Play guitar in a small band (or jam sessions)
- Take better care of our car
- Read books on writing and investing
- Organize a badminton league

As you can see from that list, several of my interests could encompass huge amounts of time. When recording music on my guitars and keyboard, I usually get so engrossed that hundreds of hours pass before completing a cassette tape (and now I need to learn how to record music on our computer). Combine that with daily walks, bike rides or hikes for exercise, occasional tennis, concerts, lectures, movies, plays, and lots of reading, and it's easy to see how the days pass quickly. Time flies faster than ever since we retired and each new day involves challenges and activities that *we choose*. That's what makes retiring young fun and rewarding.

Has my list been exhausted after more than eight years? Hardly. In fact, I have not started half of them, a few have been dropped, and some will be ongoing for the rest of my life. In the meantime, new activities of interest have been added. The Internet has opened the world to us and can occupy far more time than one might think. Writing this book has also encompassed hundreds of hours and promoting it may involve even more. Perhaps another will follow.

Early retirement for us was a smooth transition; however, after reading several books on the subject, it appears that not having enough to do can be a definite problem for some. If you are retiring to get away from something, rather than retiring to do things you want to do, that could be an issue.

STARTING ON THE MOVE

If you are planning to retire young and are wondering about making the transition from working full-time to maybe not working at all, perhaps describing how we handled the first few months will give you some additional ideas and strategies. Unlike myself, Kris was not retiring because she had so many things to do that she couldn't wait to start. She was not burned out on her career like I was and her first self-employment venture was only three years old. (That probably has a lot to do with Kris picking up a part-time accounting job eight months later). She retired because I did and because we were ready for a change in our lives. We wanted to relocate and experience a new geographic area of the country.

Kris believed a long "vacation" would be the best transition to retirement because traveling would keep her busy and she would not have to contend with past clients continuing to call for assistance. A week after we retired, and after first helping a friend paint his new store, we set off on a 6,600-mile auto trip to see some sights, visit friends we hadn't seen in years, and spend time with our families in Wisconsin; we returned to California six weeks later. The trip was fun for both of us and it provided the opportunity Kris was looking for to unwind while also constructively filling the time she otherwise would have been looking to fill.

It also gave us the opportunity to stop in St. George on our way back to California and find a place to live. By the time we returned to the coast, we knew how much space we had in our rental and could make some decisions on how much we could take with us when we moved. While that was the end of our planned travels for transitioning into full-time retirement, we found ourselves on the move a lot more than we anticipated.

Within a week or so of returning to California from that six-week trip, we relocated to Utah with the goal of settling into retirement in a new geographic area. But a mere 17 days after we listed our California house for sale, it sold and back we went. We had three weeks to move our remaining possessions and tenant out of the house. This provided the perfect opportunity to decide what was most important to keep and what could be sold. We were already living in a townhouse in Utah less than half the size of our California home and had decided that, whether we continued renting or later purchased a home, our retirement house would be considerably smaller than the one we sold in California. There was no point in paying to move everything we owned because we didn't have room for it anyway. We also still had business assets that would have been impractical to keep and store.

Three weeks and three garage sales later, our possessions were considerably thinner and we had amassed a couple thousand dollars more in retirement income. Though we retired the end of May, by the end of September we had only been in Utah for approximately three weeks. Then, after being in our new townhouse for just three consecutive weeks, it was back to California again to settle a health insurance issue (which provided another opportunity to stay and visit with friends and family). In reality, we did not get settled into our new retirement home until the third week of October—over four months after we locked our office doors for the last time. With all that activity, time passed quickly and I had barely started on my list of things to do in retirement. But that was okay, since I had a whole lifetime ahead to get to them.

SETTLING IN

By the first of November we had settled into retirement. We walked two to five miles most days, played tennis two or three times per week, went to movies regularly, read voraciously at home and/or at the library, played Scrabble and worked crossword puzzles together, started going to concerts and plays, and enjoyed doing the things we had retired to do. By the first of December, I was fully immersed in recording a Christmas cassette tape for family and friends. For Christmas we drove to California again, joined up with friends, rode the train from Santa Barbara to San Diego, rented a car, and spent our first holiday in Mexico. Life was good, it was fun, and it was truly turning out to be what I had sought for a long time—a genuine pleasure to wake up to each morning. (But we were getting tired of driving back and forth to California!)

For the first time in our married lives we had cable TV (it came with the townhouse) and we found all sorts of interesting things to watch. The opportunity arose to catch as much NFL football as I wanted to and I enjoyed every minute of it. To learn more about various companies so I could make a little extra money trading stocks, CNBC became a staple a couple of hours per day. (Of course, as you read earlier, that idea didn't pan out.) And, like many things, watching TV eventually got old and our viewing time decreased. We were pleased to have more visitors in the first year of retirement than any other year in our married lives. Perhaps it was easier for others to visit because we finally had the time to accommodate them.

Although we liked our townhouse, we were not particularly excited about the neighborhood. It was close to Interstate 15 and there was an old farm within a hundred yards of our door. We were trying to adapt to roosters crowing all hours of the day and night, a group of barking dogs penned outside, and the smell of horses and cattle on various days when the wind blew from the west. Having lived in a single-family home for the previous 15 years, we were not used to multi-tenant housing. The noise from the kids screaming and playing directly outside our windows, and the number of cars and people coming and going, was a factor leading to the search for other housing. Some people do fine in apartments and condos, but we were not two of them. We spent hours upon hours searching the city for a new place to rent, as well as contemplating the economics and possibilities of purchasing a home.

We had visitors almost the entire month of April and had another 5,000-mile road trip planned for the summer. We could not believe how fast time passed. At the end of our first year of retirement, we moved into a different townhouse, this one in a quiet neighborhood comprised of almost entirely retirees that was outside the main activity of the city. Now that felt like home.

Kris secured a part-time job about eight months after retiring—primarily to fund her IRA and to earn extra money for off-budget activities and purchases. As mentioned in the previous chapter, if you choose to work part-time, do it under your terms. So did Kris accept a part-time job under her terms? She usually worked at home, went into the office when she wanted to, had no firm schedule, and worked as much or as little as she wanted to (within reason, of course, to get the job done). Now that seems to fit the criteria for almost the perfect job.

But as discussed earlier, competent workers get more offers and before long they find themselves working more than they would like. After seven years of working that part-time job (which grew from a few days per month to many days per month), in addition to taking on other part-time jobs as an independent contractor, last year Kris made a successful effort to get back down to a few days each month. There has been a need for her skills and experience and Kris has a hard time turning people down. That's how a few days can turn into a lot of days. But at least the jobs she picks up are by choice, not necessity. And that makes all the difference.

NEARLY NINE YEARS LATER

As I update this in January 2002, nearly nine years of early retirement have flown by. We still work part-time (as much as we want to but with the number of hours decreasing as time passes) to fund our off-budget expenses and contribute to our future retirement via SIMPLEs or IRAs. We have not traveled much so far—seeing the country or the world has not been one of our priorities. Most of our travel has been to visit friends and family or to see sights within a couple of days of our home.

Our long-range plan has us traveling more when we get into our mid-50s; no particular reason, it just seems like it would be a good time. We want to try a cruise and group bus travel tours. Neither of us likes to drive much so bus tours may provide an appealing alternative. In the meantime, we have cherished the last eight-plus years and look forward to our years ahead. Life is good, life is fun, and it's relatively stress-free. Who could ask for more?

We have had no difficulty filling the 60-plus hours per week we used to work with activities of our choice. While part-time work fills some of that time, what that does is give us more financial flexibility. Were we more into traveling, we could easily occupy all the time we wanted to. We know of others who retired young and spend months each year traveling throughout the world. Some move to an area of the country (or world) and live there long enough to fully explore it; then it's on to the next geographic area. Now that would certainly be one way to keep life exciting!

So many activities exist in the St. George area (and probably in most communities) that we cannot imagine someone not having enough to do. Of course, you have to have the interest and motivation to participate. When you choose to retire young, select an area to reside where you have access to the types of activities you like to do. And here's one other thing you may not have thought about: For the first time in many years, you will have control over your time. You no longer have to rush here or there to meet someone else's demands or schedule. Your days can be more relaxed and the pace slower; things will get done as *you* choose to do them. You can enjoy the leisure that early retirement allows.

Because every day is ours to spend however we wish, we have turned our schedules around from when we were working full-time. We had no choice then. Like most people, we worked all week and did any shopping or entertainment/recreational activities on the weekends along with everyone else. Now we go out and do as many things as we can during the week while everyone else is working, and usually stay home on the weekends when everyone else is out. Weekdays, and especially off-season weekdays, are a particularly good time to travel—motel rates are cheaper and destinations are less crowded. When you've got the time, it only makes sense to seize the opportunity.

You may have a long list of activities to do when you retire. But if you are unsure about transitioning into early retirement, you might try getting in your vehicle and driving 6,000 miles to visit friends and family you haven't seen for a long time. You'll surely get away from your job, your time will be constructively filled, and you won't have to be concerned about your old clients (or employer) still pursuing you for help. It worked for us and it may work for you.

Chapter Seventeen

Retirement or Merely a Respite?

Retiring young will give you control—of your time and of your life. But frankly, not everyone is going to be able to constructively fill 24 hours a day, seven days a week with meaningful activities. This may be an issue for those who are used to working 40, 50, or 60-plus hours per week and have never developed sufficient hobbies or other leisure activities to adequately replace those hours. If that turns out to be true for you, go back to work. However, depending upon how many activities you have found that you do enjoy, maybe part-time work will fill the gap. It may be the solution for filling just enough hours in your week to keep you busy, while still allowing sufficient time to do the other activities you didn't have time for when working full-time.

It has been my intention throughout this book to convey my feelings about retiring young; we only live so long, so make the most of it. If you work right up until the day you die, you will never realize how much fun not having to work can be. But early retirement will also not necessarily be appropriate for everyone.

What if it's not right for you? Or what if you decide you want a better lifestyle than retiring young has afforded you? Then by all means, go back to work until you are ready to retire and/or you have amassed the net worth that will support the lifestyle you want.

Had we worked eight years longer as originally planned (since our initial goal was to retire when I turned 50), we would have been able to move to St. George and buy a larger and more luxurious house, purchase one or two new vehicles of choice, increase our annual budget, and spend more money at a whim. But did we need all that, or could we be happy with less?

We decided that simplifying our lives and quitting full-time employment in our early 40s made more sense (and frankly was more of a challenge) than continuing to work for the sole reason of being able to purchase more material possessions. Nearly nine years later, we have definitively answered the question above; yes, we can be happy with less. But that will not be true for everyone. If you're not sure it is for you, here's one other consideration. There's always the possibility that during those additional eight working years, something could have happened that would have prevented us from being able to retire young and healthy. The same applies to you. Why take that risk if you can afford not to?

TAKE ADVANTAGE OF LIFE

Several times throughout this book the issue has come up of retiring before you die, contract some dread disease, or suffer some disability that will never allow you to enjoy retirement in the same way you could without those issues in your life. Why do I feel so strongly about that? It has a lot to do with my 17-year career in the field of vocational rehabilitation working with hundreds of disabled individuals. Having personally interacted with people whose lives were changed in an instant of time—from living the life they enjoyed and doing the things they liked to do, to taking medication and suffering perpetual pain—made an indelible impression on me.

It takes but a split second to experience an injury that can change your life forever. How many automobile accidents are there each year, week, or day? Surely you know people whose lives have been changed forever as a result. And how many people do you know who have contracted cancer, heart disease, or any multitude of other illnesses? Working with disabled people on a daily basis for 17 years cannot help but influence one's thinking.

It was those experiences, and the death of my dad from a heart attack at age 52, that had a significant impact on my life and helped me clarify and solidify my philosophy on retiring young so that we can enjoy life as long as possible. We never know what the future holds. While I endorse retiring at the earliest opportunity, so must that retirement be all you want it to be. If you find it is not what you expected or desired, then returning to work either part-time or full-time is always an alternative.

THINKING AHEAD

Should you decide to return to work after attempting early retirement, what concerns might you have? Prior to retiring in our early 40s, we contemplated the ramifications of taking a respite for one to five years. At first, we discussed taking one year off—basically a break from the day-to-day routine that had begun to wear on us after eight years of working an average of 60 hours or more per week. But what if that turned into two or three years or longer before we decided to again return to work full-time?

What might be the consequences of not working for one to five years? Would employers understand our taking a respite in the middle of our careers? Would we be perceived as irresponsible or lazy? Would changes in our career fields during that time leave us like dinosaurs in the modern world? Given those perceptions by a future employer, would anyone hire us? On the other hand, were we to return to work in some capacity of self-employment again, would it make any difference how long we took off?

You need to consider those possibilities before deciding to retire young. If the ramifications within your career field could be significant, then you need to take more time to think through those issues. However, as former employers ourselves, and based on the positive reactions from friends when we decided to retire early, we believed there would be employers in the future who would hire us as long as we did not fall too far behind in the critical aspects of our professions. Besides, we could always argue that we were refreshed and eager to return to work (contrary to being burned out as I was at the time of retiring).

The one primary concern that needs to be addressed is how quickly one could fall behind in a rapidly-changing career field, such as anything technology oriented; you could be at a major disadvantage if you chose to return after an absence of two or more years, maybe less. At the same time, you could use early retirement to continue studying your career field and to stay abreast of changes, in case you decided to return. You could also consider working part-time in your field to stay current. Of course, returning to work after a period of early retirement may also present the perfect opportunity to change careers, if that is something you are considering. Either way, early retirement needs to be carefully contemplated and planned prior to taking that major step.

Two years ago, a high school classmate I hadn't seen in several years stopped by for a short visit. He had quit his job of 23 years in one career field and was taking some time off to travel and have fun while reassessing his employment options. Currently in his fifth carefree month, the question arose as to how long he could take off and still be employable. With a background in human services and grant writing, we assumed that his success in the latter would be sufficient for a return to his career field even after an absence of a couple of years or longer. Plus, his master's degree and management experience should provide transferable skills for other career fields if he ultimately chooses to try something new.

This is a good example of an individual being able to take a respite without damaging his future return to work when the time seems right. In this case, the key is probably the fact that careers related to human services do not undergo the rapid changes that we see in technology-oriented fields. As it turned out, my friend secured a teaching position at a college in California. Taking a respite from full-time employment was a good thing for him personally, and it did not preclude his being able to return to work in a new career field when he was ready.

DOWNSHIFTING/VOLUNTARY SIMPLICITY

While wandering around the Minneapolis International Airport in the fall of 1995, I found a copy of the September *Worth* magazine. Paging through it led to an article titled "Downshifters" by John Brant. The article grabbed my attention because it began describing a trend called "voluntary simplicity" where people were choosing to work less and buy less. That sounded like the choice we had made two years earlier to simplify our lives and retire younger, rather than continue the full-time employment rat race for the mere purpose of chasing more money than we needed. The article presented several examples of people who had downshifted and learned to live with less so that they no longer had to work the long hours required of their previous lifestyles.

In 1995 The Harwood Group was commissioned by the Merck Family Fund to conduct a survey of Americans' thinking toward a variety of issues related to our society (titled "Yearning for Balance: Views on Consumption, Materialism, and the Environment"). Some interesting results emanated from that survey. One question focused on what would make people more satisfied with their lives. Of the six options presented, three being material and three non-material, all three non-material options scored significantly higher. The three options that would make people more satisfied with their lives were: being able to spend more time with family and friends, having less stress in their lives, and being able to do more for their communities. The three options that would not make people more satisfied with their lives were: a more luxurious car, a bigger residence, and more luxuries in their homes.

Consistent with that trend toward less materialism was an expressed desire for a simpler life. In fact, 62 percent expressed an interest in simplifying their lives; that increased to 72 percent of those in the 40–49 age group. Comparing themselves with their parents at the same age, 72 percent owned more material goods, 66 percent felt more secure financially, 61 percent had a nicer residence, and 58 percent thought their careers were more successful. But only 49 percent believed they were happier.

Downshifting was also addressed as 28 percent of the respondents claimed they had made some attempt to simplify their lives in the past five years. Of that downshifting group, the majority did so to pursue more balance in their lives—to allow more time for themselves and their families and to reduce the stress in their lives.

The Merck-sponsored survey was found on a Web site operated by The Center for a New American Dream. According to their home page (www.newdream.org), the nonprofit organization is dedicated to helping "individuals and institutions reduce and shift consumption to enhance our quality of life and protect the environment." There were numerous links and information items on the Web site that you may find helpful in your effort to simplify your life, either as an early retiree or in an effort to become one.

Downshifting is an attempt to balance people's lives—to retreat from a hectic, time-consuming, stressed-out life, to one that involves far less of all of those. But in order to have that, people must learn and embrace frugality and saving. A major factor in Americans' increased consumption of products and services over the past 20 years has been the continuing need to keep up with (or get ahead of) the Joneses. People's identities and self-esteem are often determined by their possessions. But the fact remains, we are who we are, not what we spend.

Downshifters are learning that material possessions do not necessarily equate with satisfaction. The price that is paid for bigger and better homes and vehicles, and all the new technological wonders, is longer hours, more stress, and less enjoyment of life. For many, the material assets do not compensate for the time lost not being able to do the things that are most important—like having more quality time to spend with spouses, children, and friends.

As you have read throughout this book, many of the changes one makes to simplify life and allow one to downshift or retire young are not that big of a deal when you look at the total picture. Downshifters, as well as many early retirees and those planning for it, adopt a less hectic and expensive lifestyle. What may seem like a big change at first gradually turns into an accepted manner of doing things. And the reward comes when you have less stress and more time to do those things that genuinely count in your life.

Each individual needs to decide what is most important in his or her life. This book was written around our decision to kiss the 65-hour workweeks good-bye and enjoy life in a more simplistic manner—to better appreciate what we have, not what more we could have. The accumulation of net worth is essential until the day you have enough to meet your needs. After that, the rest is excess. But then, each of us has different needs.

If you are in your net worth accumulation phase, you need to decide how much will be enough for you; this book should help you figure that out. Once you have enough, then downshifting or early retirement becomes a potential alternative lifestyle for you. If you are less than confident about early retirement, you might opt for downshifting first. That could mean working less hours on your present job, changing careers to something less hectic and stressful, or perhaps attempting a self-employment venture (although speaking from experience, that could end up being more stressful and hectic than what you left).

If you have calculated a net worth sufficient to meeting your needs (your budget), and you are looking forward to having the freedom to do whatever you want to do each day, then early retirement is the favored alternative. Look at your options, consider the ramifications of your decision as discussed before, and make your move. The worst that could happen is you might end up going back to work some day. The best that could happen is you might begin experiencing the most enjoyable years of your life.

Several articles I read while pursuing the topic of downshifting referred to the book *Your Money or Your Life*, and I have also recommended it. What seems to impress most people is the manner in which it relates life experience to work, how much we earn on our jobs (or especially second jobs), and how we can learn to live differently. While you may find it a little slower going in parts than some other books, many ideas presented should be beneficial if you are serious about retiring as young as possible. And assuming you are serious, this last chapter focuses on you.

Chapter Eighteen

The Choice

Early retirement is not for everyone. Some people genuinely enjoy the work they do while others find the money and/or the challenge of their careers unrivaled. There are those who would like to retire early but who cannot make the commitment to simplify their lives, embrace financial self-discipline, and invest wisely. And there will always be some who simply see today more clearly than they see tomorrow.

If you derive a high level of satisfaction from your job or career, then by all means, continue doing what makes you happy until you no longer have that passion and drive. But when the time comes that going to work day after day is a chore, not a joy, you will want to be in a financial position of being able to either walk away altogether, or to at least cut back to part-time work doing something you find more to your liking.

On the other hand, if working full-time is already surpassed by nearly everything on your list of preferred things to do, then you can't begin planning for early retirement any too soon. We started preparing 24 years before we expected it to happen. As it turned out, and much to our delight, we were able to make it a reality several years earlier than planned.

SETTING YOUR GOAL

Where you are in your life cycle, and how well you have positioned yourself to this point, will serve as the baseline for determining how realistic early retirement is for you. If you are already 50 years old with $400,000 to $500,000 in net worth, or if you have a substantial employer-funded pension to look forward to, you may be in a position to retire now. If you are 30 and have nothing invested, but you have a strong motivation to retire by age 50 or 55 and you earn enough money, you should certainly be able to accomplish your goal.

But if you are in your 20s, you have it made. With the opportunity to take full advantage of tax-deferred compounding, you can either invest smaller amounts and watch that money grow into a huge sum years later, or you can invest larger amounts and give yourself the option of retiring much earlier. With sufficient motivation and success at following the 3 Keys to retiring young, you will have a choice in your 40s or 50s that few others will—to either continue working, or retire and do whatever you want.

Nearly nine years after retiring at age 42, I can offer this: If you are burned-out on your job or career 20 or 25 years from now, you will relish the opportunity to walk away and do something you find more enjoyable. And you'll appreciate that option even more when you see everyone else your age trudging into their offices day after day (longing for their next weekend, holiday, or vacation) because they have no other choice—they didn't start preparing in their 20s and let the power of tax-deferred compounding work for them the way you put it to work for you.

Unless you plan to receive some kind of windfall, get a healthy pension, or marry into money, achieving your early retirement goal is going to depend on this sage advice: The less you spend, the more you save, and the earlier you start investing it, the faster your investments will grow and the closer you will be to attaining your goal of retiring as young as possible. As obvious as that statement is, most people fail to heed its advice. For those who want to retire early, it's obvious advice that cannot be casually dismissed.

Retiring young requires a vision for the future and the ability to establish long-range goals and devise strategies to accomplish them. Some people seem to have a knack for setting and fulfilling future goals while others do not. If you fall into the latter category, all is not lost. Long-range planning has never been one of my stronger points—with one exception. At age 26, I set a goal of retiring at 50, and for the next 16 years we worked hard and saved even harder in an effort to fulfill that vision. We accomplished it shortly after I turned 42. We still don't have any real visions for the future, but we fulfilled the one that genuinely counted. With similar motivation and effort, so can you.

GUIDING PRINCIPLES

Accumulating the net worth necessary for retiring as young as possible can be accelerated by establishing priorities, making rational trade-offs, and following a number of guiding principles that we successfully used over the years.

- If it's not on sale, don't buy it.
- If it *is* on sale, and you need it, buy in quantity.
- Establish spending priorities based on your future goals.
- Make rational trade-offs in spending and save the difference for retirement.
- Take bonuses, raises, gifts, tax refunds, and other "extra" money and invest it in your retirement accounts. (It's hard to miss money you never had and it will compound into a significant sum over time.)
- Buy basics, not trends.

- Shop the clearance sections of stores for discounts of 50-75 percent (sometimes more).
- If you can't afford to pay cash, you can't afford it (exceptions: your house and probably your vehicle).
- Don't pay interest on loans; collect interest on savings.
- Buy used if it hasn't been abused.
- Don't buy from vending machines or convenience stores.
- On big-ticket items, do your research and buy reliability.
- Take advantage of off-peak discounts for such things as dining out, travel/recreation, movies, and seasonal items.
- Buy less and go for better quality—unless you don't want it to last a long time.
- On big purchases, ask yourself, "Is buying this item worth retiring later or going back to work to pay for it?"
- Occasionally reward yourself for living by these guiding principles most of the time.

In the long run, not having to get up (especially if you're not a morning person) and go to work every day can be far more rewarding than owning a house full of depreciating assets you don't need. Choose to live with an emphasis on tomorrow rather than today so that you, too, can retire in your 40s or 50s (or as soon as possible), take control of your life, reduce your stress level, and have the freedom to do what you want to do. Give yourself the choice—to work or not to work—that *can be* the question!

AND A LITTLE LUCK

In addition to focus, determination, and a concerted effort, your path to retiring young can benefit from a little luck in the areas over which you have little or no control. We feel fortunate to have had no serious accidents, illnesses, or injuries that could have totally altered our plans. I hope you are equally lucky.

The same can be said for your investment portfolio. From 1995–1999 we saw unprecedented growth in the stock market. Whereas we retired with just enough money to last the rest of our lives (as long as we didn't live past about 85), after almost nine years of early retirement, we feel fortunate that our net worth has grown to where we now have more options. We can:

- Boost our annual expenses (which so far we've done minimally).
- Invest more conservatively to decrease our portfolio volatility (our main strategy so far).
- Live longer without having to worry about running out of money (always a welcome result).

Had we started off in a bear market our first few years, we might not have felt as confident about retiring young. But with a good bull market start, we were strongly encouraged. We initially planned our retirement in 1993 anticipating historical stock market growth over the long term (which at the time was about a 10 percent average annual return); what we experienced these past eight years was far better. But all stock market investors must be prepared for volatility. Whether you choose to manage your own investments or hire the job out, the gains of today can be gone tomorrow (at least on a temporary basis) and that, in turn, can change your early retirement plans.

We still expect to achieve stock market returns over the next 30 to 40 years reasonably consistent with the past 76, but we can live on considerably less as long as we continue to observe the 3 Keys. Our goal is to die broke, so we will adjust our retirement plan annually to reflect and achieve that objective. And what's the worst that can happen to us and ultimately to you? Barring serious medical problems, if the U.S. stock market were to tumble like Japan's and not recover for decades, we could potentially see ourselves *having to work part-time*. Even then, we would still be better off than most people. No one can predict the future; we can only plan for it as best we can. What is predictable, however, is that following the 3 Keys will allow you to retire younger with more money so that you, too, can enjoy the best years of your life.

If you earn an above-average income, you can conceivably retire in your 40s or 50s. If you earn less than the average (or have many dependents), you may not be able to retire that young, but you still want to be able to retire as young as possible with the financial resources to make that retirement all you want it to be.

EARLY RETIREMENT AND CHILDREN

Not much has been written in this book specifically concerning early retirement and children. That's because the concepts and strategies being advocated apply to all people, whether single or married, with or without children. Obviously if you have dependents to take care of (whether they are children, elderly parents, or ten pets), it's going to cost more to live and your budget is going to be higher. Given that, it would appear you have four choices:

- Earn more money.
- Retire later, or not at all.
- Figure out how to save even more of what you earn.
- Plan to supplement retirement with part-time work.

While conducting research for this book, numerous examples were seen of families with and without children who managed to save an unusually large percentage of their incomes—15 to 45 percent. What common characteristics did these families share? They established future goals (usually retirement, in addition to college educations for their children), paid themselves first (often through payroll deduction plans or electronic deductions from checking or savings accounts into investment portfolios), simplified their lives and cut expenses, saved more as their incomes increased, and invested in mutual funds. In other words, they followed the 3 Keys to retiring young!

Chapter 17 discussed downshifting and voluntary simplicity. Of the numerous articles I read on the subject, most of the examples were of families with children. Downshifting was the parents' attempt to give their children the one thing money could not buy—quality time together. But to give their children quality time, tradeoffs had to be made. In all cases, the parents gave up: (1) high-powered, time-consuming jobs, or (2) the continued acquisition of material possessions that required too much of their time to buy and maintain. Some gave up both.

Apply the same rationale to your situation. How many assets do you *need?* How many possessions do your children *need*? Do you have to keep up with the Joneses? Are you gaining more by working longer hours so that you can afford to buy everything you and your children want, or would it be better to buy less and have more time to spend with your family?

Many parents feel it is their responsibility to pay for their children's college education. But one couple we know has chosen a path that I think makes more sense. They are allowing their kids the opportunity to work their way through college. Between part-time jobs and school loans, their kids will pay their own way. Our friends' philosophy is that if their children need help paying back those loans after graduating, they will then provide assistance. But if their children secure good jobs and can manage on their own (the first child obtained a job starting at $60,000 per year!), then all the better; our friends will be one step closer to retirement.

Having also worked my way through college, I support and commend the parents for adopting this philosophy. And, just in case you are wondering, yes, our friends could afford to fully pay for those college educations if they wanted to; that is not the issue. These friends are continuing to instill in their kids the work ethic, and few could successfully argue that we don't try harder, and appreciate more, the things we have to work for and earn ourselves.

Another issue is whether you need to leave an inheritance for your offspring, or whether you should plan to die broke and spend the money you've earned for your own retirement. Once you have raised your kids and they are independent functioning adults, is it your obligation to make sure they are rich when you die? Some think so, but do you? For most parents, such decisions will significantly impact their potential to retire (and whether that occurs when they are younger or older). If you want to give away all your money, that's fine—but then plan on retiring later, or maybe never.

If you are convinced that retiring younger is suited to you, then you must think about yourself, as well as your kids. Let your children make their own way through life as much as possible and concentrate on building your net worth to the point where you can retire early. Then you will have more time to spend with your children and grandchildren. When it comes right down to it, what matters most—time spent with your family or owning more things? Again that's a choice only you can make.

HOW TO RETIRE YOUNG

The time has come to answer these questions. Would you like to have less stress in your life and more time for yourself, your friends, and your family? Would you relish the opportunity to choose whether you want to work or not? Would having the freedom to do whatever you want, whenever you want, appeal to you? If your answers are yes, then this book has given you the strategies needed to begin your quest toward early retirement. What you must do next is implement the 3 Keys to retiring young:

Simplify Your Life
Embrace Financial Self-Discipline
Invest Wisely

With a bit of luck to go with your efforts, you CAN retire young. For most people it will not happen overnight and it will require some changes in current lifestyle. You must decide, the sooner the better, whether the necessary trade-offs—which mostly involve saving rather than spending—are worth it. For most people, they clearly are not. But whether you retire early or later, applying the 3 Keys will significantly impact your future.

The traditional three-legged stool is wobbly; you should not rely on it for your future support. And you don't have to. By following the philosophy and strategies in this book, you will have the option later to fully retire, work part-time, or not retire at all. Give yourself the choice that few others—who won't follow the advice and guidelines presented herein—will give themselves. Statistics reveal that most Americans want to retire young. Those same statistics indicate that most people are living for today rather than tomorrow. That incongruity must be resolved for those who truly want to retire in their 40s or 50s.

Since May 1993 we have fielded countless questions on how we managed to retire so young, and many people suggested I write a book about it. That was my intention upon retiring at 42 and the results are finally in your hands. Now that we have completed almost nine blissful years, it seems an appropriate time to share our rationale, strategies, and experiences so that others can follow suit.

In this book I told you why we retired young (and why others should, too) and I presented the detailed budgets we have successfully lived with for the past eight full years. Although that budget works well for us and would be suitable for many others, it will not meet the needs of everyone. It requires making trade-offs and choices based on priorities that emphasize future goals. Not everyone wants to do that, and not everyone *can* do that.

You were also given many of the strategies and techniques that helped us focus on and achieve our dream of retiring young. The question now becomes: Is retiring young your dream, too? If it is, then simplifying your life, embracing financial self-discipline, and investing wisely will be your 3 Keys to turning that dream into reality. Follow our lead and you, too, will be able to leave the hectic, stressful, workaday world behind.

There is another choice, though. You can spend all your money as fast as you earn it to buy everything you want. That may mean never being able to retire, but if that makes you happy, then keep on spending. We can't afford to have everyone retire young anyway. As a nation, what would we do if no one worked? Who would pay all the income and FICA taxes? And the fact is, consumer spending does fuel two-thirds of the U.S. economy. But our philosophy is this: let *other people* work, pay most of the taxes, and fuel the economy—we prefer retiring young.

FORGET THE ROCKING CHAIR

Some people perceive retirement as quitting work to spend the rest of their lives in a rocking chair on the front porch. For those who retire old, that may be the case. But for those retiring young, that's merely one of many options—and not the one most will choose. Early retirees exit full-time employment to pursue the interests and activities they most enjoy. Life is too short not to, for we never know what the future has in store for us.

That sums up our early departure from the full-time workforce. Retiring young has given us exactly what we were seeking—freedom and control over our lives. There hasn't been one day since the end of May 1993 that I have been bored, and not a single day goes by that we don't fully appreciate the situation we're in. The number of additional assets we could have owned over the years, those trade-offs we made to save more money, could not begin to compensate for the enjoyment we have experienced since retiring in our early 40s.

SOMETHING TO LOOK FORWARD TO

Whether you are working or retired, you want your life to be a happy one. And what comprises happiness? Our former stockbroker used to provide a periodic reminder by reciting a modified quote from Joseph Addison (English writer, 1672–1719):

> The happy person needs three things:
> Something to do,
> Someone to love,
> And something to look forward to.

If you are working full-time, you certainly have something to do. And, hopefully, we all have someone to love. That leaves having something to look forward to. If what you most look forward to is your time away from work and the freedom and opportunity to do the things you would rather be doing, then it's time to start down a path where work becomes optional, not mandatory. You *can* retire young if you make the right choice below and put forth the effort necessary to turn that dream into reality:

- You can live for today and hope that, someday in the future, you will be able to retire and not fall below the poverty line.

Or

- You can live with an emphasis on tomorrow, follow the 3 Keys to retiring young, and give yourself the future option of working part-time, working full-time, or not working at all.

The choice is up to you. I wish you well.

Index

Appendix

Supplemental Reading

Books

A Kick in the Assets by Tod Barnhart (New York: Perigee/Penguin Putnum, 1998)

Bogle on Mutual Funds: New Perspectives for the Intelligent Investor by John C. Bogle (Burr Ridge, Ill: Irwin, 1994)

Cashing In on the American Dream: How to Retire at 35 by Paul Terhorst (New York: Bantam Books, 1988)

Common Sense on Mutual Funds: New Imperatives for the Intelligent Investor by John C. Bogle (New York: John Wiley & Sons, Inc., 1999)

The Courage to Be Rich by Suze Orman (New York: Riverhead Books/Penguin Putnam, 1999)

Die Broke: A Radical, Four-Part Financial Plan by Stephen M. Pollan and Mark Levine (New York: HarperBusiness, 1997)

Earn More (Sleep Better): The Index Fund Solution by Richard E.

Evans and Burton G. Malkiel (New York: Simon & Schuster, 1999)

Financial Peace by Dave Ramsey (New York: Viking Penguin, 1997)

Get A Life: You Don't Need A Million to Retire Well by Ralph Warner (Berkley: Nolo Press, 1998)

Getting Rich in America: 8 Simple Rules for Building a Fortune and a Satisfying Life by Dwight R. Lee and Richard B. McKenzie (New York: HarperBusiness, 1999)

Getting Started in Mutual Funds by Alvin D. Hall (New York: John Wiley & Sons, Inc., 2000)

How to Retire Early and Live Well With Less Than a Million Dollars by Gillette Edmunds (Holbrook: Adams Media Corp., 2000)

How to Retire Young and Rich by Joseph S. Coyle (New York: Warner Books, 1996)

Let's Get Rid of Social Security: How Americans Can Take Charge of Their Own Future by E. J. Myers (New York: Prometheus Books, 1996)

The Millionaire Next Door by Thomas J. Stanley, Ph.D. and William D. Danko, Ph.D. (Atlanta, Georgia: Longstreet Press, Inc., 1996)

Never Pay Retail: How to Save 20% to 80% on Everything You Buy by Sid Kirchheimer (Emmaus, Pennsylvania: Rodale Press, Inc., 1996)

Ordinary People, Extraordinary Wealth by Ric Edelman (New York: HarperBusiness, 2000)

The New Rules of Money by Ric Edelman (New York: HarperPerennial, 1998)

The Only Investment Guide You'll Ever Need by Andrew Tobias (San Diego: Harcourt Brace, 1996)

Personal Finance for Dummies by Eric Tyson (San Mateo, CA: IDG Books Worldwide, Inc., 1994)

The Retirement Myth by Craig S. Karpel (New York: Harper-Collins, 1995)

The Simple Living Guide by Janet Luhrs (New York: Broadway Books, 1997)

Take Control by Michael A. Janke (Maryland: Madison Books, 2000)

The Tightwad Gazettes, Vols. I, II & III by Amy Dacyczyn (New York: Villard Books, 1992, 1993, 1996)

You Can Retire While You're Still Young Enough to Enjoy It by Les Abromovitz (Chicago: Dearborn, 1999)

Your Money or Your Life by Joe Dominguez and Vicki Robin (New York: Penguin Books, 1992)

You've Earned It, Don't Lose It by Suze Orman (New York: Newmarket Press, 1998)

Web sites

American Bankruptcy Institute at http://www.abiworld.org/

American Chamber of Commerce Researcher's Association at http://www.accra.org/

American Credit Consumer Counseling at http://www.abiworld.org/consumer/

American Savings Education Council at http://www.asec.org

Bloomberg.com at http://www.bloomberg.com/

Bond Market Association at http://www.investinginbonds.com/

Bureau of Economic Analysis at http://www.bea.doc.gov/

Bureau of Labor Statistics at http://www.bls.gov/

CBS MarketWatch at http://www.cbs.marketwatch.com/

Center for a New American Dream at http://www.newdream.org

Cost of Living Comparison Calculator at http://www.bankrate.com/ndo/movecalc.asp

Debt Relief Clearinghouse at http://www.debtreliefonline.com

Employee Benefit Research Institute at http://www.ebri.org/

Fidelity Investments at http://www.fidelity.com/

Forbes at http://www.forbes.com

InvestorWords at http://www.investorwords.com/

Kiplinger's Personal Finance Magazine at http://www.kiplinger.com/

MSN Money Central at http://www.moneycentral.msn.com/

Money Magazine at http://money.cnn.com/

Morningstar at http://www.morningstar.com/

Motley Fool at http://www.fool.com/

Mutual Fund Investor's Center at http://www.mfea.com/

Mutual Funds Magazine at http://www.mfmag.com/

National Center for Policy Analysis at http://www.mysocialsecurity.org/

National Foundation for Credit Counseling at http://www.nfcc.org

Pension Benefit Guaranty Corporation at http://www.pbgc.gov

Quicken at http://www.quicken.com/

Retire Early Home Page at http://www.retireearlyhomepage.com/

Smart Money Magazine at http://www.smartmoney.com/

Social Security Administration at http://www.ssa.gov/

State Public Interest Research Group at http://www.truthaboutcredit.org

T. Rowe Price at http://www.troweprice.com/

U.S. Census Bureau at http://www.census.gov/

U.S. Department of Commerce at http://www.doc.gov

U.S. Department of Housing and Urban Development at http://www.hud.gov

U.S. Securities and Exchange Commission at http://www.sec.gov

Vanguard Group at http://www.vanguard.com/

Acknowledgments

Numerous people contributed in one way or another to the completion of this book and I want to express my appreciation to all who gave of their time and talents:

My wife, Kris, for tolerating the hundreds of hours I sat at the computer writing and researching when her first choice would have been for us to have been doing something else together, and for providing statistical assistance and offering suggestions on content and format. But more importantly, thanks for sharing a vision and working together to fulfill our dream of retiring young—these past nine years have been the best.

Kevin Berg, a long-time friend, for his ongoing enthusiasm and support as I wrote this book, and for his comments and suggestions on the final draft prior to sending it to American Book Publishing. Thanks to both Kev and Sharon for proofing the final manuscript.

Susan and Jack Buchanan, for introducing us to *Cashing In on the American Dream* in 1992, without which we probably would not have realized the feasibility of retiring in our early 40s. I hope this book has the same impact on others.

The design and production staff at American Book Publishing and especially my editor, Shannon Murdock, and copy editor, Margie Schlatter, for all of their assistance and helpful comments, corrections, and suggestions.

Thank you to the businesses that cooperated in surveying their employees, and to family and friends in various states who surveyed their friends and coworkers so that the 2-Minute Survey on Work would have wide representation. These businesses, friends, and family include:

Harmon's—Michelle Laumatia and Rick Burger
Skywest Airlines—Brad Gale
Southern Utah Title Company—Joseph McPhie
The Spectrum—Bonnie Thompson and Kim Hafen
Zions Bank—David Clark
Kevin Berg, O.D.
Bill and Patti Bettale
B.H.S. 25th Class Reunion
Shirley Ferstenou
Bob Hause, Jr.
Lee Kroenke
Craig Marvin
Susan and Joe Murray

Thank you to the hundreds of individuals who were willing to take time to fill out the 2-Minute Survey on Work, including the employees at the businesses above; the many friends and coworkers of friends; the waiting passengers at the Minneapolis International Airport; and the patrons at the Eau Claire, Wisconsin and Bensenville, Illinois public libraries. To all of these survey respondents, your willingness to share your feelings about work and retirement provided the foundation and support for this book.

About The Author

When it comes to retiring young, Larry Ferstenou has done more than talk. He left the full-time workforce at age 42 and has been enjoying the freedom of not having to work for nearly nine years. But not only did Larry and his wife Kris (who was 40 at the time) retire young, they did it without any lottery wins, inheritances, million-dollar stock options, or employer-funded pensions. In fact, their combined after-tax income over the course of their careers averaged only $47,300 per year including interest, dividends, and capital gains—yet, they retired in 18 years.

In order to quit working in their early 40s without any windfalls or pensions, Larry and Kris had to figure out the "3 Keys" to retiring young and then prove those keys work—and that's what they did. Now, after almost nine terrific years of early retirement, Larry has written *You **CAN** Retire Young!* to share the time-tested, practical strategies that will make it possible for others to also retire young without being rich.

Larry grew up in north-central Wisconsin where he earned a B.S. degree in psychology from the University of Wisconsin-Eau

Claire, followed by an M.S. degree in vocational rehabilitation/evaluation from the University of Wisconsin-Stout. A 17-year career in the field of vocational rehabilitation, and an unexpected family death, were central to forming Larry's philosophy on retiring as young as possible.

After spending 25 years in Wisconsin, Larry and Kris moved to Kansas for three years, then the central coast of California for 14 years, and finally retired to southern Utah in 1993 where they continue to enjoy their early retirement dream. For more information, please check out www.youcanretireyoung.com.

FOR A LIST OF ALL ORDERING OPTIONS, GO TO:

www.youcanretireyoung.com

ORDER FORM

(Please photocopy this form)

Want to purchase copies for friends and family? Here are three easy-order options for your convenience.

Telephone: (801) 463-3942
Have your credit card ready.

Internet: http://www.pdbookstore.com
Click on "Personal Finance."

Mail: **New: Publisher Direct**
P.O. Box 65624
Salt Lake City, UT 84165
(801) 486-8639

Please send ___ copies of *You **CAN** Retire Young! How to Retire in Your 40s or 50s Without Being Rich* by Larry Ferstenou. I have enclosed $19.95 plus $4.85 (and $1.75 for each additional book) for Priority Mail shipping. Rush my books to: (please print clearly)

Name: ____

Address: ____

City: ______________________ State_____ Zip__________

Telephone Number: __________________________________

Payment:

___Check ___Visa ___Master Card ___AMEX ___Discover

Card Number: _______________________________________

Expires: _____/_____ Signature: _______________________

THANK YOU FOR YOUR ORDER

Price and shipping subject to change without notice.